THIS BOOK ... ER THE
... ERSITY
... ARIES

D0793948

SUBVERSIVE VIRTUE

SUBVERSIVE VIRTUE

Asceticism and Authority in the Second-Century Pagan World

James A. Francis

The Pennsylvania State University Press
University Park, Pennsylvania

Library of Congress Cataloging-in-Publication Data

Francis, James A., 1954–
    Subversive virtue : asceticism and authority in the second-century
pagan world / James A. Francis.
        p.   cm.
    Includes bibliographical references and index.
    ISBN 0-271-01304-4 (alk. paper)
    1. Asceticism—History. 2. Ascetics—Rome. 3. Ethics, Ancient.
4. Rome—Civilization. I. Title.
BJ171.A82F73 1995
111'85—dc20   93-21081
                                                                    CIP

Copyright © 1995 The Pennsylvania State University
All rights reserved
Printed in the United States of America

Published by The Pennsylvania State University Press,
University Park, PA 16802-1003

It is the policy of The Pennsylvania State University Press to use acid-free paper
for the first printing of all clothbound books. Publications on uncoated stock
satisfy the minimum requirements of American National Standard for Information Sciences—Permanence of Paper for Printed Library Materials, ANSI
Z39.48–1984.

11899050 02547

APR 7 1995

UNDERGRADUATE

To the memory of my father
and
the love of my mother

CONCORDIA UNIVERSITY LIBRARY
PORTLAND, OR 97211

Contents

Acknowledgments

This book grew out of my graduate work in the Department of Classical Studies and the Department of Religion at Duke University. Therefore, I must first of all thank my professors there, particularly Elizabeth Clark, Diskin Clay, and Robert Gregg (now of Stanford University), and most especially my *Doktorvater* Kent Rigsby for his continuing advice and direction. I would like to single out for special thanks two faculty colleagues from Rollins College: Catherine Higgs, for her friendship and understanding, and Patricia Marshall, for her encouragement and consummate devotion to scholarship. A special debt of gratitude is owed my research assistant, Kim Peterson, an alumna of the Rollins Classics Program, whose energy, abilities, and perseverance proved invaluable in the completion of this project. I must also recognize the extraordinary care, diligence, and expertise of Paul Harvey of The Pennsylvania State University in reading the manuscript in preparation for publication and express my gratitude for his sound judgment and recommendations. In the same vein, I wish also to thank Timothy Barnes of the University of Toronto for reading and making helpful suggestions on Chapter 4. For financial support in research and preparation of the manuscript, I am grateful to the Charlotte W. Newcombe Foundation, the Woodrow Wilson National Fellowship Foundation, and to Rollins College for a generous Critchfield Faculty Development Grant. I would also like to recognize the libraries that assisted me at various points in my research: Smathers Libraries of the University of Florida, Wilson Library of the University of Minnesota, Weyerhauser Library of Macalaster College, the library of Luther-Northwestern Seminary, with special thanks to the staff of Olin Library at Rollins. I cannot express enough gratitude to my parents, who made it all possible. Finally, I thank David for bearing up with me.

Abbreviations

AAR	American Academy of Religion
ANRW	W. Haase and H. Temporini, eds., *Aufstieg und Niedergang der römischen Welt / Rise and Decline of the Roman World* (Berlin and New York, 1972ff.).
CIL	*Corpus Inscriptionum Latinarum*
CQ	*Classical Quarterly*
CR	*Classical Review*
GRBS	*Greek, Roman, and Byzantine Studies*
ILS	H. Dessau, ed. *Inscriptiones Latinae Selectae*, 3 vols. in 5 (Berlin, 1892–1916)
JBL	*Journal of Biblical Literature*
JHS	*Journal of Hellenic Studies*
JRS	*Journal of Roman Studies*
JSOT	*Journal for the Study of the Old Testament*
JTS	*Journal of Theological Studies*
LSJ	H. D. Liddell and R. Scott, *A Greek-English Lexicon*, 9th ed. revised and augmented by H. S. Jones, with a supplement by E. A. Barber et al. (Oxford, 1968).
PBSR	*Papers of the British School at Rome*
RE	A. Pauly, G. Wissowa, and W. Kroll, eds., *Realencyclopädie der klassischen Altertumswissenschaft* (Munich, 1893–1980).
SBL	Society of Biblical Literature
TAPA	*Transactions of the American Philological Association*
Vig. Chr.	*Vigiliae Christianae*

Introduction

Deviance is a fact of life. In any human community exist those who simply will not conform to prevailing standards. I find historical inquiry the most satisfying when it explores such phenomena of human nature, especially when that nature is writ large in that complex corporate organism we conveniently term "society." The way in which a society uses its authority to deal with dissenters offers an intimate glimpse into its inner workings—its values, assumptions, and spirit. Confronting dissent not only provides a measure of a society's tolerance, but also of its vitality and creativity in the techniques it chooses for defending its culture and norms. The issue becomes more intriguing when deviance is manifested in behavior that appears innocuous or even laudable, at least when viewed in isolation. Ascetic behavior presents just such a case of subversive virtue.

This book examines the conflict between asceticism and authority in one of its most dynamic periods. It centers upon the balmy late afternoon of Rome's classical empire, from the birth of Marcus Aurelius in 121 C.E. to Philostratus's writing the *Life of Apollonius of Tyana* sometime after 217. The period offers a rich variety of characters for study: philosophers from every major school in antiquity, literary artists, religious innovators, prophets, wonderworkers, and charlatans—ranging a social scale from the emperor himself to a Jewish carpenter crucified as an insurrectionist. What holds this diverse mob together, and allows it to be viewed synoptically, is that each of these figures, either in his personal example or in his writings, speaks directly to the definition of asceticism itself and to the conflict between asceticism and authority in the second century. I have selected texts that represent the most detailed and eloquent examples of this definition and conflict.

The heart of the issue is that rigorous asceticism was deviant, and deviance was dangerous. Strident, and often obstreperous, practitioners of physical asceticism were deemed suspect by the political, social, and cultural authorities of the age, and such apprehension put the practice of physical asceticism under a cloud of suspicion generally. This mistrust of ascetics stemmed from their being perceived as radicals expressing discontent with the status quo, advocating norms and values antithetical to the accepted social and political order, and claiming a personal authority independent of the traditional controls of their society and culture. Put simply, they were seen as a threat to the continued and peaceful existence of the Roman Empire. The conflict between asceticism and authority hinged on social and cultural issues. The second century is "pivotal in the transformation of the civic person of ancient society who located authority externally, in various social institutions, into the person of late antiquity who searched within for otherworldly authority."[1] This study demonstrates that those involved in this transformation were themselves conscious of its reality. Both ascetics and authorities in the period were aware of the nature and significance of the issues involved. The former deliberately sought this transfer of authority; the latter vigorously opposed it.

Asceticism was not, in and of itself, necessarily subversive; rather, it accompanied and manifested subversion. Radical ideas tend to cluster about the ascetic. Yet, the issue is not black and white, especially since the educated and ruling classes of the empire professed admiration for ascetic ideals. Marcus Aurelius could both embrace rigorous self-denial as a youth and thank the man who taught him not to display himself as an ascetic. The poet Lucian could mercilessly excoriate the practices of one Cynic, Peregrinus, while lauding those of another, Demonax, as an example for all philosophers. Asceticism and authority manifest contradiction and paradox. Authority drew a line at which esteem for ascetic principles abruptly stopped, precisely where asceticism crossed into social dissent and radicalism. Finding and describing this line advances a fertile and difficult area of historical inquiry: the discovery of the unwritten, but very real and often inflexible, codes that circumscribe the limits of social tolerance.

The sheer number and variety of sources from this period demonstrate the pivotal importance of the second century in both defining and developing the limits of acceptable ascetic behavior. Controversy and polemic abound, both on the subject of asceticism itself and on the constellation of related issues that revolve around the ascetic. While scholars have examined many of these topics, given the growing interest in the second century over the past several years, few have recognized the central importance of asceticism or the watershed significance of the second century in the ascetical controversy.

Scholarship on this period has given attention to the related issues of prophecy, miracle working, charismatic leadership, marriage and sexuality, and the role of women, among both pagans and Christians.[2]

1. J. Perkins, "The 'Self' as Sufferer," *Harvard Theological Review* 85 (1992): 247.
2. P. Cox, *Biography in Late Antiquity: A Quest for the Holy Man* (Berkeley and Los

While worthy in their own right, these studies offer only a partial view of a much larger phenomenon. In reality, the prophet, miracle worker, celibate, and charismatic leader are found together in one person: the ascetic described in the following pages. Through the study of the ascetic figure, all these other phenomena fall into their proper perspective as aspects of a much broader historical reality and faces, so to speak, of one type of historical individual. Asceticism thus provides the key for understanding the history of social, cultural, and religious deviance in this period, and the response of authority to it.

Studies of asceticism usually begin with the late third and early fourth centuries, the time of the flowering of Neoplatonism among pagans and monasticism among Christians.[3] This is, perhaps, understandable given

Angeles, 1983); S. L. Davies, *The Revolt of the Widows: The Social World of the Apocryphal Acts* (Carbondale, Ill., 1980); E. R. Dodds, *Pagan and Christian in an Age of Anxiety: Some Aspects of Religious Experience from Marcus Aurelius to Constantine* (Cambridge, 1965); E. S. Fiorenza, *In Memory of Her: A Feminist Theological Reconstruction of Christian Origins* (New York, 1984); E. V. Gallagher, *Divine Man or Magician? Celsus and Origen on Jesus*, SBL Dissertation Series 64 (Chico, Calif., 1982); R. J. Hauck, *The More Divine Proof: Prophecy and Inspiration in Celsus and Origen*, AAR Academy Series 69 (Atlanta, Ga., 1989); A. B. Kolenkow, "A Problem of Power: How Miracle Workers Counter Charges of Magic in the Hellenistic World," *Society of Biblical Literature Seminar Papers* 1 (1976): 105–10; R. MacMullen, *Enemies of the Roman Order: Treason, Unrest, and Alienation in the Empire* (Cambridge, Mass., 1966); E. H. Pagels, "Adam and Eve, Christ and the Church: A Survey of Second Century Controversies Concerning Marriage," in *The New Testament and Gnosis: Essays in Honor of Robert McL. Wilson*, ed. A. H. B. Logan and A. J. M. Wedderburn (Edinburgh, 1983), 146–75; R. Reitzenstein, *Hellenistische Wundererzählungen*, (Leipzig, 1906; repr. 1974); H. Remus, *Pagan-Christian Conflict over Miracle in the Second Century*, Philadelphia Patristic Monograph Series 10 (Cambridge, Mass. 1983); M. Smith, *Jesus the Magician* (New York, 1978); and G. Theissen, *Sociology of Early Palestinian Christianity*, trans. J. Bowden (Philadelphia, 1978). See also the bibliographical notes found at the beginning of each chapter of this book and the notes to the discussion of the "holy man," Chapter 4, pages 118–26.

3. A historical bibliography of scholarship on asceticism would be voluminous. Significant studies in this century include R. Arbesmann, "Fasting and Prophecy in Pagan and Christian Antiquity," *Traditio* 7 (1949–51): 1–71; K. S. Frank, *Askese und Mönchtum in der alten Kirche* (Darmstadt, 1975); J. Leipoldt, *Griechische Philosophie und frühchristlichen Askese* (Berlin, 1961); B. Lohse, *Askese und Mönchtum in der Antike und in der alten Kirche*, Religion und Kultur der alten Mittelmeerwelt in Parallelforschungen 1 (Munich, 1969); A. Meredith, "Asceticism—Christian and Greek," *JTS* 27(1976): 313–32; P. Nagel, *Die Motivierung der Askese in der Altenkirche und der Ursprung des Mönchtums*, Texte und Untersuchungen zur Geschichte der altchristlichen Literatur 95 (Berlin, 1966); H. Strathmann, *Die Askese in der Umgebung des werdenden Christentums* (Leipzig, 1914); and A. Vööbus, *A History of Asceticism in the Syrian Orient: A Contribution to the History of Culture in the Near East*, 3 vols., Corpus Scriptorum Christianorum Orientalium (CSCO) 184, 197, 500; Subsidia 14, 17, 81 (Louvain, 1958–88). Useful bibliographies are found in V. L. Wimbush, ed., *Ascetic Behavior in Greco-Roman Antiquity: A Sourcebook* (Minneapolis, 1990), 484–87, and P. R. L. Brown, *The Body*

the widespread popularity of ascetic ideals and practices in this period. Starting at this point, however, conveys the impression that the rise of asceticism was in some way natural, inevitable, and welcome. At the same time, and for the same reason, scholars generally concentrate on the study of Christian asceticism, noting pagan doctrine and practice only as they were borrowed and incorporated into the Church. Again this leaves the impression that Christian asceticism was a natural development influenced by pagan philosophy, and that pagan intellectuals found it congenial to their own ethical ideals. This study of *pagan* attitudes and practices regarding asceticism in the *second* century (a century before most studies of asceticism begin) demonstrates that quite the opposite was true.[4] Asceticism was held suspect until proved otherwise. To view the great popularity of asceticism in the later period correctly, it is vital to understand the sort of suspicion and opposition that had to be overcome to allow the flowering of the fourth century to occur.

The *legenda* of Apollonius of Tyana, a first-century Pythagorean ascetic, encapsulate this development. In life, Apollonius was a wonderworker, religious nonconformist, and political demagogue—a social deviant of the first rank. By the early third century, he was a heroic paragon of the established order. This transformation marks the trajectory of asceticism in the second century: a progression of conflict, change, and continuity that established the definition, character, and function of asceticism in the centuries that followed.

I should note at the outset that I have deliberately confined this study to literary evidence. An examination of, for example, the inscriptions and papyri on this topic would constitute a separate work of equal if not surpassing length. The questions and methods applied to most of the texts discussed here are new, as is the synoptic treatment of this evidence as a whole. My aim in this work is to consolidate a foundation and establish a fresh approach, on the basis of which the more difficult species of evidence may be treated.

The nature of literary evidence imposes a certain limitation. Most of these texts were written by members of the educated, upper classes—

---

and Society: Men, Women, and Sexual Renunciation in Early Christianity (New York, 1988), 449–93.

4. There have been precious few works devoted to pagan asceticism, and none are inclusive and synthetic. Two fine studies are M.-O. Goulet-Cazé, *L'Ascèse Cynique: Un Commentaire de Diogène Laërce VI.70–71*, Histoire des doctrines de l'antiquité classique 10 (Paris, 1986), and B. L. Hijmans, *ΑΣΚΗΣΙΣ: Notes on Epictetus' Educational System*, Wejsgerige teksten en studies 2 (Assen, 1959). Though concerned with a different topic, P. Rabbow, *Seelenführung: Methodik der Exercitien in der Antike* (Munich, 1954) devotes a good deal of attention to asceticism in his examination of spiritual exercise.

men who would have little sympathy with radical social ideas. This is simply characteristic of the study of antiquity; the educated class were those who wrote, and so the only view that comes down to us in texts speaking in the first person is that of this class. Many of the ascetics themselves were of a lower class, indeed, to believe what some said of them, from the lowest. Certainly most did not belong to the class of educated writers; if some did, their writings have not survived. The ascetics seldom speak in their own voice. It would be dangerous, therefore, to typify more radical forms of asceticism as a lower-class phenomenon. Class consciousness and distinction certainly played a role in the conflict between asceticism and authority, but to view the socially deviant aspects of asceticism as a "cry of the oppressed" is incorrect. Careful perspective is essential, and I prefer to be more strictly bound by the evidence when dealing with class issues in antiquity.

The approach I have taken to this study actually capitalizes on upper-class domination of the evidence. My purpose is precisely to illustrate in what ways this class found ascetical practices objectionable and threatening. It was the forces of authority, embodied in this class and in its attitudes and opinions, that established the issues and parameters of the conflict. Challenges to these attitudes and opinions impelled the forces of authority to articulate the values and assumptions that undergirded their society—a society in which they, by definition, were the arbiters of political, social, and cultural standards.

Throughout this study, I use two crucial and troublesome words taken from Greek that require clarification. The first is the most important in this entire book: *askesis* (ἄσκησις). The word is often difficult to translate, due primarily to its range of meaning.[5] Initially found as an adjective describing an object as "having had much effort put into its making," as a noun it took on the meaning of "prolonged effort" or "training." Its use to denote military or athletic training and, hence, "discipline" in general, expanded to include interior or moral exertion and discipline. From these definitions, the word came to connote the self-denial such regimens required. In the texts studied here, the word can possess any or all of these meanings, dependent upon context.[6] I have often rendered it simply by the transliteration (*askesis*), so as nei-

---

5. Fortunately, the use of the word has already received a detailed analysis in H. Dressler, *The Usage of Ἀσκέω and its Cognates in Greek Documents to 100 A.D.*, Catholic University of America Patristic Series 78 (Washington, D.C., 1947); see also Hijmans, 55–63.

6. A fine and potentially universal translation as "training in denial" is given, almost incidentally, by D. Clay, "Lucian of Samosata: Four Philosophical Lives (Nigrinus, Demonax, Peregrinus, Alexander Pseudomantis)," *ANRW* II.36.5 (1992): 3412.

ther to prejudice or confuse the reader with modern, Christian concepts of asceticism.

The second problematic word is *goes* (γόης), with its cognate *goeteia* (γοητεία). The former is often used to mean "magician" or "sorcerer," the latter "magic" or "sorcery." These words do indeed have these meanings, but they also carry clear and distinct connotations of an impostor or charlatan, of trickery or fraud.[7] The English word "mountebank" is an excellent translation of *goes*, though unfortunately archaic. Again, I most often transliterate the word to avoid excluding its full range of meaning in the original.

In speaking to friends and colleagues about my work, I was surprised to hear a number of them remark on its timeliness and relevance to contemporary society. I must admit that this was not my intent in writing on this topic, but I nevertheless welcome any such interpretations. If this book, in some way, contributes to an understanding of the dynamics of power in our own society and the ways in which it seeks to control and confine those it labels "deviant," it will serve a purpose far nobler than that of simple erudition.

7. For the history, development, and use of the word γόης, see W. Burkert, "Γόης. Zum griechischen 'Schamanismus,'" *Rheinisches Museum* 150 (1962): 36–55.

C h a p t e r   O n e

STOICISM

Setting the Norm

IN HIS *MEDITATIONS,* the emperor Marcus Aurelius (121–180 C.E.) states that one of the valuable lessons learned from his tutor Rusticus was: "Not to display oneself as a man keen to impress others with a reputation for asceticism or beneficence."[1] The sentiment is paradoxical. Ascetic self-discipline (τὸν ἀσκητικόν) and public-minded benefaction (τὸν εὐεργετικόν) would be desirable qualities in a ruler, particularly in a monarch of a world empire. Aurelius himself certainly embraced these virtues; yet he praises the man who taught him to restrain them. Virtue, it seems, has its limits.

It is surely difficult for an emperor to be a monk, but Aurelius's restraint springs from a deeper source than his social position. Aurelius was a Stoic. Stoicism dominated the intellectual life of the second century. It so permeated the culture that those possessed of learning absorbed in their education that it became a sort of ethical *koine.* Accepted standards of behavior, including ascetic behavior, were either established by this philosophy or articulated and justified in its terms. Immediately prior to the passage above, Aurelius had thanked Rusticus

---

1. μὴ . . . ἢ φαντασιοπλήκτως τὸν ἀσκητικὸν ἢ τὸν εὐεργετικὸν ἄνδρα ἐπιδείκνυσθαι (I.7).

for teaching him to avoid sophistry, theoretical speculation, and sermonizing. Stoicism, as practiced by the Romans, professed aversion to intellectual conceit, impracticality, and empty words.

The limit imposed upon asceticism and benefaction concerns display: attaining a popular reputation by parading one's good works, whether of personal or social virtue. Such conspicuous behavior is excessive and violates *decorum*. It is also suspicious, for virtue is a means to power. On the personal level, the word used for benefaction, *euergesia,* implies indebtedness to the benefactor for a favor received. On the political level, the term carries connotations of *philotimia,* undertaking works to benefit the community for the sake of the status and notoriety gained thereby. In both cases, the benefactor gains the esteem of others and binds them to himself by a debt of social obligation. Popular reputation translates into personal power.[2] In the same way ascetics, on the basis of their austere and self-disciplined lives, could challenge the authority of political leaders, social norms, and cultural traditions, and set themselves up as authorities in their own right.

The Evolution of Stoicism

The very philosophy that, in Aurelius's day, preached restraint and conformity originated in dissident asceticism and social radicalism.[3] Stoicism was not born to be the congenial appanage to an imperial society it became after encountering the Roman aristocracy. The Early Stoa, from its founding by Zeno around 300 B.C.E. through the death of Chrysippus in 207 B.C.E., espoused several radical doctrines regarding politics, slavery, sexual morality, and religion, argued on the charac-

2. Latin conveniently distinguishes between the power or authority a person possesses as an individual, *auctoritas,* and the legal or constitutional power conferred upon him, *potestas.* The former is closer to "influence" or "clout" in English.

3. A useful introduction to and survey of Stoicism is found in A. A. Long, *Hellenistic Philosophy: Stoics, Epicureans, Sceptics,* 2d ed. (Berkeley and Los Angeles, 1986), 107–222. See also J. M. Rist, *Stoic Philosophy* (Cambridge, 1969); A. Erskine, *The Hellenistic Stoa: Political Thought and Action* (Ithaca, N.Y., 1990); and, in full detail, M. Pohlenz, *Die Stoa: Geschichte einer geistigen Bewegung,* 2 vols., 4th ed. with corrections and additions by H.-J. Johann (Göttingen, 1970). R. MacMullen, *Enemies of the Roman Order: Treason, Unrest, and Alienation in the Empire* (Cambridge, Mass., 1966), chap. 2, 46–94, provides a good survey of the issues relevant to Stoicism discussed in this work. See also the bibliographical notes at the beginning of Chapter 2. For a good, brief review of philosophy in general in this period, see B. P. Reardon, *Courants littéraires grecs des IIe et IIIe siècles après J.-C.,* Annales littéraires de l'Université de Nantes 3 (Paris, 1971), 31–61, and J. M. André, "Les Ecoles philosophiques aux deux premiers siècles de l'Empire," *ANRW* II.36.1 (1978): 5–77.

teristically Stoic bases of nature and reason. Zeno had once been the pupil of the Cynic Crates, and the Early Stoa approved and assimilated doctrines that would continue to characterize Cynicism: complete independence of the wise man from outside authority, manifest indifference to social conventions, and rational skepticism regarding the gods. With the advent of the Middle Stoa under the teachings of Panaetius (c. 185– 109 B.C.E.), the school began a drastic shift toward social respectability, and the radical teachings of the earlier period were forgotten, or remained only as a source of embarrassment. Attempts were even made to expurgate Zeno's writings.[4]

Whereas the dominant virtue in Cynicism had been the courage of one's beliefs, and in Early Stoicism the wisdom to discern the true workings of nature and reason, with Panaetius a new emphasis appears on *sophrosyne* (sobriety, discretion, self-control), which came to be identified with *decorum* in the Latin ethical vocabulary. To the sacrifice of traditional Stoic ethics, Panaetius presented his philosophical system in a form that recommended itself to the ethical traditions, moral sense, and practical reason of the new masters of his world—the Roman aristocrats with whom he associated.[5]

This work of revisionism was further advanced by Posidonius (c. 135–c. 51–50 B.C.E.), a friend of Cicero and Pompey. The earlier belief in the perfectibility of the human person, based on a unitary concept of the soul, was discarded. Posidonius abandoned the earlier explanation of human frailty and error as a weakness or defect in reason, which had been the sole attribute of the soul, and posited instead an active conflict between two elements within the soul: reason and passion. Given this conflict, no human action could ever be morally perfect. It therefore became the obligation of the individual not to aim at perfection, but to perform the duties nature set out before him to the best of his ability. For this reason, the good man will not change the rules of his life or society decreed by nature, but rather obey them all the more strictly. After Posidonius, Stoicism tends to degenerate into mere moralizing.[6]

Coming into the second century, Epictetus (c. 55–c. 135 C.E.) could thus state that the first and foremost area of philosophy lay in the prac-

4. Rist, *Stoic Philosophy,* 79ff. Erskine, 211–14 (appendix), gives a brief biography of Panaetius, with careful citations from the sources.

5. P. Scipio Aemilianus and, through him, P. Rutilius Rufus, C. Laelius, Q. Aelius Tubero, and Q. Mucius Scaevola; E. V. Arnold, *Roman Stoicism* (Cambridge, 1911), 103, 381–84. See Erskine, 150–80, on the place of Stoicism in Late Republican policy and politics.

6. Rist, *Stoic Philosophy,* 201–18. For a discussion of the relation of Panaetius's and Posidonius's teachings to the development of Stoic asceticism, see M.-O. Goulet-Cazé, *L'Ascèse Cynique: Un Commentaire de Diogène Laërce VI 70–71,* Histoire des doctrines de l'antiquité classique 10 (Paris, 1986), 172–82.

tical application of its principles and that all theorizing merely serves this highest purpose and end (*Ench.* 52.1). A philosophical doctrine could hardly be found more congenial to the notoriously practical Romans. Indeed, the transplanting of Stoicism to aristocratic Roman soil resulted in the unquestioning acceptance of the customs of the upper class, customs that were, after all, the lot nature had accorded to them. Practices of social etiquette became subjects of moral precepts; the Romans made duties of their own conventions. The use of Stoic doctrines and the weight of the Latin term *officium* (duty as an ethical imperative) turned traditions and social and political functions into moral obligations, and the so traditionally Roman veneration of the "ancestral ways" (*mores antiqui*) into the foundation of philosophy.[7] In defining the work of the philosopher, Epictetus gives equal weight to accepting the will of fate free from pain, fear, and perturbation and to maintaining the social relationships of son, father, brother, citizen, wife, neighbor, fellow-traveler, ruler, and subject (*Epict. Diss.* II.xiv.8). Even in the sphere of religion, the skepticism of Early Stoicism was replaced with support of traditional religion, so that Roman Stoics felt a particular pride in their city's devotion to piety. L. Annaeus Cornutus (c. 20–66 C.E.) sealed this development in his *Summary of the Traditions Concerning Greek Mythology,* in which he reconciles the ancient myths with Stoic doctrine by means of etymology and allegory.[8]

Stoicism not only provided a rationalization of Roman traditions and mores, but a justification for the Roman Empire itself.[9] The Early Stoic position was that empire was a form of slavery, an unjust imposition of rule of one set of rational human beings over another. This position began to change in the mid-second century B.C.E., again with Panaetius. He was the first Greek intellectual to offer a philosophical justification for the Roman Empire. Essentially he argued that the rule of Rome was that of the better over the weaker, and therefore natural, exercised in the best interests of its subjects, therefore rational. How well this argument could validate and merge with Rome's own view of her historic role and destiny is seen in that "sacred text" of empire:

Remember, Roman, that you are to rule the nations with authority.
These will be your arts: to impose the ways of peace,
To spare the vanquished, to cast down the proud.[10]

7. P. A. Brunt, "Stoicism and the Principate," *PBSR* 43, n.s. 30 (1975): 12–16.
8. Arnold, 112, 233f.
9. Erskine, 192–204, with discussion of the history of scholarship on the topic and bibliographical notes. See 215–23 for useful general bibliography.

10. tu regere imperio populos, Romane, memento

Epictetus further illustrates how far Stoicism had come from any practical application of its earlier contention that the wise man must be genuinely autonomous and, therefore, the only true "king." In defining the calling of a citizen, this Stoic freedman states that all must be done in reference to the whole of the state, and that the individual must never act for the sake of personal gain or detached from social responsibility. This accords with nature, for just as the whole is more sovereign than the part, so the state is more sovereign than the individual citizen (*Epict. Diss.* II.x.5).

E. V. Arnold gives a succinct, if unflattering, description of the development of Stoicism after Panaetius and Posidonius: "The door is thrown open for convention, opportunism, and respectability. The daring moral theories and bold paradoxes of the founders of Stoicism tend to disappear from sight, and are replaced by shrewd good sense and worldly wisdom."[11] No scholar doubts that Stoicism in this period had fallen from the intellectual vigor and fervor of its youth. It would however be incorrect, if not sanctimonious, to label Stoics after Panaetius and Posidonius either hypocrites or opportunists. On the surface of it, there is as much to be said for a philosophy that addresses the pursuit of moral action in the world as it exists, as for one that seeks to change the world. If nothing else, Stoicism in its middle and later Roman periods, concentrating as it did on practical moral action, offered a stunning rebuke to those critics of philosophy who, since Aristophanes' *Clouds,* viewed the discipline simply as the pursuit of arcane and irrelevant knowledge.

There is also another side to the evolution of Stoicism that must be taken into account, both for the sake of fair representation and for an understanding of those formed by its principles. In retreating from radical social doctrine and theory and placing emphasis on practical morality, Stoicism shifted the emphasis in philosophy from—to use broad definitions—politics to psychology. Focus is drawn away from externals, such as the social and political structure, and placed on the internal dynamics of the individual: motivation, intent, integrity, and self-possession. The chief concern of Roman Stoicism was with individual ethics and with the individual per se.[12] It is only through an appreciation

---

(hae tibi erunt artes), pacique imponere morem,
parcere subiectis et debellare superbos (*Aeneid* VI.851–53).

11. Arnold, 303.

12. Rist, *Stoic Philosophy,* 92. This corresponds to an even broader cultural movement in this period that M. Foucault identifies as a new emphasis on "the care of the self"; see *The History of Sexuality,* vol. 3, *The Care of the Self,* trans. R. Hurley (New York, 1986), 29–68.

of this emphasis that the Stoics can be judged on their own terms, and
the careers of a Seneca in the first century or a Marcus Aurelius in the
second—men who pursued philosophy from the heights of wealth and
power—be understood.[13]

Philosophy in Opposition and Opposition to Philosophy

Not all schools of philosophy were so accommodating to the Roman
order as Stoicism, nor did all Stoics simply acquiesce in every action of
the political authorities. Philosophers provided a source of political resistance to the emperors, most notably to Nero and the Flavians in the
last half of the first century. This resistance accounts, in part, for political authorities' suspicion of ascetics, many of whom were or affected
the appearance of being philosophers.[14]

The Pisonian conspiracy against Nero, in 65 C.E., and its aftermath
offer the most eminent example. As depicted in Tacitus, *Ann.* XV.48–
XVI.34, the growing opposition, for a variety of reasons, to Nero's
tyranny and personal excesses coalesced around Gaius Calpurnius Piso,
and a plot was hatched to kill the emperor. This was uncovered and, as
a result, Nero lashed out against all his opponents, especially those vo-
cal critics who professed allegiance to the Stoic school.[15] Tacitus does
not connect most of these men directly with the conspiracy, seeking
instead to portray them as (relatively) innocent victims of imperial cru-
elty and martyrs to philosophy, though there can be little doubt of their
involvement at some level. The Stoic *eques* Musonius Rufus was sent
into exile, as Tacitus states, because of his distinction as a philosopher
(*Ann.* XV.71). Foremost among the emperor's critics were two Stoic
senators, Thrasea Paetus and Marcius Barea Soranus. In destroying

13. For an insightful, balanced portrait of Seneca and the apparent contradictions in his
life and career, see M. T. Griffin, *Seneca: A Philosopher in Politics* (Oxford, 1976), esp.
175ff.; also S. Dill, *Roman Society from Nero to Marcus Aurelius*, 2d ed. (London, 1905),
294–333, with copious references to the ancient sources.

14. See MacMullen, *Enemies*, 46–94, and D. R. Dudley, *A History of Cynicism from
Diogenes to the Sixth Century* (London, 1937), 125–41.

15. Those who suffered execution or exile include: Seneca and his nephew, the writer
Lucan; Persius and his teacher Verginius Flavus; Annaeus Cornutus, teacher to both Lucan and Persius; Musonius Rufus and his pupil, Rubellius Plautus, with three of
Rubellius's relatives; Thrasea Paetus, his daughter, her husband Helvidius Priscus, and
another relative, Anteius Rufus; Barea Soranus, his son-in-law Annius Pollio, and the
latter's brother.

these men, Tacitus writes, Nero aimed at the destruction of virtue itself (XVI.21). In a speech the historian puts into the mouth of the vindictive Cossutianus Capito, Thrasea's opposition is likened to that of Cato and Brutus—unflatteringly, since the reprobate Capito deprecates those paragons of Republican political virtue (XVI.22). Charges were also brought against Thrasea's son-in-law, Helvidius Priscus, also a Stoic (Tac., *Hist.* IV.5). He was sent into exile. Yet all the aristocratic Stoics did not present a united front. Soranus's prosecutor, Publius Egnatius Celer, professed the school as well (*Ann.* XVI.32).

Resistance continued under the Flavians, partly as a senatorial vendetta. Upon his return from exile under Galba, Helvidius proceeded to impeach Thrasea's prosecutor, Eprius Marcellus (*Hist.* IV.6) while, later, Musonius secured the conviction of Publius Celer (*Hist.* IV.40). Helvidius, in his own right, became a vociferous critic of Vespasian (Dio LXV.12.2). Exiled once again, he was ultimately executed under the same emperor in 74 C.E. (Suet., *Dom.* 10; Tac., *Agr.* 45). Under Domitian, two other Stoic aristocrats were executed on a charge of *maiestas,* ostensibly for lionizing the resistance: Q. Arulenus Iunius Rusticus, who wrote an account of Thrasea's death, and Herennius Senecio, the author of an account of the death of Priscus.[16] Philosophical opposition had thus become "canonized," and philosophers in general were repeatedly banned from Rome under the Flavians.[17]

The alliance between Stoicism and the Roman aristocracy blurs the issues involved here. From Tacitus's own narrative, it is clear that Nero's opponents possessed various motives, and that the philosophical doctrine they espoused may not have been a deciding factor, even among those opponents who professed Stoicism. The familial and political connections among the various parties, and the systematic prosecution of their enemies, presents an appearance of factional infighting among the aristocracy more than a philosophical struggle for principle. Certainly Tacitus's own bias is to portray the history of the period as a trial of strength between the emperor and the senate, so that the degree to which the opposition was motivated by their being members of the political aristocracy, as opposed to being Stoics, cannot be determined. This is true of the aristocratic Stoic opposition as a whole. D. R. Dudley has rightly pointed to the twofold nature of the opposition to the emperors, noting that senators of republican sympathies were generally put to death while philosophers (both Stoics and Cynics) and lesser aristo-

16. Rusticus: Tac., *Agr.* 2; Suet., *Dom.* 10; Dio LXVII.13.2. Senecio: Tac., *Agr.* 2, 45; Pliny, *Ep.* III.11.3, VII.19.5; Dio LXVII.13.2.
17. Dio LXV.13, LXVII.13; Tac., *Agr.* 3; Pliny, *Ep.* III.11.

crats were usually exiled. Dudley holds that this difference in the punishment accorded these two elements shows how the emperor estimated
the relative degree of danger they represented.[18] That philosophers were
perceived as dangerous seems certainly to be true, but it is important to
remember that the heart of this danger lay in their providing dangerous
ideas to dangerous men, that is, to the senatorial aristocracy who possessed the resources to take effective action.[19]

The consensus among scholars is that the Stoics of this period had no
objections to political authority, or even to monarchy as such, but
rather only to those rulers who could be termed tyrants by virtue of
their conduct.[20] It is in their opposition to tyranny that the aristocratic
Stoic "martyrs" of the first century were quickly turned into heroes.[21]

This is not the case with those perennial champions of classical anarchy, the Cynics. Though far less influential, and certainly less respectable, than their counterparts from the Stoa, the Cynics were often the
loudest critics of authority of any kind.[22] The Cynic Demetrius was a
contemporary of Thrasea and Helvidius. Praised by Seneca for his strict
asceticism (*Ep.* 20.9), he was exiled after declaiming publicly against
the luxury of Nero's new baths (Philostr., *VA* IV.42). Apparently re-
called at Vespasian's accession, he appears in Rome in 70 C.E. in the
curious position of defending Publius Celer against Helvidius's prosecution (Tac., *Hist.* IV.40). Exiled again under Vespasian's ban on philosophers, he reappears in an anecdote from Suetonius, being rude and abusive to the emperor responsible for his unwilling departure from the
capital (*Vesp.* 13). Two Cynics in the reign of Titus, Vespasian's son,
publicly condemned his relationship with Berenice. One was flogged,
the other executed (Dio LXV.15.4). Dio Chrysostom, in exile at the
time and styling himself a Cynic, is credited with being active in plots
against Domitian (Philostr., *VS* 488).

One philosopher persecuted by both Nero and Domitian merits particular consideration: the Pythagorean Apollonius of Tyana, to whom a

18. Dudley, 128. See also the analysis of the Stoic opposition in M. T. Griffin, *Nero: The End of a Dynasty* (New Haven, 1985), 164–77.

19. MacMullen, *Enemies,* 46, 70.

20. Arnold, 396f.; MacMullen, *Enemies,* 62f.; Brunt, "Stoicism," 9.

21. The distinction is not merely semantic, for in the next century a Stoic monarch would himself cite Thrasea and Helvidius as exemplars in his own political education and place them, as Tacitus did, among the company of Cato and Brutus; see M. Aurelius, *Med.* I.14.

22. See Chapter 3, pages 61–64. Brunt, "Stoicism," 29, has suggested that one element involved in the downfall of Thrasea was a deliberate misrepresentation of his philosophical beliefs, claiming that his Stoic devotion to so-called liberty was but a cover for Cynic anarchy.

lengthy portion of this work is devoted. Hearkening, no doubt, to the models of the first-century Stoics, Philostratus declares that the conduct of philosophers under tyranny is the surest test of their character (*VA* VII.1). To adumbrate an important theme in Apollonius, Philostratus states that Nero was antagonistic to philosophy because he suspected its devotees of being addicted to magic, and of being diviners in disguise (IV.35). Accusations of magic and divination had also entered into the trial of Soranus (Tac., *Ann.* XVI.31). To "give witness" to philosophy, even to the point of martyrdom, Apollonius enters Rome despite warnings (*VA* IV.36 and 38). While in the city, however, he does not openly criticize the emperor (IV.43), and is ultimately released after questioning by the magistrate (IV.44).

Apollonius encounters two other philosophers while in the city. The Cynic Demetrius, a relentless critic of emperors soon to be exiled by Nero (*VA* IV.42) and later again by Vespasian (Dio LXV.13.1–3), disobeyed Nero's ban and came to Rome specifically to court Apollonius's approval (*VA* IV.42). Apollonius also exchanged letters with Musonius Rufus, who was languishing in prison at the time (IV.46). As no confrontation, or even meeting, with Nero occurs, it appears that this episode serves only to establish Apollonius's credentials as the respected equal of those philosophers persecuted by Nero, even if he himself did not suffer. This attests to the power these figures of resistance still retained at the time of Philostratus's writing, nearly two centuries later. In the *VA*, this episode serves merely as a prelude to the real test Apollonius would undergo with another emperor.

Domitian is Apollonius's true nemesis, but in this case it is not only the emperor who takes the offensive against the philosopher. Apollonius himself is credited with stirring up rebellion in the senate, among provincial governors, and at the Panathenaic Festival (*VA* VII.4). He is portrayed as an active partisan, and again journeys to Rome of his own will to confront the emperor, even before the warrant for his arrest could be served (VII.10). Apollonius is brought to trial. A familiar motif recurs as he is accused of magic, specifically of performing divinatory rites regarding Domitian's future and Nerva's chances for the throne (VII.11–15). With some justification, the philosopher is also accused of actively plotting with the latter. At one point, an imperial official reveals Domitian's real motive in bringing Apollonius to trial—to gain evidence for condemning certain consulars for conspiracy (VII.18). Later, Domitian himself confirms this to Apollonius privately (VII.32f.). As in the case of the Stoic opposition to Nero, the persecution of philosophers was merely an adjunct to the prosecution of the emperor's real enemies, aristocrats who enjoyed the moral and political support of these intellectuals.

The political leaders of the second century had ample precedent in the immediate past for suspecting the political motives of philosophers. The latter became associated with, even symbols of, political opposition. Though effective political change always remained in the hands of the aristocracy, philosophers were ready at hand to provide the intellectual justification for such a change. Apollonius himself had done so for the "good" emperor Vespasian upon his assuming the purple (*VA* V.35f.). Philosophers were also easier targets for a suspicious monarch to hit, lacking the social status and political and military power of their senatorial opponents.

The imperial court was not the only place philosophers could prove unpopular. In broader and less exalted social circles, the issue was not so much resistance to authority as censure of commonly accepted behavior, either in the howling diatribe of the Cynic or the haughty reserve of the Stoic.[23] Seneca advised the student of philosophy not to flout social conventions (*publici mores*), lest philosophy become even less popular among the people than it already was (*Ep.* 14.14; cf. 73.1 and Epict., *Ench.* 32.8–36). Dio, speaking approvingly of their banishment in 71 C.E., states that philosophers despise everyone alike, calling the wellborn a mollycoddle, the lowborn a half-wit, the handsome immoral, the ugly simple, the rich grasping, and the poor servile (LXV.13.1). Lucian, whose opinion of the philosophers of his day was notoriously low, believed that most were simply too confused to help the common man.[24] Epictetus could baldly declare: "If you yearn for philosophy, prepare at once to meet ridicule" (*Ench.* 22; cf. *Epict. Diss.* III.xv.10f., IV.viii.9). In general, he advises his reader never to call himself a philosopher in public and to keep his philosophical principles to himself (*Ench.* 46).

Far from being a member of a profession bringing automatic esteem, the devotee of philosophy in this period carries an aura of suspicion. Some could be lionized, such as Thrasea and Helvidius, for their courage in opposing tyranny, but most—to take Epictetus at his word— would find their profession unwelcome. Second-century ascetics, many of whom styled themselves philosophers, faced a society that already held a prejudice against them. If, in turn, they compounded this with an ostentatious asceticism and novelties of social and religious doctrine,

23. Brunt, "Stoicism," 8.
24. From the numerous occurrences throughout Lucian's works, see especially *Menippus* 3–4 and *Philosophies for Sale* 20.

further alienating them from the mores of their society, an even harsher judgment could be expected.

Musonius Rufus and Epictetus

One of the Stoic heroes themselves has handed down a detailed ascetical teaching: Musonius Rufus (before 30 to before 101–2 c.e.), whom Nero and Vespasian exiled. Musonius taught Epictetus (c. 55–c. 135 c.e.) who, in turn, framed his own teaching, which profoundly influenced the thought of Marcus Aurelius. Significantly, it was the same Rusticus responsible for teaching Aurelius ascetical restraint who introduced him to Epictetus's writings (*Med.* I.7). These Stoics established the definition of asceticism held by the adherents of that philosophy which dominated the intellectual life of the educated and ruling classes of the time and, thereby, its definition among the representatives of social and cultural authority.

Musonius himself is just such a representative, a public figure and conspicuous participant in public life, actively concerned with the problems of his day. As an aristocrat, he does not disapprove of the accepted conventions of civilized life; but as a Stoic, he criticizes the waste and extravagance that seemed to characterize the members of his class.[25] Yielding neither to passive pessimism nor to invective, his philosophical doctrine recommended a positive approach to creating a morally healthy, rational individual and society.[26]

This positive approach is particularly evident in his treatise *On Askesis* (περὶ ἀσκήσεως). Musonius defines asceticism as the practical application of the lessons of philosophy: "Therefore upon the learning of the lessons appropriate to each and every excellence, practical training (ἄσκησιν) must follow invariably, if indeed from the lessons we have learned we hope to derive any benefit" (Musonius, VI; Lutz, 52).[27] This is a particular necessity in philosophy, since in other professions the mind is not corrupted beforehand by being taught the opposite of

---

25. C. E. Lutz, "Musonius Rufus: 'The Roman Socrates,'" *Yale Classical Studies* 10, ed. A. R. Bellinger (New Haven, 1947), 116–27. For further background, see Lutz's introduction; R. Laurenti, "Musonio, maestro di Epitteto," *ANRW* II.36.3 (1989): 2105–46; and A. C. van Geytenbeek, *Musonius Rufus and Greek Diatribe*, rev. ed., trans. B. L. Hijmans (Assen, 1963), esp. 96–123 on asceticism.

26. Lutz, 24 and 29 n. 128.

27. Translation by C. Lutz; all subsequent translations are taken from this edition. The text is that of Lutz, largely following that of O. Hense, *C. Musonii Rufi reliquiae* (Leipzig, 1905).

what it will need to learn. Philosophy, therefore, requires greater application (*askesis*). Musonius offers a summary of this sort of practice: "The person who is in training (τὸν ἀσκοῦντα) must strive to habituate himself not to love pleasure, not to avoid hardship, not to be infatuated with living, not to fear death, and in the case of goods or money not to place receiving before giving" (VI; 56). The overall impression is rather mild. The ideal is one of hard work and self-discipline, a "stoic" ideal in the popular sense of the term, equivalent to traditional Roman *sobrietas*.

It is important to note that emphasis here is on internal attitude rather than external practice; the essence of ascetic training lies in love, aversion, fear, and desire. The focus is more on the disposition of the mind (or soul, ψυχή) and less on that of the body (σῶμα). Musonius, in fact, distinguishes between two types of asceticism: one concerns both mind and body, the other is particular to the mind alone.[28]

> Now there are two kinds of training (ἀσκήσεως), one which is appropriate for the soul alone, and the other which is common to both soul and body. We use the training (ἄσκησις) common to both when we discipline ourselves to cold, heat, thirst, hunger, meagre rations, hard beds, avoidance of pleasures, and patience under suffering. . . . Training (ἄσκησις) which is peculiar to the soul consists first of all in seeing that the proofs pertaining to apparent goods as not being real goods are always ready at hand and likewise those pertaining to apparent evils as not being real evils, and in learning to recognize the things which are truly good and in becoming accustomed to distinguish them from what are not truly good. In the next place it consists of practice in not avoiding any of the things which only seem evil, and in not pursuing any of those things which only seem good; in shunning by every means those which are truly evil and in pursuing by every means those which are truly good. (VI; 54)

The value of those practices that apply to both mind and body, tolerance of privation and patience under suffering, lies in the discipline they give to the mind. Physical hardship is not a good in and of itself, but only in the lessons it teaches the mind—through the body—that "not all apparent evils are evil." Nor does it appear that such physical deprivation is to be deliberately sought out as a permanent feature of life. It is even possible to construe this asceticism of mind and body as a temporary period of training for the neophyte philosopher, to be pursued

28. See also Laurenti, 2113–19.

only until the mind is sufficiently trained to look upon externals with indifference. Seneca had recommended just this sort of temporary physical training for youth, to inculcate the lesson that physical deprivation cannot harm the soul.[29]

The important *askesis* is that of the mind; without it, physical asceticism is pointless. Immediately before distinguishing between the two types of asceticism, Musonius states: "Since it so happens that the human being is not soul alone, nor body alone, but a kind of synthesis of the two, the person in training (τὸν ἀσκοῦντα) must take care of both, the better part, the soul, more zealously, as is fitting, but also of the other, if he shall not be found lacking in any part that constitutes man" (VI; 55). Asceticism is, thus, primarily a mental and moral discipline, a matter of knowledge and ethics that consists in training the mind to discern true good from true evil and to act accordingly.

The profession of the philosopher does not lie in externals, and there is no need for the practitioner to wrap himself in the traditional worn cloak (*tribon*), go without a tunic underneath, grow his hair, or deviate from the ordinary appearance of the average person (XVI; 106). Emphasis on internal discipline thus also offers a rationale for social conformity, or at least the avoidance of those practices that set the philosopher apart and make him a target for derision.

Moderation is the hallmark for Musonius. While he believed that "the beginning and foundation of temperance (τοῦ σωφρονεῖν) lay in self-control (ἐγκράτειαν) in eating and drinking," his recommendations are far from extreme. With regard to food, the reasons for moderation are physiological: a vegetarian diet is natural to human beings, while eating meat is bestial and its heaviness hinders the mind (XVIIIA and B; 112f. and 116). So too with regard to clothing and shelter, simplicity is more healthful and more practical; it is also more commendable, since money spent on luxury is better given to help one's fellow citizens (XIX; 120–23). In asceticism, the practice of "decorum and moderation" (κόσμου τε καὶ μέτρου) is essential (XIX; 120).[30]

Some elements of Musonius's teaching, however, could appear subversive or radical. One deals directly with authority: "Whether one's father or the archon or even the tyrant orders something wrong or unjust or shameful, and one does not carry out that order, he is in no way disobeying, inasmuch as he does no wrong nor fails of doing right. He only disobeys who disregards and refuses to carry out good and honor-

29. *Ep.* 18.5–13.
30. Musonius's ideal here is a traditional one of "simplicity" or "having few needs" (ὀλιγόδεια); see Geytenbeek, 112ff. Note also how Musonius invokes traditional civic benefaction as an argument for simplicity in the previous citation.

able and useful orders" (XVI; 103). This is the principle that justified opposition to Nero, Vespasian, and Domitian. Emperors, at least, would consider such a doctrine dangerous.

Musonius also enunciates the principle that sexual intercourse is justified only in the context of marriage and for the purpose of begetting children (XII; 86). Such constraint is rare, and radical, in antiquity. At the same time, however, Musonius makes clear that marriage itself constitutes no disability to leading the philosophical life. In fact, it is a positive benefit. The philosopher must lead in all things according to nature, and marriage is manifestly according to nature. Marriage is the foundation of the state; thus anyone who destroys marriage destroys the whole human race (XIV; 92; cf. XIIIA–XV; 88–101). Though perhaps prudish on the subject of sex, Musonius clearly upholds the classical dictum that many children are good for both the individual and the state (XV; p. 96–101).[31]

Another seemingly radical doctrine is Musonius's insistence that women, too, should study philosophy (III–IV; 38–49). Though revolutionary at face value, this recommendation should not be pressed too far. It is superfluous to teach women skill in public speaking and adroitness in argumentation, since they will only use philosophy in their traditional roles (εἴπερ φιλοσοφήσουσιν ὡς γυναῖκες), and not shrink from their duties and run off practicing speeches and acting like sophists (IV; 49). Philosophy will make a woman a better housekeeper, more economical, more chaste and self-controlled, a blameless life-partner, wife, and mother, "willing to serve her husband with her own hands, and willing to do things which some would consider no better than slave's work" (III; 38–42). So much for the revolution.

Epictetus shows himself the apt pupil of his teacher in articulating

31. Much recent work has been done on the Roman family: see B. Rawson, ed., *The Family in Ancient Rome: New Perspectives* (Ithaca, N.Y., 1986); K. R. Bradley, *Discovering the Roman Family: Studies in Roman Social History* (New York, 1991); and S. Treggiari, *Roman Marriage: Iusti Coniuges from the Time of Cicero to the Time of Ulpian* (Oxford, 1991). Arnold, 347ff., would see movement here toward an ideal of chastity among Stoics generally; his argument is overstated and incorrect. R. Lane Fox, *Pagans and Christians* (New York, 1987), 349, validly raises the simple, practical question as to whether anyone outside a narrow philosophical circle ever listened to such moralizing about sex. See also the seminal work of M. Foucault, *The History of Sexuality*, vol. 3, *The Care of the Self*, which concentrates on the second century and the writers discussed in this work, esp. 72–80, 150–85. A brief, general summary of pagan Roman attitudes toward marriage, sex, and bearing children may be found in P. R. L. Brown, *The Body and Society: Men, Women, and Sexual Renunciation in Early Christianity* (New York, 1988), 5–32. For a recent introduction to the topic of family life, see P. Veyne, ed., *A History of Private Life*, vol. 1, *From Pagan Rome to Byzantium*, trans. A. Goldhammer (Cambridge, Mass., 1987).

similar definitions of asceticism.[32] For him, too, *askesis* involves the practical application of the lessons of philosophy, but he distinguishes it from mere "practice": "Because of this, the philosophers enjoin not to be content with learning alone, but to add to it practice (μελέτην) and then training" (ἄσκησιν, *Epict. Diss.* II.ix.13). The term conveys the sense of a "drill," that is, a more intense, regular, and specific form of exercise: "It is necessary to set up an opposite habit to this habit, and where it is a matter of slippery sense-perceptions, there training exercise (τὸ ἀσκητικόν) must be set in opposition" (III.xii.6). The examples Epictetus then gives make the meaning clear. If one is inclined to pleasure, *askesis* should take the form of bodily mortification; if one is inclined to avoid hard work, his *askesis* should be strenuous labor (III.xii.7–12). Asceticism is thus defined as a physical discipline that aids in the correction of a mental attitude: "Who then is the one in training (ἀσκητής)? The one who practices not feeling desire (ὀρέξει) and practices developing aversion (ἐκκλίσει) only to those things that lay within his moral choice, especially those things that can be attained only with a great deal of toil" (III.xii.8).[33] Epictetus also gives the impression that this sort of physical drill is characteristic of the beginner in philosophy (III.xii.12). In discussing practice and drill, Epictetus makes a fundamental distinction between true philosophers and those who mouth and teach its principles without putting them into practice. Against these latter sham philosophers, Epictetus pours out invective.[34]

Yet, even though training or drill must be present, it must never take exaggerated forms. This is the first principle of Epictetus's own treatise *On Askesis* (*Epict. Diss.* III.xii): "Training exercises (τὰς ἀσκήσεις)

32. See B. L. Hijmans, *ΑΣΚΗΣΙΣ: Notes on Epictetus' Educational System,* Wejsgerige teksten en studies 2 (Assen, 1959), esp. 64–91. An excellent annotated bibliography and survey of scholarship on Epictetus can be found in J. Hershbell, "The Stoicism of Epictetus: Twentieth Century Perspectives," *ANRW* II.36.3 (1989): 2148–63.

33. The Greek term τὰ προαιρετικά, translated here as "moral choice," has a precise technical meaning in the Stoic vocabulary and is difficult to render in English. Basically, it refers not simply to having the power to choose generally, but to the uniquely human faculty of making *moral* choices and decisions. The first step in this is to determine whether the matter involves a moral choice between good and evil or whether it is outside of it (τὰ ἀπροαίρετα) and, therefore, indifferent (*Ep. Diss.* III.iii.14–19, III.viii). Inevitably, matters of moral choice are internal; that is, matters of will and the state of mind with which one confronts the whole of reality outside the self (I.i.7–28, I.iv.18–27, I.xxx). Thus, what lies outside this realm are "externals" (ἔξω). The essence of moral choice lies in the discipline of the fundamental dynamics of the will; namely, desire and aversion, and in their application only to their proper objects of moral choice. See Hijmans, 24–27 and 64–68.

34. *Epict. Diss.* IV.viii, II.xix.20–28, and II.ix.20f., where he colorfully refers to such philosophers as "counterfeit Jews."

must not be performed which are opposed to nature and aberrant, since then we who call ourselves philosophers would be in no way different from wonderworkers (III.xii.1)."[35] The statement is of cardinal importance. First, it makes clear that the performance of ostentatious feats of physical asceticism is unbecoming to a philosopher (cf. III.xii.3). Second, it characterizes such performance as typical of "wonderworkers" (θαυματοποιῶν), evoking images of the wandering prophets, magicians, and demagogues who were the standard-bearers of dissidence and subversion in the second century. Here is the first evidence connecting these figures with the practice of rigorous physical asceticism. As seen in Aurelius, the connection concerns display. The "wondrous feats" of the mountebank or the ascetic manifest extraordinary personal power and demand attention. Epictetus has no time for either ascetical severity or ostentation.[36] Any form of physical asceticism must not be undertaken for the sake of display: "Should you wish to engage in harsh practices (ἀσκῆσαί ποτε πρὸς πόνον), do so for yourself and not for others" (Ench. 47; cf. Epict. Diss. III.xiv.4–6).

Epictetus does not make Musonius's distinction between an askesis of mind and body and that of the mind alone. His use of the term applies to both physical and mental disciplines equally. (His use of the word above has been exclusively connected with physical practices.) Yet it is just as clear that, as with Musonius, the internal, mental aspects are of greater importance and give meaning to the physical discipline: "In conclusion, whatever disciplines are practiced upon the body by those engaged in exercise may themselves be considered training, provided they are concerned with desire and aversion in some way. If, however, they are concerned with display, they indicate one who has turned outward from himself and is hunting for something else, seeking spectators who will proclaim: 'Oh, what a great man!'" (Epict. Diss. III.xii.16f.).[37] Those who undertake physical disciplines (τῶν γυμναζόντων) practice askesis (τὰ ἀσκητικά), only if their exercises touch upon the dynamics of the mind (desire and aversion—πρὸς ὄρεξιν καὶ ἔκκλισιν, the same impulses characteristic of Musonius's askesis of the soul). It is the inter-

---

35. τὰς ἀσκήσεις οὐ δεῖ διὰ τῶν παρὰ φύσιν καὶ παραδόξων ποιεῖσθαι, ἐπεί τοι τῶν θαυματοποιῶν οὐδὲν διοίσομεν οἱ λέγοντες φιλοσοφεῖν.

36. Such as throwing one's arms about statues in winter (III.xii.2 and Ench. 47; cf. Diogenes Laertius VI.23). Epictetus also devotes an entire discourse to cleanliness (IV.xi), castigating "philosophers" who refuse to bathe or make themselves socially presentable.

37. καὶ λοιπὸν ὅσα τῷ σώματι προσάγεται ὑπὸ τῶν γυμναζόντων αὐτό, ἂν μὲν ὧδέ που ῥέπῃ πρὸς ὄρεξιν καὶ ἔκκλισιν, εἴη ἂν καὶ αὐτὰ ἀσκητικά· ἂν δὲ πρὸς ἐπίδειξιν, ἔξω νενευκότος ἐστὶ καὶ ἄλλο τι θηρωμένου καὶ θεατὰς ζητοῦντος τοὺς ἐροῦντας "ὦ μεγάλου ἀνθρώπου."

nal aspects that give definition to the external. This is clearly stated in another passage where, after elaborating the internal dynamics of resisting base temptations, Epictetus defines the true ascetic: "That one is truly in training who exercises himself against such impressions" (*Epict. Diss.* II.xviii.27).[38]

Unique to Epictetus is his delineation of three areas (*topoi*) of *askesis* that further underscore the overriding importance of internal psychic dynamics (*Ep. Diss.* III.ii.1–6). The first of these areas concerns desire and aversion (τὰς ὀρέξεις καὶ τὰς ἐκκλίσεις). The object is control of the emotions and passions. No feeling becomes unbearable and overwhelms reason unless it stems from a failure of desire to obtain, or of aversion to avoid, its object. By training desire and aversion to keep only to their proper object, moral choice, the tumult of passion is avoided. The second area deals with choice and refusal (τὰς ὁρμὰς καὶ ἀφορμάς) or, in other words, duty (τὸ καθῆκον). Balancing, in a way, emotional control, attention to duty compels the individual not to be "unfeeling" (ἀπαθῆ) like a statue, but to recognize social obligations and ties to the gods, family, and state. The third involves matters to which assent has already been given (τὰς συγκαταθέσεις), and has as its object avoiding error and rashness in judgment. This requires the rigorous testing of all sense impressions; most important, the judgments of the mind that, as we in our age would say, stem from the ego. Put simply and generally, Epictetus sees *askesis* as the control of all impulses, including the will, and its subject as the mind or "ruling reason" (τὸ ἡγεμονικόν).[39]

The way in which the physical may serve this *askesis* of the mind is given in another passage. Here, the purpose of physical discipline is to develop an indifference to the vicissitudes of fate:

> Would you wish me poverty? Bring it on, and you will know what poverty is when the part is played well. Would you wish me power? Bring it on. Would you wish me stripped of power? Bring it on. But what if you wish me suffering? Bring suffering on too. But what if you wish me exile? Wherever I go it will be well with me, for it is so here where I am. It is well with me not because of the place where I am, but because of my beliefs, which I am certain to carry with me since no one is able to take

---

38. οὗτός ἐστιν ὁ ταῖς ἀληθείαις ἀσκητής ὁ πρὸς τὰς τοιαύτας φαντασίας γυμνάζων ἑαυτόν. See Hijmans, 78–91, that the objects of *askesis* are entirely internal: desire, grief, fear, duties, passions, etc.

39. Hijmans, 64; *Ep. Diss.* III.iii.1. This concept and term "ruling reason" will play a large part in the discussions in Chapter 2.

these away. They are the only things that are mine and cannot be taken away by any means, and it is sufficient for me to possess them wherever I may go and whatever I may do. (*Epict. Diss.* IV.vii.14)

This indifference is directly connected to the development of the proper internal attitude; it is better to die of hunger free from grief and fear than live richly with a troubled mind (*Ench.* 12.1). It is the mark of the stupid to exercise a great deal of time and effort on the body. The body must be attended to in moderation, but all attention must be focused on the mind (*Ench.* 41).[40] If asceticism turns outward toward externals, it will fail, as Epictetus makes clear in *On Askesis:*

> For since desire (τὴν ὄρεξιν) will not be rightly directed nor will aversion (τὴν ἔκκλισιν) be sure of its step without great and constant *askesis,* realize that if you allow your *askesis* to turn outward towards things that are not proper objects of moral choice, you will have neither your desire successful in its aims nor your aversion on a sure footing. (*Epict. Diss.* III.xii.5)

In terms of day-to-day practice, Epictetus shows himself actually less demanding in his counsels than Musonius. Again, moderation is the rule: "In things that pertain to the body, partake only according to bare necessity of such things as food, drink, clothing, shelter, and household slaves; draw the line at everything which tends to display or luxury" (*Ench.* 33.7). The parameters are quite broad. The same is true regarding sex: "Be as pure as is within your ability before marriage; and should you indulge, partake in those things which are customary and lawful" (*Ench.* 33.8). Epictetus is adamant regarding marriage and raising children as a social duty (*Epict. Diss.* III.vii.19–23).

Epictetus does more than simply defend traditional social duties, as Musonius had done. He raises them to the level of moral imperatives.

> So also in the case of a man, it is not his physical nature that must be prized, his bits of flesh, but his principles. What are these? Citizenship, marriage, begetting children, worshipping God, caring for parents, in sum, desire, aversion, choice, refusal (ὀρέγεσθαι, ἐκκλίσεις, ὁρμᾶν, ἀφορμᾶν), doing each of these

40. Hijmans, 4f., "Musonius does not despise the body to the same degree as Epictetus seems to do; he does not, as Epictetus, use denigrating expressions for it, but it is on the other hand quite clear, that the body for Epictetus is not in principle a hindrance."

things as they ought to be done, as we were born by nature to do them. (*Epict. Diss.* III.vii.25f.)

The all-important internal dynamics of desire, aversion, choice, etc. are primarily to be exercised in the maintenance of traditional social relationships. The preservation of these relationships is, in and of itself, a good (*Epict. Diss.* III.iii.8). More than that, it is a *duty*—an example of the second area of *askesis* (III.ii.4). Another entire discourse (*Epict. Diss.* II.x) is devoted to determining the nature of individuals' duties precisely from an examination of their social roles: father, son, town-councillor, etc.[41] In this way, Stoicism turned the maintenance of the prevailing social and political order into a command of reason and nature hallowed by the dictates of philosophy.

Stoic teaching set the norms and limits of acceptable ascetical practice in the second century. Because of Stoicism's fundamental emphasis on interior disposition, it defined asceticism less as a discipline of the body than of the mind. Physical practice is certainly required, but gained meaning only as it related to the development of internal discipline. Once such mental discipline was attained, all externals became indifferent and physical exertions, for the most part, lost their significance.[42] Moderation is essential. Rigorous or ostentatious feats of physical discipline are unbecoming to the philosopher, and hold undesirable associations with the sort of wonderworkers and demagogues that, as will be seen later, infested the streetcorners and marketplaces of the second-century empire. Moderation is also the hallmark of the positive practices recommended by this philosophy. The Stoics disparaged extremes of poverty and abstinence, advocating instead avoidance of excess and enslavement to physical desires. Above all, no practices are countenanced that might conflict with traditional social obligations. Along with vigilant self-restraint, it is incumbent upon the philosopher to maintain and uphold his social duties both to his family and his state. Indeed, it is by his ascetical practice that he is able to fulfill these duties more assiduously.

41. This subject will be taken up in greater detail in Chapter 2.
42. See Goulet-Cazé, *L'Ascèse,* 182–90.

Chapter Two

❧

MARCUS AURELIUS

Rational Asceticism and Social Conservatism

IN THE SECOND CENTURY, asceticism ascended to the very apex of Roman society. In contrast to the philosophy-hating tyrannies of Nero and Domitian, Marcus Aurelius ruled with the reputation of a philosopher-king[1] and, to a certain extent, that of an ascetic. Although much has been written examining the precise nature of the emperor's philosophical tenets, the character of his asceticism has remained ill-defined and in need of detailed study.[2]

1. Among pagan sources, both Dio (LXXI.1.1) and the *Historia Augusta* title Aurelius "the philosopher." *HA* M.A. I.1: "A man who pursued philosophy all of his life and who surpassed all rulers in the purity of his life"; *HA* M.A. XXVII.7: "The saying of Plato was always on his lips, that nations flourished if either the philosophers ruled or the rulers pursued philosophy"; cf. XVI.5, XIX.12. Even Christians readily attribute the title to Aurelius: Justin, *1 Apol.* I; Athenagoras, *Leg.* I; and Melito in Eus., *HE* IV.26.9–11, where also Nero and Domitian are singled out specifically as the only emperors who persecuted, while Aurelius is described as holding opinions "both more philanthropic and philosophic" than even the beneficent Hadrian and Pius.

2. For bibliography, see R. Klein, ed., *Marc Aurel.*, Wege der Forschung 50 (Darmstadt, 1979), 503–29, and F. H. Sandbach, *The Stoics*, 2d ed. (Bristol, 1989), 179–82. Establishing a detailed definition of Aurelius's philosophy, beyond matters that touch upon asceticism, would both be redundant and lie outside the scope of this work. Much more so would any discussion of his "personal commitment" to his beliefs. This question

Paradoxically, Aurelius's reputation and that of the entire Antonine period make this task more difficult. Gibbon's characterization set the tone for most of modern scholarship: "But his life was the noblest commentary on the precepts of Zeno. He was severe to himself, indulgent to the imperfections of others, just and beneficent to all mankind." It is not surprising that immediately after his description of Aurelius, Gibbon penned his famous phrase that the Antonine age was "the most happy and prosperous" in human history.[3] Most biographies written about the emperor remain colored by this "Golden Age" *Tendenz*. Concomitant with this romanticization of the age is the denigration or dismissal of any phenomenon contrary to it, including religiosity, mysticism, miracle working, and asceticism.[4] As a result, no satisfactory general framework of the emperor's life and thought exists; it must be built up by examining the *Meditations* in the broader intellectual and social context of their author's life and times.[5]

---

is controversial and, I believe, unanswerable given the nature of the sources. The *Meditations* is not a diary, and any discussion would be based on subjective modern views of what Stoicism or the emperor *ought* to have been. On this, see P. A. Brunt, "Marcus Aurelius in his Meditations," *JRS* 64 (1974): 1–20; P. Hadot, "La Physique comme exercice spirituel ou pessimisme et optimisme chez Marc Aurèle," *Revue de théologie et philosophie* 22 (1972): esp. 239; and R. B. Rutherford, *The Meditations of Marcus Aurelius: A Study* (Oxford, 1989), 8–21. Recent attempts to read personal motivations, engendered by Stoicism, into the historical record include P. Noyen, "Marcus Aurelius the Greatest Practician of Stoicism," *Antiquité Classique* 24 (1955): 372–83; and M. Józefowicz, "Les idées politiques dans la morale stoïcienne de Marc Aurèle," *Eos* 59 (1971): 241–54. Such attempts are well refuted by G. R. Stanton, "Marcus Aurelius, Emperor and Philosopher," *Historia* 18 (1969): 570–87; and Brunt, "Marcus Aurelius." A prudent, well-balanced treatment is given by J. M. Rist, "Are You a Stoic? The Case of Marcus Aurelius," in *Jewish and Christian Self-Definition*, ed. B. F. Meyer and E. P. Sanders (Philadelphia, 1982), 3:23–45.

3. E. Gibbon, *The Decline and Fall of the Roman Empire*, Modern Library (New York, 1932), 69f., 73f.

4. Though revised, A. Birley, *Marcus Aurelius: A Biography*, 2d ed. (New Haven, 1987), still tends to romanticize the emperor. The works of Noyen and Józefowicz are positively apologetic. Ernst Renan, *Marc-Aurèle et la fin du monde antique* (Paris, 1882), most severely disparaged the "superstitious" and "credulous" tendencies of the times in contrast to Aurelius's example of enlightened rationality. Most recently, this opinion has reappeared in Rutherford, 182, 216ff. On the fallacies of the "rationalism vs. superstition" dichotomy in the period, see R. MacMullen, *Paganism in the Roman Empire* (New Haven, 1981), 70–79, and R. Lane Fox, *Pagans and Christians* (New York, 1987), 64f., 76–261 passim. A more balanced view of the age of Aurelius may be found in A. S. L. Farquharson, *Marcus Aurelius: His Life and his World*, ed. D. A. Rees (New York, 1951), 1–12.

5. Pertinent studies include the articles by Stanton, Brunt, and Rist cited above. Other important works are: J. Rist, *Stoic Philosophy* (Cambridge, 1969); P. A. Brunt, "Stoicism and the Principate," *PBSR* 43, n.s. 30 (1975): 7–35; E. V. Arnold, *Roman Stoicism*

Aurelius's asceticism, based upon Stoic principles of psychology, reason, and nature, was profoundly cerebral and markedly deemphasized the physical. At the same time and deriving from the very same principles, Aurelius's social views were equally profound in their conservatism and traditionalism. This presents a seeming contradiction. Though purporting to value ascetical ideals highly, Stoic Romans would have no sympathy with ascetics who were perceived as a threat to the social order. As the espousal of Stoic principles had long been fashionable among the Roman ruling class, Aurelius's attitudes may be taken as representative of that class as a whole. Philosophic principles thus generated both a reverence for asceticism and a justification for the status quo. In doing so, Stoicism drew a clear line at which sympathy for commonly held ideals stopped and the demand for social conformity began.

Aurelius presents a unique case, particularly worthy of study. First of all as emperor, he offers a perspective both of his own aristocratic class and of that intangible entity, the Roman "state," insofar as the perspective of the state can be defined. Second, in preserving for posterity his own musings to himself in the *Meditations,* the emperor allows a glimpse into the workings of his own thoughts, values, and inner contradictions.[6] In addition, E. R. Dodds has argued that the man himself displays an intensity of ascetical feeling, of the unreality of the world, of desolation and even resentment against the physical, uncommon in the classical world.[7] The accuracy of this extreme thesis is questionable. Yet, with the exception of Dodds, Aurelius's asceticism has simply been noted in scholarship, but not discussed in any specific way.

(Cambridge, 1911), though the reader needs to be cautious of his sources and generalizations; and E. R. Dodds, *Pagan and Christian in an Age of Anxiety* (Cambridge, 1965), also with a word of caution. R. B. Rutherford's literary study of the *Meditations* is useful in its descriptions of the broader context of Aurelius's writing, but is often diffuse on topics discussed here and, I believe, simply incorrect in its analysis and conclusions regarding the emperor's asceticism and supposed "world hatred." See P. A. Brunt's authoritative review in *JRS* 80 (1990): 218–19; and M. T. Griffin, *CR*, n.s. 41 (1991): 42–44, who though less critical rightly notes that historians will find fault with Rutherford's work. The specific difficulties in both Dodds and Rutherford will be discussed below.

6. Dodds, *Pagan and Christian,* 8 n. 1: "The personal character of his notebooks makes them better evidence for 'the feelings of the individual man in his solitude' than the letters of Seneca, the essays of Plutarch or the sermons of Epictetus, all of which were designed for a public audience." This is safe to say, but must not be overstated. Hadot, "La Physique," argues throughout that the *Meditations* are a traditional form of Stoic "spiritual exercise" that certainly reflect Aurelius's chosen system of belief but actually give precious little insight into the personal and individual character of the man.

7. Dodds, *Pagan and Christian,* 8, 21, 27f.

Aurelius as an Ascetic

Aurelius himself describes some elements of ascetical practice at the opening of the *Meditations:*

> Simplicity in manner of life far removed from the habits of the rich (I.3);
>
> To be long-suffering and have few wants, to work with my own hands and mind my own business (I.5);
>
> To desire a plank-bed covered with a pelt and whatever else that belongs to the Greek method of education. (τῆς Ἑλληνικῆς ἀγωγῆς, I.6).

These passages occur in the catalogue of the emperor's teachers and the description of his education. While it is safe to say that the virtues of simplicity and hard work continued into adult life, the physical asceticism described (such as the plank-bed) belong to Aurelius's youth, as a form of training or exercise in his early upbringing. The lines quoted from I.6 follow his mention of "composing dialogues as a boy" (ἐν παιδί), and underscore the context of youthful practice.[8] This concords with other evidence. The *Historia Augusta* states that at the age of twelve Aurelius dressed in a rough philosopher's cloak and slept on the ground.[9] These practices were meant to give the youth the bodily endurance (*tolerantia*) of a philosopher, the propaideutic physical discipline necessary to begin the study of philosophy. The overall impression is the same as in Musonius Rufus's *On Askesis,* where physical discipline is a mere preliminary to the development of the true asceticism of

8. Hence the translation of ἀγωγή as "method of education" rather than the more generic "regimen," "training," or "way of life." Such an education hearkens back to ancient Spartan models. See *LSJ,* s.v. ἀγωγή, II.3, and the notes on the passage by A. S. L. Farquharson, *The Meditations of the Emperor Marcus Aurelius* (Oxford, 1944), 1:271f., 2:442.

9. *HA* M.A. II.6. It is also stated that Aurelius's mother soon forced him to modify this discipline, persuading him to sleep instead on a couch strewn with skins—obviously reflecting *Med.* I.6. No citation of the *Historia Augusta* must go for long without some mention of the innumerable problems surrounding this document. The *HA* is a collection of imperial biographies from the period 117 to 284 C.E. As a whole, the work is notoriously tendentious, unreliable, and—in the biographies of the later or little known emperors—outright fictitious. The date(s) of composition and authorship remain in dispute. The reader is directed to T. D. Barnes, *The Sources of the Historia Augusta,* Collection Latomus 155 (Brussels, 1978) and R. Syme, *Historia Augusta Papers* (Oxford, 1983). By way of apology, it should be noted that the biography of Aurelius is considered to be one of the more factual (Syme, 35) and that here the *HA* is cited simply to amplify material from other, more reliable sources with which it agrees.

the mind or soul. Seneca, too, had recommended that a few days should be regularly devoted in the education of a youth for him to live in poverty. The object is *apatheia,* teaching that physical want, should it befall him, is nothing to be feared since such deprivation cannot harm the soul.[10] So it appears that for Aurelius the purpose and value of his early physical asceticism was also only as a propaideutic, a temporary exercise directed toward a higher goal and not an end in itself.

It would be incorrect to put too much weight on the philosophical and ascetical bent of Aurelius's education. Nothing appears out of the mainstream, much less radical, for an aristocratic Roman youth.[11] Five of Aurelius's teachers mentioned in the first book of the *Meditations* were not only senators, but consulars. Much of what the emperor learned was not concerned with philosophy, but rather with the proper conduct of a prince in society. This is particularly obvious in his veneration for Antoninus Pius and the lessons learned from him (I.16). If for no other reason, the weight of Aurelius's social class and responsibility, as well as that of his eventual high office, would have tempered any excess of philosophical or ascetical zeal.[12]

References to the adult emperor offer no evidence of continued ascetical practice beyond the training of his youth. Cassius Dio mentions that Aurelius took very little food, and that only at night (LXXII.6.3f.) But the context of this comment is the emperor's frail health, with no mention of either philosophy or asceticism. Fronto admonishes him for being too serious and disagreeable, reading books at banquets and the theater (*ad M.C.* IV.12.5). Dio states that the emperor wore himself out and destroyed his health from his excessive devotion to business and duty (LXXII.24.2, 36.2).[13] This is certainly self-sacrifice, but does it re-

10. Musonius Rufus IV, Lutz 52–56. Seneca, *Ep.* 18.5–7; see Arnold, 337f., 360–64. J. Perkins, "The 'Self' as Sufferer," *Harvard Theological Review* 85 (1992): 271f., perceives this same distinction between Aurelius's practice as a youth and adult, which she attributes to his deliberate rejection of the new and growing concern with the body in the second century in favor of traditional mental self-discipline. Her insightful and stimulating analysis avoids the pitfalls of "world hatred" theories.

11. So Farquharson, *Life and World,* 60, suggests that Aurelius's early inclination to self-discipline was probably not motivated either by specifically Stoic or even generally philosophic principles.

12. The five consulars were Cornelius Fronto, Herodes Atticus, Iunius Rusticus, Claudius Maximus, and Claudius Severus. On this point and on "princely" education, see E. Champlin, *Fronto and Antonine Rome* (Cambridge, Mass., 1980), 119; also Farquharson, *Life and World,* 13–23, 33–54. There is debate on the philosophical versus the rhetorical character of Aurelius's education and personal interests; see Birley, *Marcus Aurelius,* 69ff., 95ff. (chaps. 4 and 5, passim), and Champlin, *Fronto,* 31, 33, 106f., 121f.

13. Dio LXXII.36.2 states that Aurelius was, at one time, physically vigorous but made himself frail, ἐκ τῆς πολλῆς ἀσχολίας τε καὶ ἀσκήσεως. The word *askesis* is used, but

flect a deliberate pursuit of physical asceticism? The sources do not mention specific practices or philosophic principles. The impression, rather, is that Aurelius simply worked himself to death.[14]

In a similar vein, *HA* M.A. XV.1 also mentions his habit of attending to business at the games, but this too is in a context describing Aurelius's devotion to work and attention to the details of government. No sort of Stoic disgust at the brutality or inhumanity of the spectacle is suggested. Suetonius had said the same of Julius Caesar for the same reasons (*Aug.* 45.1).[15] *HA* M.A. XXIII.4–5 does relate an anecdote that when the emperor recruited Roman gladiators to fight in the Marcomannic Wars, there was talk that he sought to deprive the people of their amusement and thus force philosophy upon them. The import of the tale is perhaps that the emperor, and philosophers generally, were widely regarded as prudes, but scarcely more than that. The emperor sought to repair his image by seeing to it that lavish games were provided by wealthy benefactors. This and the controversial *S.C. de pretiis gladiatorum minuendis* offer clear and specific evidence that Aurelius did not hesitate to promote the spectacles, especially when his own popularity was at stake.[16] The only comment the emperor himself makes in this regard is not that the circus is disgusting, but rather simply tedious (VI.46).

Some minor passages have also been taken as an indication of Aurelius's physical asceticism. There is, for instance, the emperor's lack of

---

the text gives no indication that this refers to practices of rigorous physical asceticism. Dio first mentions ἀσχολία (lack of leisure) suggesting that *askesis* here should be taken to mean "assiduous exertion." In the immediately preceding section, Dio speaks of Aurelius's sedulous pursuit of learning in rhetoric and philosophy, so that E. Cary, in the Loeb edition, translates the passage: "As a result of his close application and study he was extremely frail in body." Perhaps echoing Dio, *HA* M.A. III.7f. states that Aurelius ruined his health as a youth by his devotion to his studies, specifically law. The precise meaning of Dio LXXII.36.2 can certainly be debated. The essential point remains, however, that if Dio is speaking of physical asceticism here, this would be the *only* passage to suggest extreme practice on the part of the adult emperor.

14. Rutherford, 120, makes an unwarranted assumption in implying that the emperor's frail health resulted from his rigorous practice of physical asceticism.

15. Aurelius may have simply been following the advice of Epictetus: "There is no need, for the most part, to go to public shows. If there should be such an occasion, however, show that you have concern for nothing other than yourself, that is, only wish for those things to happen which do happen and only for him to win who does win. Thus you will not be impaired. Refrain completely from shouting, laughing at anyone, or from great excitement. After leaving, do not speak a great deal about what happened, but only as much as contributes to your own betterment. Otherwise, it would appear that you had been absorbed in the spectacle" (*Ench.* 33.10).

16. For the text of the *S.C.*, see J. H. Oliver and R. E. Palmer, "Minutes of an Act of the Roman Senate," *Hesperia* 24 (1955): 320–49.

ostentation and avoidance of wearing the purple (*Med.* I.17.3 and Dio LXXII.35.5). Yet other Antonine emperors, most particularly Pius, were just as frugal and unostentatious for reasons having nothing to do with philosophy. Economy in the imperial household was one concern; another was the practice of imperial *civiltas*, an emperor's deliberate presentation of himself as mere "first citizen," which was particularly popular among the more constitutionally minded and conservative of the Antonines. Aurelius himself states that he learned this sort of moderation from Pius (*Med.* I.16, 17.3; VI.30).[17] The emperor also practiced sexual restraint, even as a youth (*Med.* I.17.2, 6). Yet his decision to abstain until the appropriate age and not to surrender to passion, even when the opportunity presented itself, is certainly in conformity with the moderate opinions of Musonius and Epictetus. Though Aurelius may have been more rigorous than was common in the practice of his day, his sexual continence conformed to the professed ideals of the Roman aristocracy—ideals that had been "on the books" since Augustus's moral legislation.[18]

Philosophy made Aurelius overly serious and demanding. A comment from the *HA* is telling: "Because Marcus appeared harsh both in military matters and in all parts of his life on account of his philosophical regimen, he was bitterly criticized. Yet, he replied either by word or letter to those who spoke ill of him." It is clear that he was concerned with what others thought of him in this regard, despite his own protests to the contrary.[19]

The Asceticism of Reason

Except for a period of training in his youth, Aurelius's life was not characterized by rigorous *physical* practices of asceticism.[20] It did, however, involve an amount of austerity and self-discipline that appeared more than ordinary to his contemporaries. It would be incorrect to say

17. See Farquharson, *Life and World*, 76ff.

18. Rutherford, 119, takes the points discussed here: Aurelius's diet, *civiltas*, and sexual restraint, as evidence of his "extravagant asceticism." The foregoing discussion establishes that this is not the case.

19. *HA* M.A. XXII.5–6. D. Magie in the Loeb edition notes at this passage that the emperor's critics were in the *consilium principis* itself. On Aurelius's concern for his reputation, see *HA* M.A. III.4, 6; VII.1.

20. So Perkins, 271f., rightly observes that in rejecting physical practices of asceticism in favor of internal discipline, Aurelius "maintained his adherence to traditional modes of self-mastery."

that there were no elements of asceticism in his life, but it remains to define his ascetical *gravitas* in positive terms.

The most obvious aspect of Aurelius's asceticism is precisely that it is not physical. Its focus is the mind, rather than the body; it is primarily *internal*.[21] In this regard, Epictetus had been quite insistent.

> Whatever discipline that is applied to the body by those exercising it (γυμναζόντων) may in fact be a form of *askesis*, if in some way it tends toward desire and aversion. (ὄρεξιν καὶ ἔκκλισιν, *Epict. Diss.* III.xii.16.)

> The position and character of the layman is this: he never searches for help or harm from within himself, but from things outside of himself. The position and character of the philosopher is this: he searches for all help or harm from within himself (*Ench.* 48.1).

> If you should allow your *askesis* to turn outward towards things that are not proper objects of moral choice, you will have neither your desire successful in its aims nor your aversion on a sure footing. (*Epict. Diss.* III.xii.5)

It would be appropriate to refer to this sort of discipline as the "asceticism of reason." This is consistent with the Stoic emphasis on intention as the determiner of the morality of a given act. Physical asceticism, like most if not all acts, is morally neutral in itself and, therefore, can be vicious if undertaken for the wrong reasons.[22] This emphasis results in a devaluation of an individual's acts as an accurate representation of character. A striking example occurs in a brief comment Aurelius makes regarding Socrates, the archetypal philosophic hero. The philosopher's noble death, skill at disputation, and endurance of privation are insuffi-

---

21. "The belief that underlies all others is that he should devote himself entirely to the intellect, the ἡγεμονικόν. Nothing matters except the intellect; and its activities are wholly within our power. The intellect is a deity, δαίμων, that has emanated from the universal deity; as such, it must be worshipped and kept pure by the individual, acting as a priest," E. Asmis, "The Stoicism of Marcus Aurelius," *ANRW* II.36.3 (1988): 2236. For further elucidation of philosophical concepts and technical terms in the *Meditations*, the reader may consult Farquharson's commentaries on the specific passages in his *Meditations of the Emperor Marcus Aurelius*.

22. Rist, *Stoic Philosophy*, 97–111; Brunt, "Stoicism," 12. So also B. L. Hijmans, *ΑΣΚΗΣΙΣ: Notes on Epictetus' Educational System*, Wejsgerige teksten en studies 2 (Assen, 1959), 55, notes that for Epictetus "to act virtuously without the right state of mind is no virtue at all," and traces the source of this opinion back to Democritus. Arguing that intention is not the sole determiner of morality: I. G. Kidd, "Stoic Intermediates and the End for Man," *CQ*, n.s. 5 (1955): 181–194 = *Problems in Stoicism*, ed. A. A. Long (London, 1971), 150–72; see also his "Moral Actions and Rules in Stoic Ethics," in *The Stoics*, ed. J. M. Rist (Berkeley and Los Angeles, 1978), 247–58.

cient to determine the good of his character. Rather, it is necessary to view the nature of his soul. The determination rests on his possession of a catalogue of Stoic virtues: justice, piety, endurance of evil, acquiescence in fate, *apatheia*.[23] If this could be said of Socrates, it holds true for anyone.

The predominance of intention, of mind, naturally carries with it ramifications for the valuation of the body.[24] The nature of this view of the body is twofold. While Stoic psychology placed complete emphasis on will and reason, the Stoic view of nature and acceptance of the "natural" prevented it from setting the body in strict opposition to the mind. The flesh is indisputably natural, so that the duty of the wise man is not so much to vanquish, much less reject, his corporeal nature as to accept its reality and power and bring it under the command of reason. The same is true of all other aspects of human personality and life. Stoic doctrine was not strictly "dualist."[25] The body is not the enemy; it is simply unimportant. It is wrong to give the body and its desires attention beyond the measure prescribed by nature, but it is equally unnatural to disregard them entirely. At times, Aurelius states the position exactly.

> If it is to the advantage of your rational nature, keep hold of it; if to your animal nature, simply say so and quietly maintain your decision—only see to it that you make a sound judgment. (III.6)

23. VII.66: "Whether he could content himself with being just towards men and pious towards the gods, and not become rashly irritated at wickedness or thrall to another's ignorance, nor take as foreign anything allotted by the universe or suffer it as unbearable, nor turn his mind over to his paltry flesh in sympathy with its passions." This is, perhaps, the most concise description of Stoic virtue found in the *Meditations*. The same themes appear repeatedly throughout, for example, II.16; III.4; IV.31; VII.54ff.; IX.20, 28, 40, 42; X.11, 15; XII.27. Regarding this judgment on Socrates, see Rutherford, 217 n. 112.

24. This is stated most emphatically by Arnold, 286: "Virtue is a state of mind, a disposition of the soul; it is not an act. Hence the bent of the mind (*inclinatio*), its aim (*intentio*), its desire (βούλησις, *voluntas*) is everything; the performance through the organs of the body is nothing" (citing Sen., *Ep.* 95.57; *De Ben.* II.31.1; Cic., *De Fin.* III.9.32; *Epict. Diss.* I.29.1, 2).

25. See Chapter 1, pages 12–19. Such broad conceptual terms as "dualism" are notoriously difficult to define precisely, and are used most often without such definition at all. To have utility as a concept, "dualism" should require not only a distaste for physical or bodily reality, but also its clear opposition to the intellectual or spiritual. It should also imply a moral distinction: the physical is a source or locus of evil, the mind or soul of good. This opposition and moral distinction exists nowhere in the *Meditations*. So also Dodds, *Pagan and Christian*, 13: "The visible cosmos *as a whole* could only be called evil in contrast with some invisible Good Place or Good Person outside and beyond the cosmos: radical dualism implies transcendence. Stoicism recognized no such place or person: it was a one-storey system" (citing S. Pétrement, *Le Dualisme dans l'histoire de la philosophie et des religions* [Paris, 1946], 105).

Let the ruling (ἡγεμονικόν) and lordly part of your soul be unmoved by smooth or rough movements in the flesh. Let it not mingle with them but circumscribe itself, sealing off these feelings within their proper areas. When, however, they do issue forth into the intellect in virtue of that other sympathetic connection, as happens in an integrated organism,[26] then *you must not try to resist the sensation, natural as it is,* and do not let the ruling reason (τὸ ἡγεμονικόν) then add its own estimate as to *whether it is good or bad.* (V.26)

Side by side with this view, however, there also exists an apparent disgust with the physical that Aurelius makes no attempt to reconcile.

Just as bathing appears to you: oil, sweat, filth, greasy water, everything revolting, so is every part of life and everything we encounter. (VIII.24)

The rot that is the substance of everything: water, dust, bones, stench. Again, marble is but calloused earth; gold and silver are sediment; clothing is animal hair; the purple is blood; and so for everything else. The puny soul is just the same, changeable from this to that. (IX.36)

E. R. Dodds has emphasized Aurelius's disgust with the physical world and his expressions of desolation and alienation.[27] The reality of these sentiments in Aurelius's mind, and the depth of their intensity, is beyond question, but their meaning and significance remain open to dis-

26. κατὰ τὴν ἑτέραν συμπάθειαν . . . ὡς ἐν σώματι ἡνωμένῳ: the meaning is unclear and the translation above is literal. Farquharson, *Meditations,* 2:664, suggests that the "one" sympathetic connection is that of the mind down to the body, and the "other" is that of the body up to the mind. Thus, though the mind seals itself off from descending to the physical / emotional level, feelings are still able to travel up to the mind; the human being is a unity and there can be no complete severing of mind from body.

27. See above, notes 6 and 7. Aurelius is, for Dodds, a prime example of the individual in an "Age of Anxiety." This thesis has not found general acceptance. For example, R. Lane Fox, 64ff., gives a succinct and powerful critique: "Anxious individuals can be found in any age with a personal literature. . . . To sum up an age by a single emotion is to focus on a few individuals and to simplify even those few . . . and their written theories on the age-old problems of evil and its origins were neither distinctively 'anxious' nor new to the Antonine age." On the difficulties with Dodds's work in general, see R. C. Smith and J. Lounibos, eds., *Pagan and Christian Anxiety: A Response to E. R. Dodds* (Lanham, Md., 1984).

cussion. On the surface, at least, the emperor appears to be truly of two minds.[28]

J. M. Rist has suggested a more refined explanation of Aurelius's attitude toward the physical, attributing its origin to Heraclitus's teachings, appropriated either directly by Aurelius or indirectly through their influence on the development of Stoic doctrine.[29] Aurelius's feelings of disgust are not with the physical per se, but rather with physical reality as the most persistent, tangible reminder of the necessity of change and decay—Heraclitan flux. The same is true for fame, reputation, adulation, and the simple recognition of the passage of time. In the emperor's own words:

> Adopt a scientific approach to the way all things change, one into another; pay close attention and exert yourself in this area, for nothing so produces greatness of mind. Such a one has put off the body and, understanding that he must almost at once leave all these things behind and depart from among men, has devoted his entire self both to justice in his own actions and to the dictates of universal nature in whatever else comes to pass. (X.11; cf. II.14f.; III.10)

By devoted study of the passing nature of all things, the individual divests himself of the body. This is not to say that one escapes the body as a prison; rather, the individual is confronted with the reality of his own mortality, that the Heraclitan flux applies even to the self. The object is not to "flee the body" nor is it to "flee the world." This realization is

28. Dodds himself admits this, *Pagan and Christian*, 21: "He fought against the exclusive dominion of such thoughts with all the strength of his Stoic religion, reminding himself that his existence was part and parcel of the great Unity"; cf. 27f., 80f. Rutherford, 29–39, 227–47, endeavors to resurrect Dodds's view of Aurelius but fails to take sufficient account of the contrary views expressed in the *Meditations* themselves, and of the insights of Rist and Hadot, which will be discussed presently. Instead, Rutherford speaks in a general, subjective, impressionistic manner about Aurelius's feelings of "enslavement" to and "hatred" of the body (242), concomitant with the emperor's "extreme asceticism" (227), and in distinction to the views of Epictetus (246)—ignoring his own caveat (228) on comparing the two because of differences in circumstance, genre, and audience.

29. For Aurelius's use of Heraclitan imagery and language, see Rist, "Are You a Stoic?" 36–39, and Asmis, 2246–49. On Heraclitan influence on Stoicism in general: A. A. Long, "Heraclitus and Stoicism," *Philosophia* 5–6 (1975–76): 133–56. Rist considers Long's arguments on this point exaggerated. See also Arnold, 258f. who sees a particularly Roman flavor in Aurelius's opinions on the body.

rather a spur to ethical action in society and to a resigned acceptance of fate.[30]

This distinction between mind and body introduces a subject vital both to the understanding of the *Meditations* themselves and of Aurelius's concept of asceticism—the "spiritual exercise."[31] P. Hadot has outlined the process by which Aurelius moves from pessimism to optimism regarding life and the world by the repetition of fundamental Stoic dogmas.[32] This constitutes the fundamental spiritual exercise in Stoic philosophy, and the *Meditations* is essentially a handbook of such exercises. The exercise begins with pessimism, the necessity of seeing things the way they are: "dust, stench, sediment, blood." Clarity of vision and reason are the fundamentals of "greatness of mind." The purpose of the exercise is not, however, to stop here. It is only through this clear, if unattractive, vision of stark reality that the individual may see that all things are but part of nature and subject to the same universal laws, most especially those of change, decay, and death. The mind expands, and what initially appeared repulsive or depressing is now seen in a cosmic perspective as holding no cause for revulsion or fear. Optimism arises as the final phase of the exercise when all is seen to be a manifestation of the rational order of nature and, therefore, necessary and good. Thus it is that Aurelius's most positive statements refer to the grandeur and beauty of nature and the reasoned order of the cosmos, while his most negative deal with the narrow particulars of life and the world. The object of the exercise is to change the individual soul, that is, to correct one's initial, instinctive perceptions and thoughts by the continuous application of the principles and truths of philosophy. This is the asceticism of reason at work—the careful, deliberate, and repeated exertion to discipline and correct the internal attitudes and perceptions of the mind.

Nor is the soul exempt from this process: "The rot that is the substance of everything: water, dust, bones, stench. . . . The puny soul is

30. "This resolute benignity in the presence of change and death is not gained without severe discipline of the body and its passions and the mind with its shifting imaginings," Farquharson, *Life and World*, 137.

31. Fundamental to the study of this subject is P. Hadot, "La Physique"; his later works collected in *Exercices spirituels et philosophie antique*, 2d ed. (Paris, 1987); and "Les Pensées de Marc Aurèle," *Bulletin de l'Association Guillaume Budé* 1 (1981): 183–91. Earlier and more controversial is P. Rabbow, *Seelenführung: Methodik der Exercitien in der Antike* (Munich, 1954); more recently, see R. J. Newman, "*Cotidie Meditare:* Theory and Practice of the Meditatio in Imperial Stoicism," *ANRW* II.36.3 (1989): 1473–1517, on Aurelius, 1506–15.

32. See Hadot, "La Physique," 228–34. Hijmans, 78–91, outlines a similar process involving the repeated application of the χανών in Epictetus.

just the same, changeable from this to that" (IX.36). The soul is also a physical entity for Aurelius, and no matter how far he spiritualizes its qualities it cannot leave the body after death, much less be immortal.[33] It cannot be set up as the complete antithesis of the body.

For Aurelius, then, the body remains an unimportant, morally neutral instrument. It is natural; its reality must be accepted, but merely disciplining or depriving it would have no effect on the mind or soul. The asceticism of reason is, in effect, a one-way street. Discipline flows from the mind to the body, seldom the reverse. An asceticism that concentrated on the body would, therefore, be pointless. Two important points emerge. Because the body is natural, it cannot be a source or locus of evil. In addition, the body is neutral; it cannot be a battleground in the struggle for virtue. Its actions are ultimately unimportant. Virtue exists solely in the state of mind and motivation.

The asceticism of reason is, therefore, a discipline of mind and motivation: "Annihilate imagination. Block impulse. Quench desire. Keep ruling reason (τὸ ἡγεμονικόν) in control" (IX.7; cf. VII.29; VIII.29, 49; XII.25). Its privation is internal: "Therefore casting away everything else, hold on to these few things. Recall that each man lives but a short time, a brief moment; the rest has either been lived or lies in an unknown future" (III.10).[34] As such, it is the product of education, indeed, of higher education as it was known in the ancient world. It requires a carefully honed and discerning reason. It is most definitely not for the common man. This is just the opposite of the Christian practice, as Galen (129?–199), Aurelius's contemporary and court physician, noted:

33. Rist, *Stoic Philosophy*, 269ff. I would disagree, however, with Rist's calling Aurelius a dualist, for the reasons stated above in note 25. The division of the individual into mind / reason (τὸ ἡγεμονικόν), soul, and body is simply a commonplace bit of reasoning in ancient philosophy. It is the conclusions drawn from this division, the attitude toward each of the parts, e.g., whether they are "good" or "evil," that defines dualism in any specific and useful way.

34. Dodds, *Pagan and Christian*, 27f., suggests that the introjection into the self of feelings of resentment against the world, such as those found in Aurelius, results either in the mental torment of moral self-reproach *or* in physical acts of self-punishment. The asceticism of reason can certainly be described as the former. The more intriguing point is that the alternative results in the practice of that sort of intensely physical asceticism that would become so popular little more than a century after Aurelius's death. In Dodds's view, the reasoned, cerebral self-searching of the emperor and the harsh physical excess of the desert monk are but two sides of the same coin, i.e., an introvert and extrovert manifestation of some common reality. The suggestion is intriguing in itself, without one's necessarily subscribing to "world hatred" as its cause. This thesis merits full consideration from psychological, philosophical, and religious perspectives, well beyond the scope of this present work.

Just as now we see the people called Christians drawing their faith from parables [and miracles], and yet sometimes acting in the same way [as those who philosophize]. For their contempt of death [and of its sequel] is patent to us every day, and likewise their restraint in cohabitation. For they include not only men but also women who refrain from cohabiting all through their lives; and they also number individuals who, in self-discipline and self-control in matters of food and drink, and in their keen pursuit of justice, have attained a pitch not inferior to that of genuine philosophers.[35]

What amazed Galen was that the unlettered multitude could perform acts of virtue without education, or perhaps more correctly, with a false education not based on reason. As will be seen below, this rather sympathetic view can also allow a much harsher verdict. Here it is important to note that among educated pagans asceticism was purely a matter of education, philosophy, and reason. Any practices not founded on this basis were suspect, be they of the Christians or of other pagans like Lucian's Peregrinus and Alexander, who made equally irrational appeals to the unlettered and the gullible.[36]

Resignation, at a most profound level, is to be found everywhere in the *Meditations*. The asceticism of reason produces little in the way of external actions and, in some respects, negates the entire idea of effective action itself. This is seen in two related concepts: *apatheia* (VI.16), which can be described as detachment from one's internal states, and *ataraxia* (IX.31), a separation from external circumstances.[37] At one

35. Citation from Galen's lost commentary on Plato's *Republic* in P. Kraus and R. Walzer, eds., *Plato Arabus*, vol. 1, *Galeni compendium Timaei Platonis aliorum dialogorum synopsis quae extant fragmenta*, ed. P. Kraus and F. Rosenthal (London, 1943), 99; trans. Walzer, *Galen on Jews and Christians* (London, 1949), 15; discussed on 65–74. Walzer notes that the Christians' success with the multitude lay precisely in the appeal of myth and exhortation and in avoiding difficult philosophical questions. Though the results may be admirable, they are vitiated by a method that appeals to emotion and faith rather than reason. The "irrationality" of the Christians, in this narrow sense, is a constant refrain in pagan objections to the new faith. This criticism is voiced by Galen himself: "If I had in mind people who taught their pupils in the same way as the followers of Moses and Christ teach theirs—for they order them to accept everything on faith—I should not have given you a definition," Kraus and Walzer, *Plato Arabus*, 1:20; trans. Walzer, *Galen*, 15; discussed on 48–56 and passim.

36. See Chapter 3.

37. For a philosophical discussion of these terms, see M. Pohlenz, *Die Stoa: Geschichte einer geistigen Bewegung*, 4th ed., with corrections, additions, and index by H.-J. Johann (Göttingen, 1970), 1:141–53.

point in the *Meditations,* Aurelius gives this as the very definition of philosophy:

> What then can accompany man in his sojourn of life? One thing and one thing only—philosophy. And this lies in keeping the *daimon* within free from insult and injury; master of pleasures and pains; doing nothing aimlessly, deceptively, or hypocritically; independent of another's action or inaction. Furthermore, this lies in accepting whatever happens and is allotted to one as coming from that same source from which he himself came, and above all in awaiting death with an amiable attitude as nothing other than the loosing of those elements from which every living thing is composed. (II.17; cf. III.4 and Epict., *Ench.* 12.2)

Apatheia has a rational basis for "the universe is transformation and life is opinion." By virtue of Providence, all that happens is good; therefore all perturbation comes from within, from the opinion or attitude of the mind (IV.3; cf. II.15; IV.7; XII.22).

Even in regard to the gods, true piety consists in praying, not that something happen or not happen, but to be free of the desire or fear of the event in either case (IX.40).[38] *Apatheia* lies not in the suppression of emotion, not even if such emotion has an irrational basis, but of irrational *reaction* to such emotion.[39] The internal state of the philosopher, his psychological reactions, are carefully circumscribed by reason. When confronted with passion or distress, the wise man must first resignedly accept his condition and then, by applying his reason, *not* act on his feelings. The discipline required is to accept passively the decrees of fate: "At all times and in all places it lies with you to be piously content with your present circumstance" (VII.54), or again: "Accept without arrogance; let go without struggle" (VIII.33).

38. Cf. Epict., *Ench.* 14.2: "Whoever wants to be free, let him neither wish for anything nor avoid anything that is under the control of others."

39. As Aurelius states, sensation is not to be resisted. It is, after all, simply natural (V.26). I would refine Rist's comment, *Stoic Philosophy,* 25–27, 195, that *apatheia* is the suppression not of all emotion, but only of irrational emotion. Emotion is, by definition, irrational (or arational) though in some cases emotions may also have irrational, that is, logically unfounded, *causes.* Aurelius would not resist even these emotions themselves, but rather apply reason to avoid either being swept away by their very real power or acting while in the flush of passion. Hence Clement of Alexandria's contention that Christians aim to experience no desire at all, while pagans merely attempt to resist it (*Strom.* III.7.57); see P. R. L. Brown, *The Body and Society: Men, Women, and Sexual Renunciation in Early Christianity* (New York, 1988), 31f.

Some examples of *ataraxia* have already been seen in Aurelius's opinions regarding fame, reputation, and adulation. Again, the rational basis for this detachment is the passing nature of all things.[40] Life must be lived according to reason; if this results in social isolation, or even death, this too must be borne with equanimity (X.15; cf. III.4 *ad fin.*; VI.59; VII.62; VIII.52f.; IX.34). Above all, one must never desert the post in life assigned by fate (VII.45; X.25; cf. Epict., *Ench.* 22 and Plato, *Apology* 28E). Virtue lies in the acceptance and performance of duty, in acquiescence rather than action or change. This often entails merely resigning oneself to the presence of stupid and evil men, without hope of changing them (IX.20, 42; cf. V.17; VII.29; IX.38; and Dio LXXII.34.3f.). These forms of detachment offer another reason for the deemphasis of the physical in Aurelius's asceticism. Focus centers on the achievement of *apatheia,* inner detachment. Through the practice of *ataraxia,* external events and circumstances become unimportant. Again Aurelius illustrates: "Wherever it is possible to live, there one can live rightly; it is possible to live in palace, hence it is possible to live rightly even in a palace" (V.16). Physical surroundings, even the opulence of the imperial residences, are no hindrance to the achievement of the true asceticism of *apatheia.* As with physical rigor, material deprivation or its opposite need not have any impact on the mind. The practice of voluntary poverty would be pointless.[41]

Asceticism in the *Meditations* is decidedly passive. It offers no impetus to action beyond that of discerning personal morality and performing one's appointed duty. Moreover, this concept of asceticism draws clear boundaries as to the unacceptable. Stoic *apatheia* would have little tolerance for displays of enthusiasm or extremism. Excesses of emotion or display would reflect irrationality. The concept of *ataraxia* would

40. X.11; II.14f; III.10. An excellent statement on the transitoriness of life occurs in IV.32–36.

41. On the issue of wealth and the practice of philosophy, Arnold, 320f., notes that no subject would be easier on which to find conflicting Stoic views. In general, he characterizes the position in practice as "he who feels the need of wealth least, can best make use of it." Again, focus is on internal attitude; the justification of wealth lies in the intention of using it well. See Cic., *de Off.* I.68 and *Epict. Diss.* IV.ix.2. Rist, *Stoic Philosophy,* 189f. comments on a "notorious" proposition of Panaetius, mentioned in Diogenes Laertius 7.128, that virtue alone is insufficient to secure happiness, but that health, *property,* and strength are *required* as well. Material want can be a constant distraction to the mind, and a certain amount of substance is necessary to secure the *otium* needed to pursue philosophy. See also Dio Chrysostom, *Or.* 20.11–18, 26 (περὶ ἀναχωρήσεως), where he argues that true withdrawal is within the mind and that physical surroundings are neither a help nor a hindrance to one determined to live philosophically.

make the physical privations of Christian, Cynic, and Pythagorean asceticism appear ludicrous.

Asceticism and Personal Authority

Another characteristic of this view of asceticism is that it conveys no extraordinary authority, moral or otherwise, on its practitioner. Aurelius does not make his own experience a paradigm for the instruction of humanity. In this, he is simply following Stoic doctrine as it had developed from the time of Panaetius (c. 185–109 B.C.), whose psychology carried to the extreme the Stoic emphasis upon motivation as the determiner of the morality of a given act. By insisting on absolute purity of motive, Panaetius banished the true Stoic sage into the realm of the hypothetical. The ordinary individual (ὁ προκόπτων, "the one making progress") was left only to strive toward virtue by the performance of his duty (καθήκοντα, *officia*) as a rational and social being.[42] The "holy man" does not exist for Aurelius, nor for his Stoic contemporaries, and one can only assume a very negative reaction if such a one presented himself to the emperor or other like-minded individuals.[43]

One passage in the *Meditations* might be taken to indicate otherwise: "Therefore such a man, now no longer putting off being among the best, is a kind of priest (ἱερεύς τίς) and servant of the gods, utilizing that which is set within him" (III.4). The reference to priesthood is, first of all, a simile (τίς). It is simply descriptive, not a claim to spiritual authority. The wise man is like a priest because he attends to the cult, or cultivation, of his particular god. For the wise man, this is his own *daimon* within, his ruling reason (τὸ ἡγεμονικόν), which is a part of the divine reason of the cosmos. Every human being has this divine spark, so the philosopher is not unique in its possession, but only in its cultivation. This passage goes on to state that the cultivation or use of the deity within produces a whole catalogue of Stoic virtues. Exactly the same effect results from the right use of reason and from following nature.[44] The cultivation of the *daimon* generates internal moral virtue, not external miraculous power. Here lies another motive for the suspicion of self-styled holy men, wonderworkers, and theatrical ascetics:

42. Rist, *Stoic Philosophy*, 186ff., 197; Arnold, 101f., 302. See below, page 43.

43. Lucian expresses precisely this reaction to Peregrinus and Alexander, while evidence for such a reaction against Apollonius of Tyana is found in Philostratus's *Life of Apollonius*. See Chapters 3 and 4.

44. For a succinct explanation of Aurelius's equation of nature, fate, God, reason, and the *daimon*, with citations from *Meditations*, see Brunt, "Marcus in his Meditations," 15.

cion of self-styled holy men, wonderworkers, and theatrical ascetics: their works are outside the "normal" course of relations with the divine. From this it is a short step to adduce a sinister source for such extraordinary feats.[45]

A worthwhile comparison can be made with the later development of Neoplatonism in the writings of Porphyry. His mentor Plotinus's guardian spirit is no mere *daimon*, but a god himself (*Vit. Plot.* 10). Porphyry states that it is the Supreme God himself who is established within the inward parts of the philosopher (*de Abst.* II.52). His comments regarding the philosopher as priest go far beyond Aurelius. The simile is gone. The philosopher *is* a priest, and not just of any particular god, but of the Highest God. He is knowledgeable in all things pleasing to the Supreme Divinity (*de Abst.* II.49f.) and thus can claim ultimate religious and philosophical authority.[46] In comparison, Aurelius's simile is feeble indeed. Elsewhere in the *Meditations,* Aurelius accepts with resignation the fact that those closest to the gods in life meet with the same fate of oblivion in death as the rest of humanity.[47]

Though Aurelius's pursuit of philosophy endowed him with no special personal authority, it is possible that it colored his exercise of authority as emperor. An obvious place to look is in the field of politics, law, and society, where the emperor's views could find their most direct application.

At first glance, the *Meditations* suggest that the emperor's beliefs would have a positive impact. Justice or the obligation to social activity or "conduct becoming a rational, political being" is mentioned more than one hundred times.[48] In addition to this general concern is the Stoic doctrine of the unity of humanity, which finds its *locus classicus* in IV.4: "If this is so, we are citizens; if so, we share in some political entity; if so, the universe is like a state—for to what other political entity can one say that the whole human race belongs?" (cf. IV.3; VII.9). Humanity is united by its common reason into a commonwealth with common laws. Finally, there are Aurelius's comments regarding his own political education, invoking the names of Thrasea, Helvidius,

45. Hence Philostratus's concern to portray Apollonius as a devout worshiper of the traditional gods, as opposed to a *goes* conjuring up *daimones;* see Philostr., *VA* V.12; VIII.7.2, 9; and Chapter 4, page 97.

46. Cf. Apollonius's own claims to religious authority, Chapter 4, pages 108–12.

47. XII.5: "How could the gods, having arranged all things artfully and benevolently towards men, have overlooked this one thing: that some men who were particularly good and had, so to speak, the closest relations with the divine—having become intimate with divinity through pious acts and worship—should, once dead, never again come into being but be utterly extinguished."

48. Brunt, "Marcus in his Meditations," 7.

Cato, and Brutus and ideals such as equality of rights, equity, freedom of speech, and liberty.[49]

The meaning behind the emperor's words is another matter. Despite Aurelius's repeated emphasis on the performance of social acts, he gives no concrete examples of the sort of acts of which he is speaking. Given the nature of the *Meditations,* it may be that Aurelius had no need to remind himself of the specific acts he had in mind.[50] In either case, he assumes them. The key point is that the definition of "acts becoming a social being" is *not* contained in Aurelius's philosophy. It must be provided from the outside, from the prevailing norms of society. Rather than providing a critique of society, Aurelius's Stoicism provides a philosophical justification for the status quo. If the path of virtue lies in the performance of duty and acceptance of the decrees of fate, the wise man will not seek to alter or abandon either his society or his position within it. Seneca had already said as much, adducing the Stoics as an example: "The philosopher (*sapiens*) will not upset accepted customs (*publicos mores*), nor turn public attention to himself by some novel manner of life (*Ep.* 14.14, cf. 73.1).[51] This conclusion is consistent with the almost complete emphasis on the internal dynamics of the personality mentioned earlier. Stoic morality and ethics were essentially individual concerns. Justice, social activity, and political conduct are meant to be guides for individual action, not items on a social agenda.[52] When

---

49. ἰσονομία, ἰσότης, ἰσηγορία, and ἐλευθερία (I.14). There is also a certain irony in Aurelius's mention of these names of antityrannical heroes of the Roman past. Stoicism, by his day, no longer offered a platform for rebellion or revolution. It had become so entrenched in the imperial status quo that an emperor could feel safe in mentioning the names of those who plotted against his predecessors; see Brunt, "Stoicism," 29f.

50. Stanton, "Emperor and Philosopher," 579, holds that Aurelius's references to social acts are nebulous because they lie purely in the realm of theory and carry no effective practical import. Against this view Brunt, "Marcus in his Mediations," 6, argues that Aurelius knew quite well what actions were required of him in his position and would not have bothered to elaborate upon them in writing. This latter view is, in my mind, the more correct. Aurelius assumes the definition of social acts from the commonplace accepted norms of his society.

51. Brunt, "Stoicism," 32: "The historian can note that what the Stoics supposed to be right, what they could conscientiously devote or sacrifice their lives to doing, was largely settled by the ideas and practices current in their society, and that a Helvidius or a Marcus was inspired by his beliefs not to revalue or reform the established order, but to fulfill his place within that order, in conformity with notions that men of their time and class usually accepted, at least in name, but with unusual resolution, zeal and fortitude."

52. Rist, *Stoic Philosophy,* 92: "Throughout our investigation of Stoicism we find a concern for the individual case, and in ethics with the individual per se." See also his "Stoic Concept of Detachment," 264ff.

Aurelius addresses the point directly, he must admit that Platonopolis cannot be built (IX.29).

As for the unity of mankind and the world state, scholars have already made short shrift of the practical import of these ideas.[53] One further observation should be added. Aurelius's cosmopolitanism, in comparison with Epictetus's for example, gives particular emphasis to reason and law.[54] This emphasis has the ability to transform this benign, philanthropic doctrine into a potent weapon. Those who do not conform to the mores of the world state can be branded irrational (i.e., insane or malevolent) or outlaws (i.e., traitors to the state). When theory is brought down to the level of reality, the world state of the Stoics does not possess its own laws, but can only appropriate them from the customs and codes of existing society.

The political ideals mentioned by Aurelius bring up the question of law and legislation. Here scholarly opinion differs sharply. At the extreme are the generalizations of E. V. Arnold, who attributes the "humanity" of the whole of Antonine legislation to Stoic influence, whether or not those identified with the legislation were professed Stoics.[55] P. Noyen is more specific, arguing that laws such as the *S.C. Orfitianum* and the *Constitutio divi Marci ad Aufidium Victorinum* bear the personal mark of Aurelius's philosophical beliefs. He describes the former law as "revolutionary and progressively feministic" and the latter "the culmination of legislation in favor of the destitute."[56] Such views are not only exaggerated; they are fundamentally incorrect.

---

53. Brunt, "Stoicism," 16 n. 49: "It is a misunderstanding to ascribe to this metaphysical doctrine political or practical import." Stanton, "Emperor and Philosopher," 579: "For in his view the task of the citizen of the universe is to work from observation to theory and not from theory to practice."

54. G. R. Stanton, "The Cosmopolitan Ideas of Epictetus and Marcus Aurelius," *Phronesis* 13 (1968):192.

55. Arnold, 402: "This legislation is not entirely the work of professed Stoics; it is nevertheless the offspring of Stoicism." Concomitant with such a view is an overstatement of Stoic ideals and their practical effects: "The practical statesmen who set about to re-create Roman law on the principle of substituting everywhere human rights for class privileges were men thoroughly imbued with the Stoic spirit, whether or not they were avowed disciples of this philosophy" (281). Such statements are particularly surprising since Arnold elsewhere agrees that Stoicism, by this time, has lost its moral vitality and had settled into a conventional respectability (303).

56. Noyen, 375ff.; cf. "Divus Marcus, princeps prudentissimus et iuris religiosissimus," *Revue internationale des droits de l'antiquité*, 3d ser., 1 (1954): 349–71. Noyen admits that his motivation in this study is to come to a judgment about Aurelius's personality; that is, did he practice what he preached? On the fallacy of such an approach, see above, note 2. For the laws themselves, see Paul., *Sent.* IV.10; Ulp., *Reg.* XXVI.7; *Inst.* III.4; *Dig.* XXXVIII.17.9 (Gaius), 17.6 (Paul.), 17.7 (Paul.); *Dig.* XXIII.2.59 (Paul.); *Dig.* XXXVII.7.9 (Tryph.); *Dig.* XXV.4.1.pr. (Ulp.).

Noyen limits himself entirely to Aurelius's laws. His thesis lacks context. If these laws bear the imprint of Aurelius's own Stoicism, they must be shown to be significantly different from the laws of other emperors. M. Hammond, in surveying the entire Antonine era, emphasizes the continuity of "humane" legislation throughout the second century and, in some cases, even under the principate as a whole.[57] G. R. Stanton, arguing directly against Noyen, notes that Aurelius's legislation is equal in volume to that of his predecessor, and in many cases simply develops existing laws of Hadrian or Pius. Specifically he notes that the *S.C. Orfitianum* was of only indirect benefit to women. The earlier *S.C. Tertullianum* under Hadrian or Pius actually did more.[58] Aurelius was, in fact, no innovator but rather continued the trends of the second-century imperial administration.[59]

A unique perspective on this problem comes from the studies of W. Williams who, independently of the issues discussed here, searched for signs of individuality in the imperial constitutions from Hadrian to Commodus. Of the laws which, in Williams's view, carry marks of Aurelius's personal intervention, only two coincide with those Noyen lists as bearing the emperor's philosophical stamp; while Williams finds no evidence of Aurelius's intervention in the pieces of legislation Noyen considers to be most characteristic of the emperor's personal philosophic influence.[60]

57. M. Hammond, *The Antonine Monarchy*, Papers and Monographs of the American Academy in Rome 19 (Rome, 1959), 331 and nn. 18–21.

58. Stanton, "Emperor and Philosopher," 571, 571 n. 6, and 573–75. For the *S.C. Tertullianum: Inst.* III.3.2; cf. *Dig.* XXXIV.5.9.1, XXXVIII.17.2.9 (Pius); Zonaras 12.1.

59. G. R. Stanton, "Marcus Aurelius, Lucius Verus, and Commodus: 1962–1972," *ANRW* II.2.2 (1975): 500f., wherein he cites the opinions of J. Bleicken, *Senatsgericht und Kaisergericht: Eine Studie zur Entwicklung des Prozeßrechtes in führen Prinzipat*, Abhandlungen der Akad. der Wiss. in Göttingen, Philol.-Hist. Klasse, Folge 3:53 (Göttingen, 1962), 118–20; R. P. Duncan-Jones, "The Purpose and Organization of the *Alimenta*," *PBSR* 32 (1964), 123–46; P. D. A. Garnsey, *Social Status and Legal Privilege in the Roman Empire* (Oxford, 1970), passim; A. R. Hands, *Charities and Social Aid in Greece and Rome* (London, 1968), 111–15; and H.-G. Pflaum, "Tendences politiques et administratives au IIe siècle de notre ère," *Revue des études latines* 42 (1964): 112–21.

60. W. Williams, "Individuality in the Imperial Constitutions. Hadrian and the Antonines," *JRS* 66 (1976): 67–83. The two examples of legislation coinciding with Noyen are on insanity: *Dig.* I.18.14, and on the status of freedmen: *Dig.* XXXVII.14.17.pr. Williams's criteria pertain to the style of the documents. He argues that Aurelius's hand (rather literally) manifests itself in four characteristic traits: (1) painstaking attention to detail, (2) insistence on obvious or trivial points, (3) linguistic purism, and (4) attitudes expressed toward the Greeks. On the basis of these criteria, Williams is careful to conclude that *some* (Williams's emphasis) constitutions demonstrate the personal intervention of the emperor. On the emperor's personal involvement in framing law generally, see the more detailed study of F. Millar, *The Emperor in the Roman World* (Ithaca, N.Y. 1977), chap. 5, 203–72.

Aurelius's legal *acta* simply do not demonstrate any particular Stoic *humanitas*. In certain instances even the opposite is true, especially when property rights and civil order were at issue. For example, Ulpian cites and summarizes the *generalis epistula* of Aurelius and Commodus on hunting down fugitive slaves. The emperors command unyielding measures in retaining captured runaways and strictly limit the rights of citizens when encountering slave-catchers (*Dig.* XI.4.1.2 *ad fin.*–5). Ulpian also notes a senatorial oration by Aurelius on the topic, stressing the same fierceness and disregard for others' rights when recovering this human property (*Dig.* XI.4.3). It is repeatedly specified that these rules are part of a general tightening of laws and procedures regarding slaves under Aurelius and Pius. The treatment of Christians offers another example. Here too, the emperor was once portrayed as mild and benevolent. Although it is probable that Aurelius did not pursue active, systematic persecution, it has become clear that he, at the least, embraced Trajan's policy of punishing confessed Christians. At the same time, when public order was threatened—as at Lyon in Eus., *HE* V.1—he could countenance severe measures.[61] It has even been suggested that the first surviving treatise attacking Christianity, Celsus's *True Doctrine*, was inspired by Aurelius and served as an exposition of his policy.[62]

Despite the repeated emphasis on society and social acts in the *Meditations*, despite all the references to politics and political ideals, there is no evidence of any positive social impact brought about specifically by Aurelius's philosophical beliefs. The Stoicism of this period, and any ascetical concepts attached to it, remain inward-looking, detached, conservative, a technique for "surviving" the world rather than reforming it.

Social Norms and Social Conformity

The conservative nature of Stoicism, and its dependence upon surrounding society for the norms to which the "social animal" must adhere, imply severe consequences for those who would not conform. Aurelius is uncharacteristically harsh in his description:

> The soul of a man does violence to itself most especially when it becomes, as far as it can, an abscess and tumor, as it were, on the universe. (II.16)

61. See below, esp. note 68.
62. M. Sordi, "Le polemiche intorno al cristianesimo nel II secolo e la loro influenza sugli sviluppi della politica imperiale verso la Chiesa," *Rivista di Storia della Chiesa in Italia* 16 (1962): 17ff.

If he is a stranger to the universe who has no understanding of the things that are in it, no less is he a stranger who has no understanding of what occurs in it. He is a fugitive, who flees the rational law of society; a blind man, who shuts the eyes of his understanding; a beggar, who is in need of another and does not have of himself all that is required for living; an abscess on the universe, who rebels and severs himself from the reason of our common nature because he is displeased at what happens, for this same nature brought this about which also bore you; a part cut off from the body politic, who cuts his own soul off from that of all rational beings, which is but one soul. (IV.29)

What specific acts could be so heinous as to make someone a festering sore on the world, a cancer in the cosmos, a stranger to the universe, a universal fugitive, blind, a cringing beggar, a social amputee? Aurelius, unfortunately, does not say. It is clear, however, how closely these words resemble the accusations made against the Christians of antisocial behavior, obstinacy, insanity, inhumanity, and treason.[63] This is precisely the point. What this line of reasoning offered was a philosophical justification for persecuting any individual or group *perceived* to be a threat to the social order either by society as a whole or by those who ruled it. The criteria for judging the case can only be taken from the norms of the surrounding society. Epictetus had already admitted this:

Our duties (τὰ καθήκοντα) are, in general, measured by our social relationships. . . . In this way, therefore, you will discover the duty (τὸ καθῆκον) owed to and expected from your neighbor, your fellow-citizen, your commanding officer, if you accustom yourself to examining your relationships with them. (*Ench.* 30; cf. *Epict. Diss.* II.x)[64]

Add to this Aurelius's own emphasis on submission, especially to the decrees of fate.[65] Anyone who is unaccepting of his lot, discontented

63. See J. Beaujeu, *La religion romaine à l'apogée de l'Empire*, vol. 1, *La politique religieuse des Antonins (96–192)* (Paris, 1955), 358, and Rist, "Stoic Concept of Detachment," 260–66. On the persecution of the Christians in general, see P. Keresztes, "The Imperial Roman Government and the Christian Church I. From Nero to the Severi," *ANRW* II.23.1 (1979): 247–315, with bibliography.

64. See Chapter 1, pages 18–19.

65. Stanton, "Cosmopolitan Ideas," 187–91. Stanton derives Aurelius's emphasis on submission from his cosmopolitan ideas. The unity of humanity under reason creates a

with his fate, is a rebel and outcast. This is the automatic verdict on the demagogue, the reformer, and the sectarian. As the lives of such dissidents as these were often characterized by conspicuous practices of physical asceticism, such practices were suspect by association. In addition, the radical ascetic, whose discipline was both physical and extreme, could be for these very reasons branded "irrational" by Stoic standards, and subjected to the penalties of those who refuse to acknowledge reason and submit to fate.

In *Med.* X.25, Aurelius repeats this theme, and connects it with the concept of law: "He who flees his master is a runaway slave, but the law is master and he who breaks the law is also a runaway." As the emperor makes clear in the following line, by law he means fate and the inexorable bonds of one's lot. Yet by drawing this analogy, Aurelius cannot but bring up ideas of social order, crime, and punishment, subjects on which he held strong opinions, as indicated by his treatment of runaway slaves. It is but a short step from the law of fate to the law of the State: "The end of rational creatures is to obey the reason and law of that most ancient of cities and governments [i.e., the universe]" (II.16). Since Posidonius, the emphasis in Stoicism had been moving from the simple following of nature to joining in the organization of nature.[66] The State, therefore, can be seen as the enforcer of the laws of nature, the guardian of the rational order. Certainly, such a view is consistent with Rome's own view of her purpose in the world and her role in history.

No amount of personal virtue or asceticism can make up for "antisocial" behavior. In one sentence, an answer is given to the Christians who demanded to know why the empire would persecute those of blameless life. As J. M. Rist has noted, people are to be valued only according to their possession of reason; if fools get what they deserve, that is no cause for pity. Stoicism, not only in spite of but actually because of its belief in the unity of humanity, the power of reason, and the supremacy of nature, can be quite harsh and inhumane to modern sensibilities.[67]

There is evidence that this line of thinking was directly applied to the

---

"type of state" with a common law (IV.4). The prime moral imperative is submission to reason and the decrees of fate (i.e., obeying the law). There is a clear unity to Aurelius's thought, connecting his psychology to his ethics and politics. Taken together, they offer a strong logical argument for social and political conservatism.

66. See M. Laffranque, *Poseidonios d'Apamée: Essai de mise au point*, Publ. de la Faculté des lettres et sciences humaines de Paris, serie "Recherches" 13 (Paris, 1964), 477–79.

67. Rist, "Concept of Detachment," 260–66.

Christians, even by Aurelius himself.[68] There once was a *locus classicus* in Aurelius's comments regarding readiness for death: "This readiness must come from one's own judgment, and not from mere obstinacy [like the Christians], but with deliberation, and dignity, and—if it is to serve as an example—without theatrics" (ἀτραγῴδως, XI.3).[69] The specific mention of the Christians is now held to be an interpolation.[70] Yet the point is still worth noting. Willingness to face death—which perhaps can be viewed as the ultimate form of asceticism—is meaningless if it springs from mere obstinacy.[71] This is consistent with the Stoic emphasis on the motivation of an act and Aurelius's comments regarding avoidance of display. The emperor, and those like him, could turn a hard face to martyrdom.[72] The issue of obstinacy is further illumined by Galen: "One might more easily teach novelties to the followers of

68. In regard to actual persecution in Aurelius's reign, sources are found in Eus., *HE* IV.9, 13, 26.3–11; and V.1 (the martyrs of Lyon), esp. V.1.45. Most scholars hold that Aurelius's policy cannot be established as any different from that of Trajan legally, and that most persecution during the period was the result of local agitation and mob violence; see Stanton, "Marcus, Lucius, and Commodus," 528–32, where scholarship from 1962 to 1972 is reviewed, and Keresztes, "The Imperial Roman Government." Note especially P. A. Brunt, "Marcus Aurelius and the Christians," in *Studies in Latin Literature and Roman History,* ed. C. Deroux, Collection Latomus 154 (Brussels, 1979), 1:484–98; also T. D. Barnes, "Legislation Against the Christians," *JRS* 58 (1968): 32–50; F. Millar, *Emperor in the Roman World,* 559f.; M. Hammond, 211f.; and R. Lane Fox, 423. On the specific issue of Aurelius's deliberate role in persecution: P. Keresztes, "Marcus Aurelius a Persecutor?" *Harvard Theological Review* 61 (1968): 321–41; M. Sordi, "I nuovi decreti di Marco Aurelio contro i cristiani," *Studi Romani* 9 (1961): 365–78, and "Le polemiche intorno." The issue of the Christians is discussed in specific detail in regard to Celsus's *True Doctrine* in Chapter 5.

69. Philostratus would later put a similar sentiment into the mouth of Apollonius; see *VA* VII.31.

70. Brunt, "Marcus and the Christians," 483ff. The argument is accepted by Rist, "Are You a Stoic?" 26 and 26 n. 15. A complete discussion of the issue is found in Birley, *Marcus Aurelius,* 263ff. (appendix 4).

71. The phrase "mere obstinacy" has been the usual translation of Aurelius's ψιλὴν παράταξιν. Birley, *Marcus Aurelius,* 154—though at the time holding the mention of the Christians to be genuine—proposes a refinement on the meaning of παράταξιν. He suggests the word is a military metaphor referring to those who have martyrdom *instilled into them* as a positive value; that is, those who are "trained to die" (in this regard, note the comments of Epictetus below). This would certainly accord better with the fact that Aurelius opposes ψιλὴν παράταξιν to death by "one's own judgment" or perhaps in this light "decision" (ἰδικῆς κρίσεως). Whichever translation is preferred, the point is that the decision to die does not come from a free, rational choice. Those who make such a decision have fled the "commonwealth" of reason, and their deaths deserve no pity. See also Farquharson, *Meditations,* 1:408, 2:858ff.

72. This attitude would, of course, not be limited to Christians. It is safe to say that the emperor would have shared Lucian's disdain for Peregrinus's theatrical suicide. D. Clay,

Moses and Christ than to the physicians and philosophers who cling
fast to their schools" (de Puls. III.3). Galen's complaint is against those
who accept dogma over logic and empiricism. The Jews and Christians offer the best example of this form of irrationality.[73] Likewise
Epictetus: "If then one can develop such an attitude toward these things
through madness and even through habit, as the Galileans do, can
nothing be taught by reason and demonstration?" (Epict. Diss.
IV.vii.6).

The connection with reason appears again in another disputed passage: "Yet to have a mind directing them (τὸν νοῦν ἡγεμόνα) toward
what appears to them to be their duties (καθήκοντα) also belongs to
those who do not believe in the gods, who betray their country, and
who do all manner of things behind closed doors" (Med. III.16). The
mention of treason, atheism, and secret abominations is clearly reminiscent of the stock accusations against the Christians. Whether Aurelius
actually had the Christians in mind at this point is less important than
the general pattern of his thought.[74] The mere possession of reason is no
proof against antisocial behavior. The characteristic of the good man is
submission, as Aurelius's next statement makes clear: "If then everything else is also common to all these types of people I have mentioned,
the one thing remaining unique to the good man is to love and embrace
whatever befalls and is spun for him by fate."

Aurelius's thought begins with the Stoic concept of the "commonwealth of reason." Citizenship depends upon the performance of social
acts, that is, obeying the law. The law is fate. Social behavior, therefore,
lies in accepting one's lot. Those who do not submit are fugitives and
outlaws who believe neither in the state, the gods, nor the norms of
society. What could be a more complete, practical description of fate
than state, gods, and society put together? To question one is to become

---

"Lucian of Samosata: Four Philosophical Lives (Nigrinus, Demonax, Peregrinus, Alexander Pseudomantis)," ANRW II.36.5 (1992): 3416f. and nn. 18f., stresses the importance of the word "theatrics" (τραγῳδία) in Lucian in terms equally applicable to Aurelius. His preferred translation of "solemn farce" would suit the passage in the
Meditations as well.

73. Trans. Walzer, Galen, 14; see also 37–45, 48–56. A stimulating discussion of
Galen's attitude toward the Christians may be found in R. Wilken, The Christians as the
Romans Saw Them (New Haven, 1984), 68–93.

74. The majority of scholars hold that the passage does not refer specifically to the
Christians: Farquharson, Meditations, 2:587; Brunt, "Marcus and the Christians," 494ff.;
Birley, Marcus Aurelius, 265. A notable exception is Rist, "Are You a Stoic?" 26 and n.
15.

an outlaw. Christian ascetics questioned all three. So did Cynics.[75] The emperor's own thinking demonstrates how the progression could be made from a seemingly detached philosophical ideal to slanders and accusations. The process has its own logic. This also explains the similarity between the accusations made against Christians, Cynics, Epicureans, *goetes,* etc. Deviance is perceived first, and the most obvious evidence of such deviance would be the practice of radical physical asceticism. By failing to comply with certain social norms, it follows that such persons believe in no norms, no laws, and no gods. The emperor could have had any or all such persons in mind when he wrote.[76]

In this light, one of the emperor's comments is particularly revealing. Among the lessons Aurelius learned from Rusticus was: "Not to display oneself as a man keen to impress others with a reputation for asceticism or beneficence" (I.7).[77] The only occurrence of a form of the word

75. Cynicism will be discussed in the next chapter in relation to Lucian and Peregrinus. A certain at least perceived relation existed between Christians and Cynics. Aelius Aristides compares the Cynics to "the impious in Palestine" (*Or.* 3.671 in Behr = *Or.* 46 in Dindorf, 2:402). Lucian relates that Peregrinus spent a few years as a Christian before his embrace of Cynicism (*Peregr.* 11–16). Thus J. Bernays, *Lucian und die Kyniker* (Berlin, 1879), 36 n. 20: "Es wird sehr begreiflich, dass ein Jude oder Christ die pseudepigraphische Maske des Kyon wählte." Christian sources, however, usually view Cynicism negatively. The Cynic Crescens is Justin's opponent in *2 Apol.* 3, 10. Hippol., *Refut.* 8.13 draws an unfavorable comparison between Cynics and Encratites; significantly, his complaint is that both are puffed up with pride because of their *asceticism.* Tatian, *Orat. ad Graec.* 19, again defames Crescens and holds him responsible for Justin's death. In 25, Tatian unleashes a general denunciation of the Cynics, specifically insulting Peregrinus's physical appearance and the Cynic "habit." Interestingly Tertullian, *ad Mart.* 4.5, speaks favorably of Peregrinus's "philosophical martyrdom."

76. In persecution trials, the fundamental issue lay in returning to Roman mores, to societal discipline and tradition. Slanders of immorality were irrelevant to the essential grounds of the trial and were simply ignored upon recantation; this appears among the earliest evidence of legal proceedings against the Christians in Pliny, *Ep.* X.96.5–7. See R. Lane Fox, 426f. and S. Benko, "Pagan Criticism of Christianity During the First Two Centuries A.D.," *ANRW* II.23.2 (1980): 1074. Roman magistrates sought worshipers of the gods, not martyrs. Their aim was to reestablish social norms first, to punish only as a last resort. It can also be said that, if the "pattern" of social deviancy is considered as a whole, a reversion to norms in one area would lead to a reversion in the others. If Christianity was a crime, it was because it stood for a complex of deviant behaviors. Thus, sacrificing to the gods or saluting the emperor's genius would suffice as evidence that the accused now accepted the whole social order. The *acta* of Christian martyrs offer abundant evidence of these "loyalty tests," for example, on sacrifice: *A. Carp. et al.* 9 (Greek), 2 (Latin); *A. Pionius* 4, 7, 9; on swearing by the emperor's genius: *A. Polycarp* 9; *A. Scillitan. Mart.* 3; *A. Apollon.* 3; and on *caerimonia* in general: *A. Cypr.* 3. For the texts, see H. A. Musurillo, ed., *Acts of the Christian Martyrs* (Oxford, 1972).

77. There is, I believe, a specific connection in Aurelius's mind between asceticism (τὸν

askesis in the *Meditations* is negative in context.[78] In the first place, not making a display of one's qualities is certainly consistent with both Stoic teaching and with traditional Roman *sobrietas* and *gravitas*.[79] Second, Seneca had already advised that a philosopher conform to outward fashion and decorum, avoiding all ascetical display, lest he make the name "philosopher" less popular than it already was.[80] Conspicuous asceticism was regarded with suspicion in and of itself.

There is another less obvious, but for the purposes of this study more important, aspect of asceticism revealed here. Diognetus, who introduced Aurelius to "the Greek method of education," also taught him "to disbelieve the tales of miracle mongers (τερατευομένων) and *goetes* about incantations and the exorcisms of *daimones*" (I.6). Some form of ascetical display could be expected of the magician or religious charlatan to impress crowds, woo the rich and powerful, and obtain contributions. Epictetus was himself aware of the problem: "Training exercises (τὰς ἀσκήσεις) must not be performed which are opposed to nature and aberrant, since then we who call ourselves philosophers would be in no way different from wonderworkers" (τῶν θαυματοποιῶν, III.xii.1). Commonly such quacks either posed as philosophers or embroidered their "medicine shows" with philosophical

ἀσκητικόν) and beneficence or philanthropy (τὸν εὐεργετικόν). In both cases, the issue is that of an act performed for the sake of drawing public attention to the doer. The latter term carries connotations of public benefaction and *philotimia,* acts of public largesse meant specifically to enhance the social standing and reputation of the benefactor. So also ascetic display can be used for the sake of attention and reputation. As will be seen in Chapter 3, Lucian constantly refers to Peregrinus's ascetical acts as performed "for the sake of notoriety" (δόξης ἕνεκα). The very publicity of such actions and the adulation they inspire are sufficient to make them ethically suspect in Aurelius's eyes.

78. Instead of *askesis* Aurelius refers to the physical disciplines of his youth as "the Greek method of education" (ἡ Ἑλληνικὴ ἀγωγή, I.6); see above, note 8.

79. Epict., *Ench.* 47: "And should you ever wish to undertake training (ἀσκῆσαι) for physical endurance, do so for yourself and not for others to see"; cf. *Epict. Diss.* III.xii.16–17. On the dangers of pride in moral achievement, *Med.* III.6.2, XII.27. Rist, "Are You a Stoic?" 26f., notes that posturing in any form is objectionable, but posing as a "moral athlete" is particularly undesirable, being merely a more sophisticated form of the crude lust for fame; see *Med.* VI.16.2. Even on the level of practical affairs and the traditional stuff of *philotimia,* doing what is necessary is more important than establishing a reputation as a benefactor, *Med.* I.16; cf. Epict., *Ench.* 24.4.

80. Sen., *Ep.* 5.2: "I admonish you, however, that you do nothing conspicuous in your dress or way of life, in the manner of those who desire not to improve themselves but to gain notoriety. Eschew unkempt clothing, uncut hair, slovenly beard, outright scorn of money, a bed placed on the ground, and whatever other conceits this perverse way entails. The very name of philosophy, even when pursued unassumingly, is already held in enough contempt; what would happen if we began to dissociate ourselves from the conventional ways of men?"; see also 5.4.

doctrine. The comparison one modern scholar has made to medieval palmers and friars is most apt.[81] One who made too much of a show, who gained an ascetical "reputation" or popular following, could lay himself open to the charge of *goeteia*.[82] A conspicuous rise in one's fortunes could be enough. Philostratus says that the sophist Hadrian the Phoenician was so favored in imperial circles that many believed he must have been a *goes* to gain such a position (*VS* 590). In his *Apology*, the same accusation is made against Apuleius by the relatives of a wealthy widow whom he had the good fortune to marry. Significantly, Apuleius maintains that he is simply a learned, curious man, interested in *philosophy*.[83] Galen stated that he did not go bragging about his cures and treatments, lest other physicians and philosophers label him a *goes* and soothsayer (μάντις, *de Praecog.* 10.15).

It seems fair then to adduce the suspicious connection between asceticism and *goeteia* as another motive for the avoidance of physical asceticism or ascetic display in Aurelius. Not that the emperor would lay himself open to such a charge; rather, the point is that such display had clear and unsavory connotations that a cultivated, philosophic gentleman would naturally avoid. An active interest in philosophy required discernment and care both against false doctrine and for personal reputation. So fine was the line between learning and quackery, "fakiry" and "fakery" so to speak, in both the popular mind and in everyday

81. R. MacMullen, *Enemies of the Roman Order: Treason, Unrest, and Alienation in the Empire* (Cambridge, Mass., 1966), 60: "They were to the ancient world what palmers and friars were to the medieval, a familiar sight everywhere, both suspect and sacred, but more rightly suspect, since the whole movement, like any vogue, drew in recruits who had the least suitable talents and motives." The situation was further confused by the inconsistent and blurred usage of such terms as: astrologi, mathematici, auspices, vates, arioli, προφῆται, magi, and γόητες—including, at times, φιλοσόφοι (128).

82. "The charge of magic is likely to be made by legitimate religious leaders against people who are viewed as threatening the social order but who have as yet done no other prosecutable criminal offense. For instance, *Mathematici*, Jews, and Christians could be seen as subversive by the Roman government, so it was logical to charge them with "magic" even though the charge might be factually groundless and impress us as absurd," A. F. Segal, "Hellenistic Magic: Some Questions of Definition," in *Studies in Gnosticism and Hellenistic Religions: Presented to Gilles Quispel on the Occasion of his 65th Birthday*, ed. R. van Den Broek and M. J. Vermaseren (Leiden, 1981), 370. This adumbrates a major theme in the following chapters.

83. Apuleius states that he is not only defending himself, but the good name of philosophy as well (*Apol.* 3). He mentions his long unkempt hair (4), and people's objections to his wallet and staff (*peram et baculum*, 25); that is, his philosopher's "habit." Note that Apuleius phrases the accusation in terms of his outward appearance as a philosopher. As will be seen in the following chapters, Peregrinus affected the same appearance at Parium while Apollonius's garb formed one of the accusations in his trial before Domitian. The case of Apuleius will be further discussed in Chapter 4.

social reality. It is no accident that the teacher who warned Aurelius away from magicians and charlatans was the same one who first introduced him to philosophy. Interest in one could lead to the other too easily in a vulnerable mind. Philostratus's comment regarding the charge made against Dionysius of Miletus of improving his students' memories by "Chaldean arts" is appropriate: "Who of those counted among the wise would be so unthinking of his reputation that, by practicing *goeteia* among his pupils, he would also taint what he taught them properly?" (*VS* 523).[84] That the emperor had direct experience with philosophical posturing and pretension is clear.[85]

The "Common Perspective" of the Educated Class

The *Meditations* reveal important evidence regarding asceticism and society in the second century. Asceticism is seen as a cerebral process of self-discipline. It is not defined primarily in terms of the physical, which Stoicism regards with a decided indifference, but rather in terms of the internal workings of the mind: motivation, attitude, and emotional response. As a discipline, it requires philosophical education and decorous moderation. It is a matter of "deportment," of producing a virtuous man according to the canons of tradition, classical *paideia*.[86] Rather than reflecting any sort of radicalism, asceticism—in Aurelius's Stoic sense—

84. It is worth comparing the use and frequency of the *goeteia* slander among such personalities as Dionysius, Hadrian the Phoenician, Apuleius, and Galen. Again, mere celebrity seems sufficient to draw down a rumor or accusation, not to mention professional and personal jealousy. In the cases of Hadrian and Apuleius, however, there appears to have been some real interest in magic on their part. As will be seen below, defining "magic" is no simple task—as evidenced by Apuleius himself in *Apol.* 25ff. Neither would it be easy in antiquity to draw clear lines between the professions of sophistry, philosophy, and medicine represented here and what we today would term "magic" or even "religion."

85. *Med.* IX.29: "How petty these politicians who, as they see it, play the philosopher. They are full of rubbish." Galen, *de Praecog.* 11.8, reports that Aurelius observed that most contemporary philosophers were not only fond of money, but contentious, ambitious, envious, and malicious. Dio LXXII.35.1–2 states that as a result of the emperor's philosophical interest, great numbers pretended to pursue philosophy, hoping that they might be enriched by him. *HA* M.A. XXIII.9 makes a tantalizing comment about men "pretending to be philosophers" stirring up trouble "for both the state and private citizens," but offers no specifics. On Galen's own low opinion of the philosophers current in Rome, see *de Praecog.* 1.13–15, 10.16. On the topic, see also Rutherford, 80–89.

86. P. R. L. Brown, "The Saint as Exemplar in Late Antiquity," *Representations* 1, no. 2 (Spring 1983): 1–4. See also H. A. Marrou, *A History of Education in the Ancient World,* trans. G. Lamb (New York, 1956), 96–101, 217–26.

was a vehicle for conforming to traditional standards of moral behavior.

For those who would not conform, Aurelius's philosophy also provided a justification for persecution. By its equation of reason, nature, and fate, and the necessity of taking its prescriptions for social behavior from the mores of its surrounding society, Stoicism could condemn dissent from prevailing norms as irrational, antisocial, and inhuman. Persons such as Cynic philosophers, prophets of new cults, miracle-working holy men, and the foolhardy atheistic followers of a "crucified sophist"[87] were thus perceived as clear and present dangers to the fabric of society itself. This was Lucian's verdict on Peregrinus and Celsus's on the Christians, while Philostratus endeavored to save Apollonius of Tyana from precisely this sort of accusation.

In writing of the end of Aurelius's reign, Dio made his famous comment that Rome descended from a kingdom of gold to one of iron and rust (LXXII.36.4). In one respect, although not one Dio intended, the process was already under way. Aurelius is both a critical Stoic thinker and a man whose thought is subject to the play of old ideas and prejudices.[88] Twice Aurelius urges himself to be a Roman (II.5; III.5). In the final analysis, it is a combination of Stoicism and *Romanitas* that best describes the emperor's character and beliefs.[89] Stoicism, stripped of its earlier radical nature, provided a justification for the status quo both of the society of the Roman Empire and of the inherited culture of classical civilization.[90] The practical application of Stoic principles: the way one behaved as a social being, how one submitted to fate, the manner of demonstrating social reason, all had to be taken from the attitudes and values of the surrounding society.

A parallel exists between the individual and society. Just as Aurelius was forced to admit the intractability of the physical and irrational side of human nature, so the social and political status quo also had to be accepted as a decree of fate. The most that could ever be done was to allow reason to maintain all the elements of both the individual personality and the social fabric in their proper place.[91] By the time of Au-

87. See Lucian, *Peregr.* 13.

88. Arnold, 217. G. W. Bowersock, *Greek Sophists in the Roman Empire* (Oxford, 1969), 74f., makes a similar judgment about Galen and the sophists of the age.

89. Rist, "Are You a Stoic?" 35; Birley, *Marcus Aurelius*, 98.

90. "Stoicism had become an authorized doctrine rather than a developing philosophical system," A. A. Long, *Hellenistic Philosophy: Stoics, Epicureans, Sceptics,* 2d ed. (Berkeley and Los Angeles, 1986), 115.

91. This parallel between the individual and society is noted by Brown, *Body,* 30f.: "Like society, the body was to be administered (by reason), not changed."

relius, Stoicism had become the philosophical justification for *Romanitas*. The emperor's philosophical beliefs neither led him to question established principles of policy nor offered him any guidance in determining the objective content of his actions. It probably never occurred to him that any such examination would be necessary.[92] Aurelius's outlook offered a strong defense for a political and social structure that was particularly conservative by nature.[93] Far from embracing any movement sympathetic to its own ascetical bent, Roman Stoicism presented a clear case for attacking those perceived as a threat to the social order.

92. Brunt, "Stoicism," 23f.
93. An excellent exposition of the "culture" of Roman conservatism is given by C. N. Cochrane, *Christianity and Classical Culture: A Study of Thought and Action from Augustus to Augustine,* revised and corrected ed. (Oxford, 1944), 114–76.

Chapter Three

LUCIAN

Ascetics as Enemies of Culture

THE CONNECTION BETWEEN ASCETICISM, philosophy, and *goeteia*, suggested in Aurelius's *Meditations*, is a pronounced theme in the satires of Lucian (c. 120–c. 180 C.E.). In moving from philosophy to literature, from emperor to artist, similar motifs appear that further describe, insofar as such a thing is possible for the historian, the "common viewpoint" regarding asceticism among the educated and cultured classes of the period.

Born in Samosata in Commagene, Lucian traveled widely practicing the art of rhetoric. At about the age of forty, after moving to Athens, he deserted rhetoric for "philosophy" and began to compose his own unique form of satirical epistolary dialogue.[1] Late in life, Lucian accepted a salaried governmental post in Egypt where, presumably, he died sometime after 180.[2] Of his more than eighty surviving works, *The Death of Peregrinus (Proteus)* stands out both as a virulent attack against a philosophic charlatan (in Lucian's point of view), and as one

---

1. Lucian, *Double Indictment* 32f. The chief autobiographical sources for Lucian are *Double Indictment, The Dream* or *Lucian's Career*, and *Apology*.
2. Lucian, *Apology* 12; cf. 1 and 11. J. vander Leest, "Lucian in Egypt," *GRBS* 26 (1985): 75–82, offers a brief review of scholarly opinion as to what office Lucian held in Egypt and advances his own arguments in favor of the post of εἰσαγωγεύς.

of only two works targeting named contemporaries. As Peregrinus was himself an ascetical Cynic, this work merits detailed discussion. The issues raised in *Peregrinus* are, in turn, further illumined by comparisons to other works of Lucian. *Alexander* or *The False Prophet*, the other work attacking a named contemporary, is an equally virulent depiction of a religious charlatan, while *Demonax* and *Nigrinus* present positive images of philosophers.

Through these writings, Lucian offers portraits of various ascetics and the society around them and polemics reflecting values similar to those of Aurelius. Lucian's perspective, however, is that of a man of refined literary culture, a gentleman of *paideia* rather than an introspective moralizing philosopher. The ideals of the writer are less rigid than those of the emperor, his appreciation of the world around him more lively. Lucian finds much to parody and ridicule in his society; he is no uncritical or resigned defender of the status quo. His allegiance to culture, rather than the norms of society, determines his ideals.

It is as an enemy of this culture that Lucian attacks Peregrinus, not only as a devotee of a philosophy that professed indifference to or rejection of the norms of civilized social behavior, but also as a self-seeking charlatan (*goes*) and self-styled "holy man," daring to exalt himself as an authority figure independent of the constraints of received culture. Nor is Peregrinus alone. Alexander the prophet and holy man as well as Jesus the "crucified sophist" and his followers come under the same condemnation for the same reasons.

In Lucian's more tendentious works, distinguishing between portrait and polemic is a problem that has beset Lucianic scholarship since the turn of the century.[3] Scholarly opinion of Peregrinus and Alexander has in the past been based upon the previous judgment of Lucian's own reliability and character; a negative appraisal of Lucian resulted in an

---

3. Trends in scholarship are reviewed in C. P. Jones, *Culture and Society in Lucian* (Cambridge, Mass., 1986), 1–5. In general, German scholarship, based on J. Bernays, *Lucian und die Kyniker* (Berlin, 1879), dismissed Lucian as an irresponsible oriental nihilist. The French, beginning with M. Croiset, *Essai sur la vie et les oeuvres de Lucien* (Paris, 1882), endeavored to rehabilitate him by focusing solely on his literary style. The result was to make him an isolated wordsmith, removed from his surrounding society. This trend culminated in J. Bompaire, *Lucien écrivain* (Paris, 1958). For history of scholarship, see also R. B. Branham, *Unruly Eloquence: Lucian and the Comedy of Traditions* (Cambridge, Mass., 1989), 219 n. 2. Bibliography in H. D. Betz, *Lukian von Samosata und das Neue Testament: Religionsgeschichte und paränetische Parallelen. Ein Beitrag zum Corpus Hellenisticum Novi Testamenti*, Texte und Untersuchungen zur Geschichte der altchristlichen Literatur 76 [5 Reihe, Band 21] (Berlin, 1961); later works in Jones and Branham. Forthcoming at the time of this writing is M. D. Macleod, "Lucianic Studies since 1930" in *ANRW*.

often uncritical positive assessment of his subjects.[4] More recent scholarship, however, has rehabilitated Lucian's veracity, while less dogmatic
approaches to his work have clearly established his value as an observer
and critic of a society in which he was fully engaged.[5] It is on this basis
that Lucian's attitude toward Peregrinus, his Cynicism, and his asceticism can be investigated. The issue is less one of finding the "historical
Peregrinus" as of examining the antecedents and context of Lucian's
opinions. Ultimately, the question is simple: What did Lucian find so
objectionable in Peregrinus? The answer, however, is complex and lies
in the number of areas in which Peregrinus crossed the boundaries of
"respectable," or at least traditional, Cynicism and violated the social
and cultural values of that educated and ruling class represented by
Marcus Aurelius and Lucian.

Peregrinus's Character and Career

In his narrative of Peregrinus's career, Lucian begins by vesting his subject with stock accusations of polemic.[6] An adulterer as soon as he came

4. Bernays, 42ff. and 52ff., that Lucian was morally and intellectually superficial and
irresponsible, incapable of understanding Cynicism, and attacked Peregrinus out of an
irrational hatred for the sect. Croiset, 87–96, 147, 189f., that Lucian is superficial, a
moral nihilist, and painted an utterly distorted picture of Peregrinus out of hostility to the
philosopher's mysticism and asceticism. M. Caster, *Lucien et la pensée religieuse de son
temps* (Paris, 1937), 243f., for a rather uncritical, positive description of Peregrinus; 88,
regarding *Alexander:* "Il contient du vrai dans la mesure où un écrit de polémique a
besoin de coïncider—parfois—avec la vérité."
    5. Fundamental to the reevaluation of Lucian is L. Robert, *A travers l'Asie Mineur:
Poètes et prosateurs, monnaies grecques, voyages et géographie*, Bibliothèque des Ecoles
Françaises d'Athènes et de Rome 239 (Paris, 1980), 393–436. Excellent modern studies
include those of Jones, Branham, and Betz above; B. Reardon, *Courants littéraires grecs
des IIe et IIIe siècles après J.-C.*, Annales littéraires de l'Université de Nantes 3 (Paris,
1971); B. Baldwin, *Studies in Lucian* (Toronto, 1973); C. Robinson, *Lucian and His
Influence in Europe* (Chapel Hill, N.C. 1979); J. A. Hall, *Lucian's Satire* (New York,
1981); and, most recently, D. Clay, "Lucian of Samosata: Four Philosophical Lives
(Nigrinus, Demonax, Peregrinus, Alexander Pseudomantis)," *ANRW* II.36.5 (1992):
3406–50. J. Schwartz, *Biographie de Lucien de Samosate*, Collection Latomus 83
(Brussels, 1965) is highly conjectural and of limited use.
    6. Though Peregrinus professes Cynicism, Lucian's depiction is entirely personal; there
is no "philosophy" to be found in the work other than a caricature of a typical Cynic.
This is hardly surprising in a work of satire. It is notable, however, that when Philostratus
comes to write his *Life of Apollonius*, which portrays its Pythagorean hero in the most
glowing positive light, the portrait is just as personal with just as little information concerning philosophical doctrine. The central issue in both cases is personal character and

of age, Peregrinus proceeded to pederasty and finally patricide, being impatient to receive his inheritance (*Peregr.* 9, 10). While such accusations are conventions (*topoi*) in this sort of writing, they do convey Lucian's fundamental attitude toward his subject. Peregrinus is portrayed as a living character type, a variation on the parvenu of dubious origins, rising by dishonest means, notoriously immoral, and profiting by ignorance.[7] This introduces a second important theme. Though Peregrinus is clearly portrayed as vicious and deceitful, he is just as clearly successful. He is believed. Concomitant with Lucian's denunciation of charlatans is his condemnation of those who believed in them.[8]

So it is that Peregrinus flees from the murder of his father to Palestine and a group of Christians. Once installed in the community he made rapid headway:

> In a short time he showed them up to be children, becoming prophet, cult leader, synagogue chief, indeed everything all rolled up in one. He not only interpreted and explained some of their books, he even wrote a number of them himself. For their part, they revered him as a god, consulted him as a lawgiver, and enrolled him as their patron and leader, second after that one whom they still worship, the man crucified in Palestine for bringing this new cult into the world. (11)

After having apparently moved to Syria, Peregrinus was imprisoned and became a confessor waited upon by pious widows and orphans (12). The Christians were easy prey, according to Lucian, because of their disregard for material goods and for their simplicity:

---

behavior rather than teaching. As Clay, "Lucian," 3411–14 and 3420–30, correctly argues, "philosophy" by this period was characterized by the philosopher's mode of life and attitude of character rather than his doctrine. This is the very definition of philosophy for Lucian. Arguments based, therefore, on the lack of "real" philosophy in any of these authors or works should be regarded warily. See also Chapter 4, pages 106–7.

7. Robinson, 18f., noting the parallel *topoi* between Peregrinus and Alexander and the character types found in Lucian's other works. Caster, *Lucien,* 245f., 249, 252, speaks of Lucian's "brutality" against Peregrinus. Robert, 407f., warns against rejecting all Lucian's accusations simply because they are *topoi,* and offers a provocative argument from epigraphical evidence confirming the historicity of certain accusations against Alexander.

8. P. de Labriolle, *La Réaction païenne: Etude sur la polémique antichrétienne du Ier au VIe siècle* (Paris, 1934), 98: "Il distribuerait volontiers l'humanité en deux classes, les dupeurs et les dupés, avec un tout petit lot d'amis sincères de la vérité et de la raison, parmi lesquels il se range. Et il n'a pas plus de considération pour les dupés que pour les dupeurs, car la sottise lui paraît encore plus pitoyable que la canaillerie." See Robinson, 34.

Those wretched creatures have utterly convinced themselves that they will be immortal and will live for all time. Because of this they scorn death, and most of them give themselves up willingly. Indeed, their first lawgiver convinced them that they would all be brothers of one another as soon as they, transgressing once for all, would renounce the Greek gods and worship instead that crucified sophist himself and live according to his laws. Thus they think lightly of everything and consider it all common property, accepting these sorts of "laws" without any solid grounds. So if any crafty charlatan *(goes)* able to profit from the opportunity should come among them, he straightaway becomes very rich in a very short time toying with simple folk. (ἰδιώταις ἀν-θρώποις, 13)[9]

Christian simplicity and communism are not admirable virtues, but proofs of stupidity and gullibility, pitiable at most. The Church offered a fertile field for the *goes*.[10]

9. Though the word used here to describe the Christians, *idiotai*, is common enough in Greek, it is worth noting that Lucian uses it repeatedly in contexts important for the matter at hand. In *Peregr.* 18, it is used to describe the "rabble" who are particularly drawn to Peregrinus's slandering of the benevolent emperor Antoninus Pius. In *Fugit.* 21, it is used to describe those who, ignorant of the truth, defame philosophy because of the outrages of runaway slaves who have proclaimed themselves Cynics. The *idiotai*, the masses if you will, represent a danger to Lucian; they are gullible, easily mislead, subject to demagoguery. Those who would lead them are a positive threat. This theme will be developed throughout this chapter. Finally, it should also be noted that Celsus uses the same word to describe the "vulgar and illiterate" Christians in *Contra Celsum*, I.27; see Chapter 5, note 68.

10. The Christians themselves realized this. The second-century Church manual, *Didache* 11–13, specifies tests and rules for itinerant apostles and prophets, describing a situation parallel to that found in *Peregrinus*. H. D. Betz, "Lukian von Samosata und das Christentum," *Novum Testamentum* 3 (1959): 229–234, discusses Lucian's attitude. He argues that Lucian was not particularly knowledgeable about the Christians, but described them on the basis of hearsay and in terms and concepts familiar to himself. S. Benko, *Pagan Rome and the Early Christians* (Bloomington, Ind., 1984), 30–53, devotes an entire chapter to describing Peregrinus as a Christian, especially noting how behavior such as his brought suspicion upon all adherents of the new faith. Though his points regarding the behavior of some Christians are well taken—the subject is discussed in Chapter 5—his confident assertion of Peregrinus's Christianity is by no means certain. M. J. Edwards, "Satire and Verisimilitude: Christianity in Lucian's *Peregrinus*," *Historia* 38 (1989): 89–98, holds that Peregrinus probably never was a Christian or, at most, had some brief connection with the sect. No Christian writer who mentions Peregrinus refers to his ever being a Christian or to his apostasy. In this passage, Lucian sought to underscore his satiric themes and description either by inventing or giving inordinate prominence to Peregrinus's Christian career. On Cynicism and Christianity in general, see M.-O. Goulet-Cazé, "Le Cynisme à l'époque impériale," *ANRW* II.36.4 (1990): 2817, 2788–2800.

Lucian puts Jesus himself in the same category as Peregrinus, referring to him as a "sophist" crucified for bringing "this new cult" (και-
νὴν ταύτην τελετήν) into the world (11, 13).[11] Christian gullibility is
based upon irrationality, their receiving novel doctrines without any evidence (13). The same theme has already been seen in Aurelius and
Galen, that even virtuous behavior not founded upon traditional education, received philosophy, and accepted reason is suspect. Lucian has no
tolerance for fools, particularly if they are organized. The Christians
appear to be a clear and extreme example of those who would follow
Peregrinus later, a possibly inoffensive but certainly unstable element in
society.[12] Christian ascetical virtue does nothing to redeem them in this
regard.

After being pardoned by the governor of Syria, Peregrinus returned to
Parium to find most of his father's possessions carried off—although
Lucian and Peregrinus's disciple Theagenes disagree as to how rich the
family was—and the suspicion of patricide still hot against him (14). In
order to deflect the charge and appease his fellow citizens, he appeared
before the assembly theatrically attired in the Cynic garb of the worn
cloak (*tribon*), wallet, and staff and bequeathed his remaining property
to the city. To no one's surprise, the people hailed him as "the one and
only philosopher, the one and only patriot, the one and only rival to
Diogenes and Crates" (15).[13] Lucian makes a comedy out of the incident. But it is obvious that, at some point, Peregrinus made a public
renunciation of his property as part of his conversion to Cynicism. He
at least made some show of being a genuine philosopher. In so doing,
not only did he adopt a highly visible ascetic practice, but one that was
common among several traditional "holy men" in the Greek world.[14]
After this incident, Lucian has Peregrinus return to the Christians, only
to be expelled for violating some dietary taboo and left with no visible
means of support (16).[15]

11. Caster, *Lucien*, 351, states that "sophist" is here a synonym for *goes*. Betz, "Lukian
u. Christentum," 235ff., that Lucian despised the new cult of Christ in the same way as
that of Alexander.

12. Labriolle, 108: "une folie de plus à ajouter à l'interminable liste des inanités humaines."

13. On the theatricality of this event and of the philosopher's appearance and Cynic
"habit," see Clay, "Lucian," 3414–20.

14. L. Bieler, ΘΕΙΟΣ ΑΝΗΡ: *Das Bild des "Göttlichen Menschen" in Spätantike und
Frühchristentum* (Vienna, 1935–36), 1:68. On Peregrinus as holy man, see below, pages
67–77.

15. Betz, "Lukian u. Christentum," 232, doubts the detail about a violation of dietary
rules. The story of this incident led G. Bagnani, "Peregrinus Proteus and the Christians,"
Historia 4 (1955): 111, to suggest that Peregrinus was an Essene Ebionite; this is un-

After forsaking the "wondrous wisdom" (θαυμαστὴν σοφίαν, 11) of the Christians, Peregrinus went to Egypt to undertake an equally "wondrous *askesis*" (θαυμαστὴν ἄσκησιν):

> After these events, he left home for a third time and went to Egypt to visit Agathoboulos in order to undertake his wondrous ascetical training (τὴν θαυμαστὴν ἄσκησιν διησκεῖτο). He shaved half his head, daubed his face with mud, and displayed what they call "indifference" (τὸ ἀδιάφορον) by erecting his member in the middle of large crowds of bystanders. In addition he gave and received blows on the backside with a fennel stalk and in many other more audacious ways performed "wonders." (θαυματοποιῶν, 17)[16]

And so Peregrinus passed simply from one inanity to another in Lucian's view. The word *askesis* again appears, again in a negative context. As with Aurelius's early philosophical education, it refers here to a period of training (διησκεῖτο), a preparation for leading a philosophical life.

Having graduated, Peregrinus embarked upon his career as a philosopher. He went to Rome and set about defaming the emperor, Antoninus Pius. The emperor dismissed his libels and "did not think it appropriate to punish on account of his words one who put on philosophy like a garment and especially one who had made a profession out of reviling" (18). Peregrinus's reputation only grew, especially among the rabble (τοῖς ἰδιώταις) and he was finally expelled by the urban prefect "because of the freedom of his speech and excessive liberties" (διὰ τὴν παρρησίαν καὶ τὴν ἄγαν ἐλευθερίαν). This only served to gain for him the reputation of a Musonius, Dio Chrysostom, or Epictetus; his name was on everyone's lips (18). After leaving Rome, Peregrinus continued to cause trouble: insulting the Eleans, urging Greeks to revolt

---

founded; see Betz, "Lukian u. Christentum," 229 n. 5. The fact that Peregrinus appears to the Parians in Cynic attire before his expulsion from the Church (15) has led to the conclusion that he embraced both Cynicism and Christianity at the same time; e.g., Bernays, 37. K. von Fritz, *RE* 19.1 (1937), s.n. "Peregrinus (Proteus) (16)," 659, holds that the expulsion came before the incident in Parium and that Lucian delayed mention of it so as to serve as the motive for Peregrinus's attempt to recover the property he gave to the city; so also Jones, *Culture and Society*, 123f.

16. I have endeavored to render Lucian's pun in English by using *wondrous* and *performed "wonders"* both in the sense of amazing and miraculous, to those who believed, and bizarre and shocking, to those who did not. The word used here for "performing wonders" is itself a double entendre; θαυματοποιῶν (wonderworking) in its various forms can also mean sorcery, conjuring, and serve as a synonym for γοητεία.

against Rome, and slandering Herodes Atticus, whom Lucian regards as "a man outstanding in culture and dignity" (19).[17] Peregrinus is revealed as a typical Cynic, gaining his reputation for fearless free speech (*parrhesia*) and denunciation of authority.[18]

Cynicism in the Second Century

The words "typical Cynic" must be used guardedly, for second-century Cynicism contains a number of paradoxes.[19] From the death of Vespasian (70 C.E.) to that of Marcus Aurelius (180 C.E.), Cynics appear in a large number of authors from Martial to Lucian, and almost always in an uncomplimentary light. Yet, only twelve are known historical figures and of these there is sufficient evidence concerning only four to say anything meaningful, while Lucian is himself virtually the only source for two of these four. With the death of Peregrinus's disciple Theagenes before the turn of the century—recorded incidentally by Galen, *de Meth. Med.* 10—our knowledge of Cynics ends, apart from a single reference, until the reign of Julian (361–363 C.E.).[20] Moreover, Lucian's scathing portrayal of Peregrinus is contradicted by the only other useful sliver of evidence: Aulus Gellius, *Noct. Att.* 8.3, in which the author visits Peregrinus in his hut outside of Athens and describes him as "a serious and disciplined man" (*virum gravem atque constantem*; cf. 12.11). Though excoriating Peregrinus, Lucian himself is unstinting in his praise of another Cynic, Demonax.[21] Throughout the literature of

17. Cf. Philostratus, *VS* 563. See W. Ameling, *Herodes Atticus*, Subsidia epigraphica 11 (Hildesheim, 1983), 1:136–51 and 2:135–38.

18. Bernays, 28–30, especially portrays Peregrinus as part of the "Cynic opposition" to Rome and Caesarism; also Labriolle, 84. C. P. Jones, *The Roman World of Dio Chrysostom* (Cambridge, Mass., 1978), 125, notes that it was no coincidence that Peregrinus, "an ardent Hellene and advocate of rebellion," was taught by an Alexandrian, Agathoboulos. On the particular significance of Alexandria, see below, and, more generally, M. Józefowicz-Dzielska, "La Participation du milieu d'Alexandrie à la discussion sur l'idéal du souverain dans les deux premiers siècles de l'Empire Romaine," *Eos* 59 (1971): 241–54.

19. The most recent survey is that of M.-O. Goulet-Cazé, "Le Cynisme à l'époque impériale," *ANRW* II.36.4 (1990): 2720–2833 with bibliography. D. R. Dudley, *A History of Cynicism from Diogenes to the 6th Century* (London, 1937) and R. Höistad, *Cynic Hero and Cynic King: Studies in the Cynic Conception of Man* (Uppsala, 1948) are also very useful.

20. Dudley, 143f., 183, and n. 1. The four are Dio Chrysostom, Demonax, Oenomaus of Gadara, and Peregrinus.

21. See below, pages 73–75.

the period there arises the repeated distinction between "true" Cynics and those who merely don the traditional Cynic habit of the cloak, wallet, and staff.[22] Rather than speak of a "typical Cynic" in this period, it is necessary to realize that the term "Cynic" covered a wide variety of persons and behaviors, some of which were not necessarily connected to philosophy at all.[23]

One important aspect of Cynicism in this regard is the tendency for "free speech" to turn into demagoguery. The Cynic, in his characteristic attire and idiosyncratic manner of life, held a particular appeal to the lower classes as a standardized symbol of opposition to convention and the desire to escape the restraints of ordered society.[24] Yet, the rugged individualism of the sect, and its lack of doctrine, offered no specific program for social reform.[25] Cynic demagogues could, at the very least, pose the threat of stirring an urban mob to violent action with only vague objectives.

22. *Epict. Diss.* III.22.10, 50; Dio Chrys., *Or.* 32.8f.; Martial IV.53; Gell., *Noct. Att.* 9.2. On the origin of the Cynic habit, see Dudley, 6f., 120ff.; on its significance, see Goulet-Cazé, "Cynisme," 2738–46 and Clay, "Lucian," 3413ff.

23. A. J. Malherbe, "Self-Definition among Epicureans and Cynics," in *Jewish and Christian Self-Definition,* ed. B. F. Meyer and E. P. Sanders (Philadelphia, 1982), 3:49, "What made a Cynic was his dress and conduct, self-sufficiency, harsh behavior towards what appeared as excesses, and a practical ethical idealism, but not a detailed arrangement of a system resting on Socratic-Antisthenic principles." So also Goulet-Cazé, "Cynisme," 2817, who states that it may be better to speak of "Cynics" rather than "Cynicism" in the period; that is, that Cynicism had become foremost an idiosyncratic *way of life* founded on asceticism.

24. Bernays, 26 and 41, views Cynicism as a protest against bourgeois society. Dudley, 143f., 146f., rejects any attempt to view Cynicism as a "philosophy of the proletariat"; see also R. MacMullen, *Enemies of the Roman Order: Treason, Unrest, and Alienation in the Empire* (Cambridge, Mass., 1966), 60f. and n. 17. Again, the varieties of Cynicism must be kept in mind. Dio Chrysostom, *Or.* 32, and Lucian, *The Fugitives,* certainly convey the impression that Cynic popular preaching held a particularly lower class appeal. Goulet-Cazé, "Cynisme," 2818, eloquently concludes: "Le cynisme fait appel en effet à une constante de l'esprit humain: face à l'ordre établi, face aux conventions, face aux contraintes quelles qu'elles soient, qu'il s'agisse de la puissance de l'argent et du pouvoir matériel, qu'il s'agisse de la pression exercée par l'Etat ou par la société, l'individu a besoin de réagir et de réaffirmer dans un surgissement rebelle sa souveraine liberté. Socrate avait soulevé une fois pour toutes les grandes questions de la philosophie; Diogène était venu témoigner que l'homme est né libre, d'une liberté absolue, indispensable à l'exercice de la philosophie; sous l'Empire romain, des Cyniques ont lancé à la face des Princes le défi de cette liberté en acte."

25. Dudley, xi: "That Cynic 'anarchy' never became so practical as to organize the murder of tyrants, and their invective against wealth was as much for the spiritual benefit of the rich as for the material betterment of the poor. Indeed, by preaching that poverty and slavery are no bar to happiness, the Cynics implied that a social revolution would be superfluous."

There is evidence of this occurring in Alexandria in the first decade of the second century, during the reign of Trajan. In his 32nd Oration, delivered at Alexandria, Dio Chrysostom addressed the issue of recent social unrest in that city.[26] Though not specifying the precise nature of the civic strife, he suggests to his audience that its cause lay with "so-called philosophers" (*Or.* 32.8). Chrysostom singles out the large number of Cynic street preachers, men whose tenets comprise nothing spurious or ignoble (Chrysostom was himself, at least for a time, a Cynic) but who choose to make a living from their soapbox.[27] He first condemns the manner of these Cynics' preaching, their low-toned and excitable appeal to the masses:

> They beguile the young and sailors and that sort of crowd stringing together endlessly jokes, drivel, and all those sorts of exhalations common to the marketplace. They therefore accomplish nothing good whatsoever, but rather the worst kind of evil, accustoming the thoughtless to deride philosophers just as someone would accustom boys to disdain teachers. And though this sort ought to have their impudence knocked out of them, these "philosophers" only further increase it. (9)[28]

The issue is not only the manner of these Cynics, but also their motivation: "If, maintaining to be philosophers, they do these things for the sake of their own profit and reputation, and not for your edification, that is a terrible thing indeed" (10).[29] The import of this statement is

---

26. The Trajanic date for this oration has been challenged by C. P. Jones, "The Date of Dio of Prusa's Alexandrian Oration," *Historia* 22 (1973): 302–9, who suggests a date c. 71–75 during the reign of Vespasian. Jones's arguments are not completely convincing and the traditional date has been well defended by J. F. Kindstrand, "The Date of Dio of Prusa's Alexandrian Oration—A Reply," *Historia* 27 (1978): 378–83, and most recently by H. Sidebottom, "The Date of Dio of Prusa's Rhodian and Alexandrian Orations," *Historia* 41 (1992): 407–19. Bibliography of the controversy in Jones, *Roman World,* 143–54, and in the notes to Sidebottom's article. Note that the discussion of this oration in Jones, *Roman World,* 36–44, presumes his earlier date.

27. E.g., *Or.* 34.2f. On Chrysostom's adoption of Cynicism and his probable later return to Stoicism, see Hans von Arnim, *Leben und Werke des Dio von Prusa* (Berlin, 1898), 245, 464; and Jones, *Roman World,* 46–49.

28. On Lucian's similar opinion about Alexander, see below, pages 69–73.

29. So also *Epict. Diss.* III.xii.16–17 regarding ascetic practices: "In conclusion, whatever disciplines are practiced upon the body by those engaged in exercise may themselves be considered training, provided they are concerned with desire and aversion in some way. If, however, they are concerned with display, they indicate one who has turned

that these Cynics scandalized philosophy by acting as entertainers or rhetoricians, plying their craft for profit and notoriety. Lucian makes the same accusation repeatedly against Peregrinus.[30]

Chrysostom, the "true" Cynic, declaims against the "false," but he was not speaking strictly for himself. The orator went to Alexandria at the behest of Trajan, at least unofficially.[31] His assessment of the unrest and its causes would have been known in the imperial court, if not adopted as the official position on the matter. Chrysostom had intimate knowledge of political danger, having been exiled under Domitian.[32] In his own career, Chrysostom serves to connect the various forms and levels of the "philosophical opposition" to the imperial status quo. His own exile from Rome was but one episode in the repeated exiles of philosophers and rhetoricians under Nero, Vespasian, and Domitian, motivated by both the Stoic leanings of the senatorial aristocracy and the street preaching of the Cynics against "tyranny."[33] In the East, opposition focused on the issues of the struggle between rich and poor and of opposition to Roman rule, both of which could easily engender feelings of "oppression" in the lower classes.[34] Witness the remark of the second-century historian Appian: "Now there are many, common and impoverished, putting on philosophy out of necessity. They bitterly denounce the wealthy and powerful and bring themselves a reputation,

---

outward from himself and is hunting for something else, seeking spectators who will proclaim: "Oh, what a great man!"

30. Lucian announces this theme (δόξης ἕνεκα, for the sake of notoriety) at the very beginning of *Peregrinus* and repeats it in 4, 8, 12, 14, 22, 25, 34, 42, and, as the motivation for Peregrinus's suicide, in 20. On the "theatricality" of the careers of Peregrinus and Alexander, and of the age generally, see the astute observations of Clay, "Lucian," 3416–20.

31. Arnim, 437; Jones, *Roman World*, 52f.

32. See Jones, *Roman World*, 45–48. The details of Chrysostom's exile are controversial. Philostr., *VS* 488, conveys the impression that it was part of the general persecution of philosophers in the period, but Philostratus's narrative can certainly be questioned on this and several other points.

33. Dio LXV.12.2 on the preaching of Helvidius Priscus in the reign of Vespasian: "He was a troublemaker and cultivated the mob, always denouncing monarchy and praising democracy." Dio LXV.15.4 on two Cynics who declaimed against Titus and Berenice; one was flogged and the other beheaded. Philostr., *VS* 488 on Chrysostom's actions in a military camp at the news of Domitian's assassination; Jones, *Roman World*, 48f., 51f., considers this story a patent fiction.

34. M. Rostovtzeff, *The Social and Economic History of the Roman Empire*, 2d ed., revised by P. M. Fraser (Oxford, 1957), 115–21. See also Dudley, 125–42, and Mac-Mullen, *Enemies*, 46–94. J. M. C. Toynbee, "Dictators and Philosophers in the First Century A.D.," *Greece and Rome* 13 (1944): 43–58, offers some important corrections to both Rostovtzeff and Dudley.

not for disdaining wealth and power, but for envying these very things" (*Mithr.* 28). M. Rostovtzeff argues that these were precisely the issues involved in the unrest at Alexandria and singles out the influence of Cynic preachers as the primary catalyst.[35]

Lucian himself presents his own example in *The Fugitives*.[36] The work opens with a reference to Peregrinus's death: that of an elderly man, "no mean wonderworker" (θαυματοποιός), whose immolation brought a foul smell to Zeus's nostrils (1). Philosophy herself enters to complain of false philosophers who have brought her name into disrepute (4, 21). The central issue becomes that of a large group of slaves and hirelings having abandoned their work to take up "philosophy." The fugitives are clearly Cynics, dressed in typical garb, howling and begging (14), refusing rational argumentation (15), claiming to follow Diogenes, Antisthenes, and Crates (16).[37] These "Cynics" seduce handsome boys and women, pretending that they are going to make women philosophers as well (18). One of them, employed in a fuller's shop, kidnapped and seduced the fuller's wife (28).[38] In the end, a divine committee descends and sees to the return of the fugitives, and order is restored. As philosophy herself makes clear at the beginning, the "Cynicism" here is false, an attempt to cloak rebellion with respectability.[39] The fugitives are portrayed with the same invective as Peregrinus. Despite a certain "theoretical" sympathy for the poor displayed in other works, Lucian's attitude becomes one of strident opposition when the poor take action.[40]

Asceticism played a key role in Cynic preaching and was fundamental to establishing the credentials of the preacher.[41] Beginning with An-

35. Rostovtzeff, 117 and n. 19, and 126. The textual basis of his argument is Chrysostom's 32nd Oration and the Acts of the Pagan Martyrs, in which he sees a predominance of Cynic themes. The force of the argument, however, lies in his historical analysis of Cynic social criticism throughout the first two centuries C.E. For the Acts, see H. A. Musurillo, *The Acts of the Pagan Martyrs. Acta Alexandrinorum* (Oxford, 1954). See also Jones, *Roman World*, 44.

36. For a similar, brief description of Cynicism, see Lucian, *Philosophies for Sale* 11.

37. In *Double Indictment* 6, Zeus again remarks: "Many, giving up the trades that they had before, dash off to don the wallet and cloak, tan their bodies in the sun the color of an Ethiopian, and go about as impromptu philosophers come from cobblers and carpenters."

38. These incidents parallel some of the stock accusations against the Christians, specifically those of Celsus; cf. *C. Cels.* III.55; see Chapter 5, pages 156–57.

39. Dudley, 147, remarks that to those of humble circumstances, turning Cynic offered "freedom from restraint, change of scene, wide tolerance of behavior, and a living (of a sort) without work."

40. Baldwin, *Studies*, 24, 64, 110f.

41. Dudley, 127: "The opponents of convention had standardized both the manner and matter of their assault into a conventional form, which demanded of its expositors no

tisthenes, renunciation opened the path to inner freedom, a freedom manifested in indifference to social mores (ἀναίδεια) as seen in Peregrinus's Egyptian training; rigorous freedom of speech especially before authority figures (παρρησία) as seen in Peregrinus's subsequent career; and the overturning of accepted social values (παραχάραξις) manifested in both ascetical minimizing of the requirements of life and in public acts meant to outrage common sensibilities.[42] For Diogenes, asceticism was the nucleus or core of his moral teaching and, thus, the very essence of Cynicism.[43] Asceticism was less a matter of battling natural instincts than of limiting their satisfaction to simple, visceral acts. The Cynics did not disparage—much less abstain from—food, drink, and sex. Rather, they abstained only from the pursuit of ever more refined and extravagant pleasure to satisfy the desire for them. By gratifying instinct immediately, simply, and naturally, the Cynic ceased to be in thrall to desire and its ever-escalating demands. In reducing the satisfaction of instinct and the requirements of life to natural essentials, the Cynic also reduced his dependence on others, and on the organization and structure of society itself, to satisfy his wants and needs. The Cynic could thus lead a life of total simplicity and independence, offering a powerful, practical witness to his words.[44]

There was no wrong in indulging one's natural desires, as long as such action would not impair these ideals. Dio Chrysostom devotes his

---

originality of thought, but rather, at best, unimpeachable asceticism and sufficient wit and rhetorical power to hold the attention of an audience." See also Croiset, 140f.

42. Bernays, 22f. and 25: "Sie hatten die Forschung grundsätzlich der Askese geopfert." Hoïstad, 10, regards Antisthenes' asceticism as merely an intensification of certain traits of a pre-Cynic, "Socratic" asceticism, to which Diogenes "contributed a number of equivocal elements which offended the ordinary man's sense of decency." Dudley, 28: "The mission of Diogenes thus became a thoroughgoing onslaught on convention, custom, and tradition in all respects. He endeavored to convert men to a truer way of life, not, like Socrates, by dialectic, nor by allegory, as did Antisthenes, but by the practical example of his daily life"; see also 30 and 95.

43. This is the fundamental thesis of another admirable work of Goulet-Cazé, *L'Ascèse cynique: un commentaire de Diogène Laërce VI.70–71*, Histoire des doctrines de l'Antiquité Classique 10 (Paris, 1986); see esp. 17–92. Forthcoming at the time of this writing is her "Le Livre VI de Diogène Laërce: Analyze de sa structure et réflexions méthodologiques" in *ANRW*.

44. See Goulet-Cazé, *L'Ascèse*, 42–52, 71–76. Perhaps the most resounding statement of these Cynic principles of ascetic simplicity is found in Pseudo-Lucian, *The Cynic*, 8–17. Dio Chrysostom, *Or.* 6.34 calls Diogenes the only free and independent man in the world and possessed of the highest happiness. For an excellent, brief discussion of Cynic freedom and independence, with sources and references to modern scholarship, see J. M. Rist, *Stoic Philosophy* (Cambridge, 1969), 58–63.

entire 6th Oration to Diogenes, particularly in his virtue of "having few needs" (ὀλιγόδεια). Chrysostom states that, contrary to popular belief, Diogenes' asceticism did not result in neglect of his body, but in better health and life and in actually *more* pleasure in food, drink, and sex than others had. In the sexual sphere, such indulgence offered stunning proof of indifference to social norms. As Chrysostom discreetly puts it: "He did not need to go anywhere to find sexual pleasure, but jokingly said he found the delights of Aphrodite everywhere and free of charge" (*Or.* 6.17).[45]

Far from Aurelius's Stoic "asceticism of reason," Cynic asceticism was directed toward external actions rather than internal motivations and was deliberately provocative in character. Whereas Stoic values came directly from society itself and were based on accepted social expectations, Cynic values were based on explicitly denying and overturning the values and expectations of society. Cynic preachers both enabled and symbolized the rejection of social norms and authorities. *Physical* asceticism, in the sense of stark "natural" simplicity, was thus the hallmark of Cynic opposition: pointing to the vanity of prevailing social norms, illustrating the viability of Cynic values, affirming the credibility of Cynic preachers, and providing startling "advertising" for the sect.[46] Yet, the nature of Cynicism remained both individual and idiosyncratic, while its goal of individual freedom would make a Cynic society a contradiction in terms. Cynicism preached not reform, but something closer to anarchy. Cynic asceticism would, quite understandably, be seen as a dangerous threat both to the empire and to the whole fabric of classical society.[47]

45. There follows in 18–20 a frank and factual discussion of the merits of masturbation. Labriolle, 84, rightly observes: "Il ne condamnait nullement le plaisir charnel, et trouvait tout simple qu'on le prît à l'occasion, selon les suggestions de l'instinct. Voilà un laisser-faire dont l'ascétisme chrétien ne se serait pas accommodé volontiers"; see also Goulet-Cazé, "Cynisme," 2817.

46. Goulet-Cazé, "Cynisme," 2811: "En aucun cas, l'ascèse cynique, dont l'originalité est d'être fondée uniquement sur des exercises de nature corporelle, ne saurait être assimilée au stoïcisme qui, tout en reconnaissant qu'il est utile d'exercer le corps s'appuie d'abord sur une ascèse de type spirituel. Certes, elle vise le même but que l'ascèse stoïcienne, à savoir la vertu; néanmois elle diffère totalement dans ses modalités, ainsi nous l'avons montré dans *L'Ascèse cynique*. Par conséquent, si l'on omet les faux Cyniques, les chalatans de tous ordres, et indubitablement il y en avait, il faut reconnaître au cynisme une existence propre fondée sur la pratique de l'ascèse diogénienne."

47. So it is that Diogenes was curtly and aptly described as "Socrates gone mad" (Σωκράτης μαινόμενος, Diogenes Laertius 6.54). Yet, it must also be noted that Diogenes was no anchorite but chose deliberately to live within his society, indicting it and giving witness to his own values; see Goulet-Cazé, *L'Ascèse*, 230. Cynicism, as such, simply cannot exist divorced from the society it criticized.

Peregrinus's Death and the Holy Man

The singular feature of Peregrinus's career was the manner of his death: self-immolation at Olympia. Lucian makes this the immediate setting and focus of his work. Peregrinus announces that after death he will become a "guardian *daimon* of the night" (δαίμων νυκτοφύλαξ) worshiped with altars and statues (27). Lucian is certain that there will be reports of cures and dream appearances, oracles, priests, and nocturnal mysteries. Theagenes, Peregrinus's chief disciple, was already quoting the Sibyl concerning him (28f.). Such a manner of death amounted to an imitation of apotheosis.[48] No sooner was the pyre cool than miraculous stories and appearances began (40), though Lucian himself claims credit for some of the inventions as his way of amusing himself with credulous fools (39). Nor did death put an end to Peregrinus's direct influence. Posthumous letters were delivered to many cities containing "certain testaments, exhortations, and ordinances" (διαθήκας τινὰς καὶ παραινέσεις καὶ νόμους, 41), which perhaps were religious propaganda directing the establishment of a cult.[49]

Opposition to this sort of idealization and apotheosis was a fundamental reason for Lucian's attack.[50] This general view can be further refined. R. Reitzenstein sees Peregrinus as part of a much larger tradition of itinerant Egyptian ascetics, prophets, and wonderworkers. In the period under consideration, men such as these tended to merge with "philosophers" in the stricter sense. Philosophers became prophets, or

48. On the strange and un-Cynic nature of Peregrinus's death, see H. M. Hornsby, "The Cynicism of Peregrinus Proteus," *Hermathena* 48 (1933): 65–84, and R. Pack, "The Volatilization of Peregrinus Proteus," *American Journal of Philology* 67 (1946): 334–45. Hornsby sees the death as reflecting a general "mystical" trend in Peregrinus's brand of Cynicism. Hoïstad, 66ff., compares Peregrinus's suicide to that of Heracles—the archetypal Cynic hero—and other Cynics, but maintains that Peregrinus's case was unique and aroused Lucian's particular disdain. Theagenes himself compares Peregrinus to Heracles in *Peregr.* 4, cf. 21, 24f.

49. Jones, *Culture and Society*, 129f., speaks of Peregrinus's movement as a "hybrid of Cynicism and popular religion"; see also Clay, "Lucian," 3432ff. Athenagoras, *Leg.* 26, mentions an oracular statue of Peregrinus at Parium. Benko, *Pagan Rome*, 45, sees parallels here with the testaments of Christian martyrs.

50. Bernays, 20, 33. Consistent with his positive view of Peregrinus, he contends that a cult was not intended by the philosopher himself, but was created by overzealous, misguided disciples who renounced the fundamental spirit of their sect. Others who focus on Lucian's opposition to a cult include Caster, *Lucien*, 69, 242f., 255, and Dudley, 179f. See also J. Tondriau, "L'avis de Lucien sur la divinization des hommes," *Museum Helveticum* 5 (1948): 124–32.

goetes to the unbeliever, and vice versa.[51] Rather than view Peregrinus simply as a Cynic, or renegade Cynic, it would appear more profitable to view him as a self-styled "holy man."[52] Seen in this way, Lucian's enmity to Peregrinus becomes the same as his toward Jesus "the sophist" and, as will be seen, Alexander. Lucian's animus is personally directed both against these individuals and against the "personality cults" that grew up around them, living or dead. Though certainly hostile to innovations in cult, credulity, the arcana of philosophers, and the miracles of prophets, these issues are ancillary—in the works discussed here—to his opposition to the "phenomenology" of the holy man himself.

Epictetus had defined the true Cynic precisely as a holy man in his highly idealized treatise: *On Cynicism (Epict. Diss.* III.xxii).[53] Upon being asked his opinion by an acquaintance who was considering taking up the Cynic life, Epictetus responds that such a weighty matter must not be taken up against the will of God (δίχα θεοῦ), lest the individual become hateful to the Divinity (2; cf. 53). He then proceeds to make the "true versus false Cynic" distinction seen above.

> Cynicism is not what you think it is. You say: "Even now I wear a worn cloak (*tribon*), and I shall have one then; now I sleep on a hard bed, and I shall sleep that way then too. I will take up a wallet and walking staff and, going about, start begging from everyone and insulting them. And if I should see some man who has depilated himself with pitch-plasters, I shall lambaste him, and do the same for coiffured hair or those who parade about in

51. R. Reitzenstein, *Hellenistische Wundererzählungen* (Leipzig, 1906), 36f., 69. See also A. D. Nock, "Alexander of Abonuteichos," *CQ* 22 (1928): 160–62.

52. This suggestion, without further elaboration, is made by Branham, *Unruly Eloquence*, 186f., citing P. R. L. Brown, *A Social Context for the Religious Crisis of the 3rd Century A.D.*, Protocol Series of the Colloquies of the Center for Hermeneutical Studies in Hellenistic and Modern Culture 14 (Berkeley, 1975), and P. Cox, *Biography in Late Antiquity: A Quest for the Holy Man* (Berkeley and Los Angeles, 1983), 45–65. Jones, *Culture and Society*, 148, makes a similar suggestion regarding Lucian's attitude toward Alexander and Apollonius of Tyana. See Betz, *Lukian u. Neue Testament*, 100–143, for a survey of the various aspects of the phenomenology of the holy man in all of Lucian's works. For a detailed discussion of the concept of the holy man, see Chapter 4, pages 118–26.

53. On this discourse, see M. Billerbeck, *Vom Kynismus / Epiktet*, Philosophia Antiqua 34 (Leiden, 1978); see also *Epict. Diss.* IV.viii: *To those who hastily put on the appearance of philosophers.* The portrait of the Cynic here is not only highly idealized, but also heavily Stoic in color. The first duty of the Cynic, for example, is to keep his "ruling part" pure (πρῶτον οὖν τὸ ἡγεμονικόν σε δεῖ τὸ σαυτοῦ καθαρὸν ποιῆσαι, 19). The Stoic psychology, ethics, and vocabulary are obvious. See Malherbe, 50 and n. 27.

scarlet clothes." If you imagine the matter to be something like this, keep far away from it. Do not come near it; it is not for you. (10–12)

This is because the true Cynic is one sent by Zeus as his herald and scout (23f.). He will not marry, lest he be deterred from his mission and purpose as devoted to the service of God, as father and brother to all and servant of Zeus, the Father of all (67–82). Every thought the Cynic thinks must be that of a friend and servant of the gods, and one who shares in the government of Zeus (95).

Epictetus draws a clear connection between the divine calling of the Cynic and asceticism. The Cynic will particularly refrain from marriage and civic life (83–85) for the sake of his mission. (The parallel with the later Christian theology of monasticism and clerical celibacy is striking.) Moreover, the mission that requires this sort of abstinence is social in character. The Cynic is to be society's conscience, showing where it has strayed in questions of good and evil (23), caring for and reproving all humanity as his children (81), engaging in a form of "politics" exalted far above simple public affairs (84). For Epictetus, the Cynic's profession is the loftiest imaginable, and one must wonder if it was meant to be attainable in the reality of this world.[54]

If a serious Stoic philosopher could make such claims—even on a theoretical level—for a Cynic, how much more likely is it that such claims would be made by one who was "more shining than the sun" and "able to compete against Zeus himself" (*Peregr.* 4). Peregrinus's apotheosis must be taken seriously. Lucian sets his entire piece in the context of Peregrinus's suicide; it begins with Theagenes' announcement and ends with the actual event and the divinization that was its immediate aftermath. All Lucian's other slanders are aimed at discrediting the suicide and apotheosis. It is this aspect of Peregrinus's career that most irked Lucian.

In *Alexander* or *The False Prophet*, Lucian presents his own negative example of a "holy man."[55] Like Peregrinus, Alexander is portrayed from the very start with an alarming array of vices. He prostituted himself as a boy (*Alex.* 5), ultimately indulging in group pederasty as an

54. Philostratus depicts Apollonius as defining his mission in much the same way; see *VA* VIII.7.7.

55. Robert's work is indispensable for the study of *Alexander*; see above, note 5. See also Branham, *Unruly Eloquence*, 181–210; Jones, *Culture and Society*, 137–42; and R. Lane Fox, *Pagans and Christians* (New York, 1987), 241–50. An example of a negative, sarcastic reference to "holy men" occurs in Dio Chrysostom, *Or.* 33.4, where sycophants and phony rhetoricians are referred to as "divine men" (*theioi anthropoi*).

adult (41), along with adultery (42), and attempted murder (56).[56] Alexander apprenticed in quackery with one of his lovers, a *goes* who purported to be a physician.[57]

Significantly, Lucian claims that Alexander's teacher was himself a pupil of Apollonius of Tyana: "His teacher and lover was born in Tyana and was one of the followers of the notorious Apollonius and was versed in all of that one's shenanigans. You can see what kind of 'school of philosophy' the man comes from" (5). After the death of his lover and the passing of his own youthful looks, Alexander teamed up with a Byzantine musician, and the pair set off with their "travelling medicine show" (γοητεύοντες καὶ μαγγανεύοντες, 6) finally coming up with a plot to enrich themselves by founding an oracle (8). Having determined their scheme, the two had to find an audience ripe for the plucking, hosts that were "both thick-headed and dim-witted"—such as Peregrinus found among the Christians. They settled upon Paphlagonia and Alexander's hometown of Abonuteichos, whose inhabitants possessed the necessary qualifications: they were equally superstitious and rich (9).

The oracle that was founded purported to be of the god Asclepius and involved a live snake with a human puppet head, manipulated by Alexander his "prophet," and named Glycon (12–18). The oracle proved immensely popular, and its name and cult spread throughout Ionia, Cilicia, Paphlagonia, and Galatia, reaching even Italy and Rome, where one particularly disastrous oracle was allegedly delivered to Marcus Aurelius.[58] Alexander knew how to run an oracle, creating a large staff and corporation to manage and expand the cult, dividing the profits accordingly (23). The basis for his success was his building on local belief—the citizens of Abonuteichos had already begun to build a temple to Asclepius when Glycon and his prophet arrived (10, 13)— and creating an institution that could take firm root.[59] Alexander became the leading citizen of Abonuteichos, responsible for defending and

56. See above, note 7.

57. A not uncommon pairing of professions, as Galen attests in *de Praecog.* 10.15.

58. On the spread of the oracle: *Alex.* 18, 30, 37; on the oracle to Aurelius: 48. Robert, 395ff. and 404, surveys the physical evidence for the temporal and geographical extent of the cult which, on the basis of coins, lasted through the reign of Trebonianus Gallus (r. 251–53) and, on epigraphical evidence, reached as far as Dacia and the Carpathians in the West and Antioch in the East.

59. Nock, "Alexander," 162, where he also discusses the cult of Asclepius in Abonuteichos established before Alexander conceived of his scheme. Construction of the temple Lucian mentions had probably already begun before Alexander's arrival to serve this pre-Glycon cult. Rather than being responsible for its construction, Alexander saw that the new building offered the perfect place and opportunity to hatch his plot.

promoting its honor and reputation. He successfully petitioned the emperor to change the town's barbaric name to the cultured and classical "Ionopolis," a role he performed in the capacity of leading citizen in a matter unrelated to his cult (58). According to Lucian, Alexander also received imperial permission to strike a coin bearing the image of himself and Glycon (58).[60] The oracle provided Alexander with social and political authority.

This authority was further cultivated and enhanced by Alexander's deliberate courting of legitimacy. He made referrals to the established oracles at Didyma, Mallos, and Klaros. By joining the ranks of the established network, Glycon became recognized by "legitimate," or at least older, religious authority.[61] Philosophy, too, added its approbation. Lucian states that while the Epicureans remained inimical to the oracle, Alexander remained at peace with the followers of Plato, Chrysippus, and Pythagoras. This is consistent with the tendency of the period for oracles, on the one hand, to become more philosophical in tone and vocabulary, even recommending certain teachers and schools; and for philosophy, on the other hand, to argue on behalf of the legitimacy and veracity of the oracles.[62] Alexander himself claimed to be like Pythagoras (4) and, in imitation of him, revealed his own golden thigh at the celebration of his "mysteries" (40). To the noble, rich, and generous special attention and privileges were given, such as hearing prophecies from the mouth of Glycon himself (αὐτόφωνοι, 26). Alexander's greatest catch among his benefactors was the consular P. Mummius Sisenna Rutilianus, a senator with a distinguished *cursus*, but nevertheless highly superstitious (30).[63] So great was his devotion to the cult that, at age seventy, he married Alexander's own daughter at the command of Glycon (35). Through Rutilianus, Glycon's prophet enjoyed no small

60. Robert, 412, regarding the renaming of the city: "Alexandre était ainsi le porte-parole d'un mouvement très ample dans tout le monde grec et sans rapport avec Glycon; Lucien a mis des oeillères à ses commentateurs"; see also Lane Fox, 81. On the coin, Robert, 400–414, states that Lucian has it quite wrong. In the first place, Alexander does not appear on the Glycon coins; instead, the reverse side bears a personification of Ionopolis. Second, no imperial permission would be required for minting the new Glycon type on a local coin.

61. On the referral network among oracles in the period and their connection with civic prestige, see Lane Fox, 202, 234, 247, 252.

62. On this new relationship between philosophy and oracles see Lane Fox, 190–97.

63. On Rutilianus, see *CIL* XIV.3601 and 4244; F. Cumont, *Alexandre d'Abonotichos: Un episode de l'histoire du paganisme au IIe siècle de notre ère*, Mémoires couronés et autres mémoires publiés par l'Académie Royale des sciences, des lettres et des beaux-arts de Belgique 40 (1887), 16 n. 2; and M. Caster, *Etudes sur Alexandre ou le faux prophète de Lucien* (Paris, 1938), 52f.

influence at court (48). The legitimation of Alexander by religious, intellectual, and social authorities—persons who unlike Christians and Paphlagonians should have known better—was particularly wrenching to Lucian.

Alexander did have his enemies as well. According to Lucian, it was the Epicureans who first detected the fraud. Alexander's response was to announce that Pontus was full of atheists and Christians, and ordered his followers to drive them away (25). Just as Aurelius's doctrines of universal reason and the unity of humanity had actually resulted in a justification for persecuting nonconformists, here Alexander bolstered his own conformity and, therefore, legitimacy by attacking highly visible nonconformist groups. Not that Alexander had the lofty philosophical motivations of an Aurelius; rather, the logic of Aurelius's conservative Stoicism and its implications for social deviance is seen here in its alternative incarnation—mass hysteria. The emperor's calm Stoic logic and the prejudices of the mob produce the same result.[64] This conflict became ritualized in Alexander's "mysteries":

> On the first day there was a proclamation, just as at Athens, but worded like this: "If any atheist, or Christian, or Epicurean is present spying upon these rites, let him depart; let those who believe in the god celebrate the mysteries with the blessing of heaven." Then, right at the beginning, there was a ritual expulsion. Alexander himself led off saying, "Away with the Christians," while the crowd in turn shouted, "Away with the Epicureans." (38)[65]

Alexander even went so far as to burn Epicurus's *Principal Doctrines* (κύριαι δόξαι) in public, an event that occasioned a paean to the philosopher's doctrine from Lucian (47; cf. 61).[66]

64. For an example of how philosophy, religion, and common prejudice were intentionally united in the Great Persecution, see R. Wilken, *The Christians as the Romans Saw Them* (New Haven, 1984), 148–56.

65. The reference to Athens indicates that this proclamation was in imitation of that at the Eleusinian mysteries, another example of Alexander's desire for legitimacy. On Epicureans and the charge of atheism, see most recently Clay, "Lucian," 3442f. and D. Obbink, "The Atheism of Epicurus," *GRBS* 30 (1989): 187–223; also A. D. Simpson, "Epicureans, Christians, and Atheists in the Second Century," *TAPA* 72 (1941): 372–81, and A. von Harnack, *Der Vorwurf des Atheismus in den drei ersten Jahrhunderten,* Texte und Untersuchungen zur Geschichte der altchristlichen Literatur 28, no. 4, n.s. 13 (Leipzig, 1905).

66. Branham, *Unruly Eloquence,* 197, notes that Lucian establishes a system of norms, here in Epicurean language, by which Alexander is judged deviant. Tranquillity (*ataraxia*)

The specific reference to Epicureanism should not be pressed too far as an indication of Lucian's specific philosophical preferences. In praising this philosophy, Lucian expresses sentiments that Aurelius would have found equally applicable to his brand of Stoicism.

> How great a source of good that book is for those who happen upon it! How much peace, detachment (*ataraxia*), and freedom it engenders within them! It frees them from terrors, apparitions, and portents, from foolish hopes and excessive desires, and instills intelligence and truth, genuinely purifying their minds not by means of torches, garlic, and other such mumbo-jumbo, but with straight thinking, truth, and frankness (*parrhesia*, 47).

For Lucian, the excellence of Epicurus's teaching lies in its ability to free the individual from superstition and the grip of primitive emotions. In contrast, Alexander's appeal—like the Cynic street preachers'—is to the emotional, irrational, excitable side of human nature.[67] He forsakes reason and by his appeal establishes, quite literally, a "cult following." It is the personal nature of this power and authority, individually derived and unchecked by religious, intellectual, and social norms—in Alexander's case even co-opted by them—that makes Alexander a threat to be exposed. Peregrinus, by attempting to give Cynicism this sort of mystery and cult, inaugurated by his public self-immolation, alarmed Lucian in the same way.[68]

This finds support in other works of Lucian. *Demonax* also offers a portrait of a Cynic, but one who was the best of all philosophers and

---

is set against Alexander's inflaming his audience with the desire for security through prophetic knowledge. At the same time, Alexander is also a veritable incarnation of sexual lust. He is the antithesis of the simple, sober realities of Epicurus, which were based on empiricism and philosophical materialism.

67. On Galen's objections to the same sort of emotional appeal on the part of the Christians, see Chapter 2, pages 33–34, 46. Also recall Chrysostom's objections to Cynic preaching discussed earlier.

68. A. D. Nock, "Alexander," 162, notes that such figures as Alexander and other *prophetai* and *goetes* constitute a new type of religious figure with proprietary rights over their unique revelation and power to employ its mysterious forces. The issue here is *personal* power and authority. I would argue that Peregrinus also constitutes such a figure, one who integrated philosophy into this religious development. Seen in this light, Peregrinus becomes a forerunner of the Neoplatonists who likewise combined a classical philosophy with personal religious revelation. In both cases the philosopher has proprietary rights over both his philosophical and his religious doctrine; indeed, it becomes quite impossible in Late Antique philosophy to separate the two.

worthy of emulation (*Demon.* 2).[69] Though Lucian comments that Demonax combined many forms of philosophy and would not reveal his
preference, in dress and life he was a Cynic like Diogenes (5) and lived a
life committed to freedom of action and speech (ἐλευθερία καὶ παρρησία, 3). He, in fact, even had the same teacher as Peregrinus—the
Egyptian Agathoboulos (3; cf. *Peregr.* 17). Unlike Peregrinus, however,
he did not carry his life to theatrical extremes: "He did not utterly
overturn the normal manner of living,[70] so as to be wondered and stared
at by those who came upon him, but lived the same sort of life and ate
the same sort of food as everyone else, possessed no shred of conceit,
and shared in social and political life" (5). Demonax led the same life
as others and, significantly, remained involved in civic society and politics.[71] Peregrinus himself is made to comment that Demonax's life was
insufficiently "doggish," prompting the retort from Demonax that Peregrinus's life was insufficiently human (21).[72] Demonax was a peace-
maker, both domestically and politically, reconciling rich and poor, urging civic harmony and patriotism according to traditional classical
ideals: "At times he calmly reasoned with excited mobs and persuaded
the majority to serve their homeland with moderation " (9). This is the
exact opposite of the Alexandrian Cynics, Peregrinus's rabble-rousing in
Rome and Greece, and the emotional appeal of Alexander.[73]

69. See also Clay, "Lucian," 3412f. and 3425–29.

70. οὐ παραχαράττων τὰ εἰς τὴν δίαιταν. The verb here, παραχαράττω, literally
means to restamp and, therefore, counterfeit a coin. It was used in a technical sense by the
Cynics to indicate their effacing the "counterfeit currency" of social convention by flouting respectable standards of behavior and adopting ascetical practices; see Diog. Laert.
VI.20, 71. Thus, the Greek here says something more specific than "Demonax did not
alter *his own* manner of life." Lucian's point, rather, is that Demonax—even though he
was a Cynic—did not practice παραχάραξις. Lucian clearly indicates that such flouting
of society is done merely for the sake of notoriety (repeating in different words the δόξης
ἕνεκα theme seen in Peregrinus) and involves rejecting customary norms and values, practicing asceticism, and abstaining from normative social and political behavior.

71. So Dio Chrysostom, *Or.* 20.1–2, notes that any conception of philosophical "retire-
ment" (ἀναχώρησις) cannot be used as an excuse for shirking political and social duties.
Those who do so do not retire; they flee and desert (φεύγουσί τε καὶ δραπετεύουσι).

72. A pun in Greek on the etymology of "Cynic" (κυνικός) from the word for "dog"
(κύων); the Cynics were so named because of their public shamelessness and notoriously
disagreeable temperament.

73. Malherbe, 46–59, discusses the split of the Cynics in the second and third centuries
C.E. between the antisocial, radical ascetics and the milder, "hedonistic" Cynics, who both
adjust to and seek to improve society. This view, which focuses on their positions with
respect to society, is preferable to Dudley's contention, 178, that Peregrinus manifests the
mystical side of second-century Cynicism, while Demonax represents the more classical
skeptical / nihilistic side. Lucian clearly portrays Peregrinus as the social nihilist, while

Moderation, avoidance of ascetical display, preservation of traditional social and political ideals are all hallmarks of Demonax's life. Though the Athenians regarded his visits to their homes "as a visitation of some god or spirit of good fortune" (θεοῦ τινα ἐπιφάνειαν . . . τινα ἀγαθὸν δαίμονα, 63) and venerated his customary seat after his death,[74] Demonax himself did not seek apotheosis in life. In this Lucian can be seen as defining a "holy man" conformable to his own ideals. Demonax is recognized as "godlike" by his preeminent display of common *human* virtues and advocacy of accepted social norms. There is no theatrical display, no claim to heroism, no miracles, prophecy, or special relationships with gods. The picture Lucian paints of Demonax's posthumous veneration is more of a spontaneous display of affection and respect from his fellow citizens for an extraordinarily gracious man than any sort of apotheosis. This is in stark contrast to Peregrinus's flamboyant immolation. Demonax is no demagogue, no radical. He did not use his manner of life to attract a popular following. He therefore poses no threat to authority. The essential elements of the phenomenology of the holy man are absent. This absence, and his clear devotion to traditional culture, make Demonax laudable. Though espousing the same Cynic ideas, he presents the antithesis of Peregrinus.[75]

Another example can be seen in *Nigrinus*. Here the philosopher embraces ascetical poverty for the sake of philosophy (*Nigr.* 12, 14), but lives a life of reclusive quiet in the midst of the vanities of Rome (4).[76] Though Nigrinus holds definite opinions regarding property and wealth, he is no radical nor is any hint of a connection made between his ideas and the actual social condition of the poor.[77] Like Demonax,

Demonax is quite the opposite, showing only a gentle, ambivalent religious skepticism at most (*Demon.* 11).

74. "To honor the man, they reverenced (προσεκύνουν) and garlanded the stone bench on which he used to take his rest when he was tired, regarding even the stone on which he sat to be sacred" (67).

75. For this reason alone, the thesis that presents Lucian as incapable of understanding Cynicism, or of possessing an irrational hatred of it, should be dismissed; see above, note 4. In his own insistent rationality, materialism, and—at times—skepticism, Lucian displays a certain affinity with Cynicism, at least in its more classical form; see Caster, *Lucien*, 68, 81ff. and Hoïstad, 64.

76. Hall, 157–64, observes that *Nigrinus* is built upon a series of opposite pairs: Rome and Athens, wealth and poverty, vice and virtue, true and false philosophy. Rome is only a convenient symbol, and the work should not be taken as an attack against the Romans as a people or against their empire. See also Jones, *Culture and Society*, 84f. and, in general, Clay, "Lucian," 3420–25.

77. *Nigr.* 4, 21, 23, 26 (theory of property), 30f., and passim. Baldwin, *Studies*, 112f., notes that neither here nor in his other works does Lucian go beyond the simple reflection

Nigrinus is a man of simple diet, moderate asceticism, plain clothes, and kind manner (26). In fact, he castigates philosophers who require rigorous asceticism from their disciples: "He clearly condemned those philosophers who suppose it to be a training in virtue (ἄσκησιν ἀρετῆς) if they discipline youths to withstand numerous privations and toils" (27). This condemnation stems from the fact that *apatheia* is created in the soul not the body (28), a view identical to that of the Stoics. Once again, virtue is an internal matter; the effect of physical asceticism on its development is limited.[78]

In his positive descriptions of Demonax and Nigrinus, Lucian is careful to point out their lack of ascetical excess. Neither of these men sought a popular following by an extreme or novel manner of life. This is in complete contrast to Peregrinus, whose every action was directed toward gaining reputation (δόξης ἕνεκα).[79] For Lucian, radical asceticism has but one purpose: to attract the attention of the crowd.[80] Lucian found such self-glorification objectionable in and of itself, and dangerous when promoted to the level of personality cult. Alexander achieved this through religious rather than ascetical means, and was equally vilified.[81]

The case of Peregrinus points to something more. By adopting the Cynics' radical freedom of speech and action (παρρησία and ἐλευθερία) Peregrinus became a demagogue and political troublemaker. The sort of threat such a one could pose is seen in Dio Chrysostom and *The Fugitives*. Demonax was a Cynic himself, but is a perfectly laudable character. Nigrinus holds strong opinions on wealth and property, but

---

that wealth and poverty are both transient, a commonplace philosophical palliative to the problem of rich and poor. Lucian will not support any reaction against authority in this regard. Baldwin rightly holds that the issue in *Nigrinus* is not wealth per se but the vulgarity and pretension of the nouveaux riches, in the manner of Juvenal and Petronius.

78. For the same reason, attempts at social revolution are futile. Wealth and poverty are passing circumstances, and a mere change of externals would produce no real benefit to the individual. The nouveaux riches of Rome whom Nigrinus so severely criticizes are sufficient proof that when the poor acquire wealth, they can actually become worse.

79. See above, note 30.

80. Croiset, 140f. Dudley, 31, on Diogenes: "There is a good deal of the showman about such actions; they were done for propaganda." See *Epict. Diss.* III.xii.16–17; Epict., *Ench.* 47; Marc. Aurel., *Med.* I.7.

81. The same is true of the more mainstream philosophers in Lucian. These men, who are expected to be superior to the ordinary man, are shown by Lucian to be quite inferior: venal, credulous, arrogant. See Robinson, 30f. and 50–54. Lucian appears inimical to anyone who sought to prove himself better than the rest of men (or perhaps, rather, *educated* men) by whatever means. His heroes, such as Demonax, seek nothing for themselves, but distinguish themselves for their simple sociability.

remains a private person and poses no threat. Peregrinus, however, sought a form of personal charismatic leadership, based upon his ascetical reputation. In doing so he crossed the line from philosopher to prophet, and set the stage for his dramatic death and apotheosis. In terms of the phenomenology of the holy man (or *goes*, depending on one's point of view) asceticism served the same purpose as prophecy or miracle working. It served to establish the credentials of the individual as superior both to his fellows and to his surrounding society.

Peregrinus combines all the worst social dangers in Lucian's mind: enmity to established and accepted norms, demagoguery, personality cultism, and religious superstition, with absolutely none of the characteristics that might redeem these excesses. Asceticism, clothed in the mantle of "traditional" Cynicism, served as both the link and expression of these disturbing phenomena. By combining all these characteristics in his person, Peregrinus is seen as the ultimate example of the *goes*.

Culture and Society

Lucian has long been characterized by scholars as a thoroughgoing conservative, a man of Isocratean *paideia* reflecting the tastes of a literary, cultivated elite. This much is true. His attitude toward culture has, however, been judged as narrow and dryly rationalist, that of a slavish bookworm, viewing his society from the perspective of fourth-century B.C.E. literary models.[82] In *The Dream* or *Lucian's Career*, Paideia herself appears to the author, splendidly dressed and opposing the squalid figure of Lucian's intended career, Sculpture. Paideia announces that by pursuing Sculpture, Lucian will merely be one of the working rabble, inconspicuous and ever cringing before and courting the eloquent (9). In pursuing her, however, Paideia promises universal knowledge, virtue, reputation, wealth, honor, and public office (10).[83] As if Lucian would

82. Consistent with the general trend of Lucianic scholarship (see above, notes 3 and 4) earlier works tend to view Lucian's conservatism negatively, as a sign of his superficiality or literary archaizing: Croiset, 101f., 142; Caster, *Lucien*, 365ff., 372 on narrow and dry Isocratean *paideia*, 388f. on viewing his society as Menander, five centuries too late; Bompaire, *Lucien*, 147, 536: "un esprit scolaire se souvenant ici et là de l'utilité des yeux." See Robert, 393, refuting those who would make Lucian "un pauvre rat de bibliothèque."

83. It may be said, of course, that Peregrinus sought similar goals for himself. Lucian does not dispute notoriety, honor, etc. as worthy goals; his point is that Peregrinus, from his youth, had been unscrupulous and contemptible in his means of pursuing them. Such is the nature of a *goes*.

need any more persuasion, Paideia takes him on a chariot ride across the world to the applause of its inhabitants. When Lucian returns, he finds himself clothed in purple (15, 16).

The piece is not so self-serving as it may appear. Men of literary education: sophists, rhetoricians, and philosophers (in the broadest sense) made brilliant careers for themselves in the service of aristocratic patrons, cities, provinces, and the imperial court.[84] Veneration for classical culture and for the person of refined literary education was universal. To note that this *"paideia* culture" was both literary and conservative is *not* to judge it moribund. It was, rather, an affirmation of the common heritage and cultural authority that made the empire a society in the first place.[85] Those who would set themselves above the "common sense" of classical culture[86] by religious enthusiasm, philosophical dogmatism, or outright rebellion, Lucian holds up as objects of laughter or, as in the case of the Christians, pity.[87] Lucian, it may be said, offers a cultured response of cultural authority against the deviant.

Culture is, of course, but one aspect of the larger reality of society as a whole. It is appropriate, therefore, to conclude this discussion with a few observations on Lucian's position within his own society. Lucian was obviously at ease with the institutions of Roman rule, as evidenced in his *Apology* and his acceptance of a governmental post in Egypt later in his life.[88] Attempts to paint Lucian as a dissident intellectual or Greek

---

84. See G. W. Bowersock, *Greek Sophists in the Roman Empire* (Oxford, 1969).

85. This positive view of Lucian's social and cultural beliefs is shared by contemporary scholars: Branham, *Unruly Eloquence*, 28–37; Robinson, 4ff.; Jones, *Culture and Society*, 151–55. P. R. L. Brown, "The Saint as Exemplar in Late Antiquity," *Representations* 1, no. 2 (Spring 1983): 1–4, offers insightful observations on *"paideia* culture." See also H. I. Marrou, *A History of Education in the Ancient World*, trans. G. Lamb (New York, 1956), 95–101 and 217–26. Any discussion of *paideia* would be incomplete without mention of Werner Jaeger's monumental and definitive work *Paideia: The Ideals of Greek Culture*, 3 vols., 2d ed., trans. Gilbert Highet (New York, 1945).

86. Croiset, 111ff., speaks with his customary derision of Lucian's "common sense" as proof of his intellectual levity. Robinson, 50–54, rightly notes how often characters in Lucian go to great lengths to find "truth," only to discover it to be commonplace. This is exactly the point; for Lucian it is simply foolish to seek answers outside of the common sense of the common classical heritage.

87. Jones, *Culture and Society,* 159, concludes that Lucian views himself as the defender of the values of *paideia* against "those who proclaimed new gods and burned the writings of philosophers, and an upstart religion [Christianity] that denied the gods and flaunted its lack of education." Given the political, military, and social troubles that began with the death of Aurelius, Jones rightly remarks on the reality of the threat perceived by Lucian. See also Branham, *Unruly Eloquence,* 187f.

88. Jones, *Culture and Society,* 84; see *Apol.* 11–13. Bernays, 44f., came to the same conclusion earlier, but with his usual *Tendenz,* viewing Lucian as a creature of Rome and exemplar of the values of "bourgeois" society.

"nationalist" have been refuted.[89] Such works as *Nigrinus* and *On Salaried Posts*, despite their scathing view of the rich, are not attacks on Roman capitalism but stock satires of the nouveaux riches.[90] In the same way, the issue of rich and poor in such works as *The Cock, Dialogues of the Dead*, and *Timon* is a standard *topos* without any necessary social or political content.[91] The frequency of this *topos* in Lucian may reflect a genuine, if purely intellectual, sympathy for the poor. It is clear, however, that such sympathy stops if the poor take action.

Lucian's conservatism is thus not only cultural in nature,[92] but social as well. Yet, presumably both for reasons of his art and his individual nature, this conservatism appears less dogmatic and self-serving than that of Aurelius's Stoicism. The emperor's beliefs are founded on a clearly defined concept of nature. As nature is by definition unchangeable, Aurelius's view of society and the duties it imposes is inflexible. Moreover, as moral duty is defined by social expectations, Stoic ethics became a bulwark not so much for the ideals of classical culture as for the structure and operation of the social status quo of the Roman Empire. Lucian, on the other hand, is anything but dogmatic. Virtually every philosophical school became a target for his satire at one time or another in his works.[93] Lucian's opinions are also clothed in satire and parody, not philosophy; they are meant to amuse first and foremost.[94] This amusement, however, is reflective of his cultural perspective. Lucian finds much in the social status quo to satirize and criticize: institu-

---

89. Foremost among these attempts are A. Peretti, *Luciano: Un intellettuale greco contra Roma* (Florence, 1946), 41–43 and 72, and M. Nilsson, *Geschichte der griechische Religion*, vol. 2, *Die hellenistische und römische Zeit*, 2d ed., Handbuch der Altertumswissenschaft, Abt. 5, Teil 2, Band 2 (Munich, 1961), 531f. A. Momigliano refuted Peretti in his review in *Rivista Storica Italiana* 60 (1948): 430–32 = *Quarto contributo alla storia degli studi classici* (Rome, 1969), 641–44. B. Baldwin, "Lucian as Social Satirist," *CQ*, n.s. 11 (1961): 199–208, also attempted to paint Lucian as a revolutionary, but later retracted this view in his *Studies in Lucian*, 107. For Lucian's ease with Roman rule, see Bompaire, 512f. and, more recently, M. Dubuisson, "Lucien et Rome," *Ancient Society* 15–17 (1984–86): 185–207.

90. Hall, 221–51; Jones, *Culture and Society*, 81f.; Robinson, 56. See above, notes 76 and 77.

91. Croiset, 153–74; Bompaire, 208–13, 357–60; Jones, *Culture and Society*, 16.

92. On Lucian's conservative tastes in literature, art, and architecture, see Jones, *Culture and Society*, 151–55.

93. Caster, 9–122, exhaustively reviews Lucian's views and criticisms of each school. See also Jones, *Culture and Society*, 24–32.

94. Branham, *Unruly Eloquence*, 129ff., correctly remarks that a fundamental question to ask when approaching Lucian's work on a literary level is, Why is it funny? There is a double nature to Lucian's art—bemused appreciation versus criticism, satire versus parody.

tions, fashions, and events that fall short of the cultural ideals professed by that same society. Unlike his Stoic contemporaries, Lucian possesses a set of norms and values independent of the structure, but based upon the culture, of his society. These norms and values were contained not in institutions but in literature, and in the process of education that expounded it.

Yet, it must also be admitted that Lucian's beliefs and values can also have their harsh side. *Peregrinus* and *Alexander* are vitriolic in tone. When culture itself is attacked, Lucian becomes adamant. Under the cloak of philosophy, Peregrinus attacked philosophy's very foundation—rationality. In defaming Antoninus Pius and Herodes Atticus, whom Lucian is careful to describe as educated, cultured gentlemen, Peregrinus attempts to stir the mob up against the embodiments of *paideia*. Alexander, likewise, seduces Rutilianus, and through him gains access to the emperor himself. His sham took in those who should have been the leaders of the educated governing class. One suspects that Lucian would also have regarded Aulus Gellius as duped by Peregrinus for his brief, positive comment in *Noct. Att.* 8.3. In appealing to the volatility, superstition, and base desires of the mob, and exalting these over the culture and education of its superiors, such *goetes* as these struck at the source of civilization itself.

An ascetic such as Peregrinus posed a threat to Lucian's culture and society. As a radical Cynic, Peregrinus professed a philosophy that deliberately set itself in opposition to convention and social restraint.[95] Asceticism was, for the Cynics, both a defiant attack against social norms and a practical proof that most of the social structure was unnecessary to support the truly free individual. Yet, as shown by Demonax and Nigrinus, a philosopher could espouse radicalism in his ideas or in the manner of his private life and still remain praiseworthy in Lucian's eyes.

What set Peregrinus apart was both the degree of his asceticism[96] and the use to which he put the personal credentials gained from it. Unlike

95. This fact had long been recognized by proper Romans; e.g., Cic., *de Off.* I.148: "The entire doctrine of the Cynics must be utterly rejected, for it is inimical to moral propriety (*verecundiae*) without which nothing can be right or good." Rostovtzeff, 126, adds an acute observation: "Another fact which should not be overlooked is that the emperors of the second century did not persecute the philosophers, not even the Cynics. The task of fighting and ridiculing them was undertaken by the loyal philosophers and sophists. In this literary strife the government did not interfere."

96. Dudley, 199: "Throughout this period [first and second centuries C.E.], then, Cynicism was a kind of radical Stoicism: the relation between the two may be likened to that between the more ascetic monastic orders and the main body of the Catholic Church." This intriguing parallel with Christianity will be taken up in Chapter 6.

Demonax, Peregrinus adopted an ascetical life that drew attention to himself and set him apart from his society. He went beyond establishing his credentials as a Cynic and sought to become a charismatic leader and "holy man," like an Alexander or Jesus. In doing so, Peregrinus set himself up as an authority outside the realm of the "received" Cynicism of Antisthenes and Diogenes, and thus outside the realm of commonly held classical culture. Peregrinus's authority was personal in nature, without the checks and restraints imposed by established and accepted tradition. For Lucian such authority figures constitute a threat. They are inherently irresponsible, as they are responsible only to themselves, and their followers constitute an unstable element in society.[97]

The capstone on Peregrinus's authority was his death. His theatrical suicide, the proclamations before, and the apotheosis after offered proofs of his claim to a superhuman nature and assured the continuance of the inanity and danger Lucian perceived.[98] After Lucian's death and at the close of the period studied here, the early third-century historian Cassius Dio (LII.36) expressed an opinion that both summarizes Lucian's view and attests to its endurance. It takes the form of a speech put anachronistically into the mouth of Augustus's adviser Maecenas at the commencement of the principate.[99] Maecenas counsels the first emperor against those who introduce strange rites and new divinities, for from them arise conspiracies, factions, and cabals dangerous to monarchy. In a sentiment that applies equally to Peregrinus, Alexander, and Jesus, Maecenas states: "Allow no one to be an atheist or *goes*." He argues that magicians (μαγευταί), by speaking falsehood, often encourage many to revolution. Completing the argument, he states: "The very same thing is done also by many who claim to be philosophers; I advise you to guard yourself against them too."

97. Goulet-Cazé, "Cynisme," 2736, notes that bands of Cynics with some sort of group identity and life, such as the runaway slaves in *The Fugitives* and Peregrinus's followers both before and after his death, signal a new development in the imperial period and constitute something substantially more than a casual group of disciples gathering around a famous Cynic, as had been the case earlier.

98. Dudley, 179ff., holds that Peregrinus's death was specifically and intentionally directed to the establishment of a cult.

99. MacMullen, *Enemies*, 156 n. 29, calls this an essentially Severan sentiment put into Maecenas's mouth. On the speech, see F. Millar, *A Study of Cassius Dio* (Oxford, 1964), 102–18.

C h a p t e r F o u r

APOLLONIUS OF TYANA
The Rehabilitated Ascetic

THE SOCIAL AND CULTURAL AUTHORITIES of the Roman Empire possessed an alternative to opposition and denunciation of ascetic radicals—assimilation. A brilliant example occurs in Flavius Philostratus's *Life of Apollonius of Tyana* (*Vita Apollonii* = *VA*). Philostratus rehabilitates an ascetic philosopher with a reputation of a *goes,* in this case a Pythagorean, into a model of classical ideals and a defender of the social order. In so doing, Philostratus admits the figure of the ascetic / wonderworker / charismatic into both the literature and society of the cultured classes. The success of Philostratus's work is attested by the fact that "his" Apollonius was later used as a bulwark for the defense of pagan religion and culture against the Christians and was set up as a pagan "rival" to Jesus himself.[1]

1. In Sossianus Hierocles' *Lover of Truth* (φιληλήθεις), parts of which are preserved in Eus., *C. Hier.*; see also Lact., *Div. Inst.* 5.2f. and *de Mort. Pers.* 16.3. Fundamental to the study of Hierocles' work is the recent critical edition of the *Contra Hieroclem* with notes, commentary, and French translation by M. Forrat, *Contre Hiéroclès*, Greek text edited by E. des Places, Sources chrétiennes 333 (Paris, 1986), and the pertinent discussions by T. D. Barnes, in both "Sossianus Hierocles and the Antecedents of the Great Persecution," *Harvard Studies in Classical Philology* 80 (1976): 239–52, and *Constantine and Eusebius* (Cambridge, Mass., 1981), 164–67. See also E. Junod, "Polémique chrétienne contre Apollonius de Tyane," *Revue de théologie et de philosophie* 120 (1988):

Philostratus is generally believed to have been born c. 170 C.E., the
Suda gives his *floruit* as 193–211 and puts his death under the reign of
Philip the Arab (244–49). As for the publication of the *VA*, a date
sometime after the death of the empress Julia Domna in 217 has long
been the *opinio recepta*. As the work was commissioned by the empress
(*VA* I.3) but not dedicated to her, it is assumed Philostratus completed
the work sometime after her death.[2] The dates of Apollonius's birth and

---

475–82; W. Speyer, "Hierokles (I) (Sossianus Hierocles)," *Reallexikon für Antike und
Christentum,* Lief. 113 (1989): 103–9; and T. Hägg, "Hierocles the Lover of Truth and
Eusebius the Sophist," *Symbolae Osloenses* 67 (1992): 138–50. In addition to reviewing
the history of scholarship and the Sources chrétiennes edition, Hägg presents new argu-
ments regarding the title of the Hierocles work (140–42), its date, that of the *C. Hier.*
(142–44), and, more important, the identity of the author of the latter work (146–50).
Hägg suggests that the *C. Hier.* was not written by Eusebius of Caesarea, but by another
Eusebius, a hypothesis that serves to resolve the problems involved in dating the work.
Professor Barnes has further informed me by personal communication of his agreement
with Hägg on this point.

For other comparisons between Apollonius and Jesus, see Porphyry, frags, 4, 60, and
63, in *Pophyrius, "Gegen die Christen" 15 Bücher: Zeugnisse, Fragmente und Referate,*
ed. A. von Harnack, Abhandlungen der königlichen preussischen Akademie der Wissenschaften, no. 1 (Berlin, 1916). T. D. Barnes, "Pagan Perceptions of Christianity," in
Early Christianity: Origins and Evolution to AD 600, In Honor of W. H. C. Frend, ed.
Ian Hazlett (Nashville, 1991), 239 and n. 32, rightly notes that this only edition of the
fragments is notoriously problematic and in dire need of revision. A. Benoît, "Le 'Contra
Christianos' de Porphyre: Où en est la collecte des fragments," in *Paganisme, Judaïsme,
Christianisme: Influences et affrontements dans le monde antique. Mélanges offerts à
Marcel Simon* (Paris, 1978), 261–75, has provided an indispensable checklist of Har-
nack's fragments and a guide to their reliability. Of the fragments concerning Apollonius
and Jesus, only no. 4 proves to be an allusion to an authentic text of Porphyry taken from
Jerome, *Tract. de Psalmo LXXXI;* nos. 60 and 63 are doubtful allusions attributed to
Porphyry by Harnack, taken from the *Apokritikos* of Marcarius Magnes.

Still, the temptation to entertain the notion that Philostratus, perhaps in some less deliberate way, was reacting to Christianity in developing his particular portrait of Apollonius
is almost irresistible. Proof positive is impossible. Yet Barnes notes the sudden intrusion
of Christianity into the consciousness of the upper classes c. 200 and its newly acquired
respectability in the Severan period; see his "Pagan Perceptions," *Constantine and Eusebius,* 126–47; and his postscript to the second edition of *Tertullian: A Historical and
Literary Study* (Oxford, 1985). The *VA* could serve as a clarion call to those members of
the upper, educated classes flirting with the new religion to come back to their social and
cultural roots. Whether Philostratus ever intended such must remain a matter for conjecture.

2. On identification, chronology, and the problems with the Philostrati notices in the
Suda, see G. W. Bowersock, *Greek Sophists in the Roman Empire* (Oxford, 1969), 2–8,
and G. Anderson, *Philostratus: Biography and Belles Lettres in the Third Century A.D.*
(London, 1986), 3–8 and 291–96 (appendix 1). Both agree that the *Suda* remains baffling
and that on many points it is "best to remain baffled." For the date of publication, F.
Solmsen, *RE* 20.1 (1941), s.n. "Philostratos (10)," 139, and G. W. Bowersock, introduction to *Life of Apollonius,* by Philostratus, Penguin ed. (Harmondsworth, Middlesex,

death are even less certain. The most that can be said is that he must have been born early in the first century C.E. and died sometime during or after the reign of Nerva (96–98 C.E.; see *VA* VIII.27).[3]

Philostratus and his work are part of a much broader cultural and literary movement known as the "Second Sophistic." The term was coined by Philostratus himself, and several of its luminaries have already been encountered in Herodes Atticus, Lucian, Dio Chrysostom, and the teachers and friends of Marcus Aurelius.[4] These "new sophists" were men of letters for whom rhetoric and the refined accomplishments of *paideia* were the acme of learning. At the same time, their literary education laid claim to a certain universality: they engaged in philosophy, intervened in and represented cities, and advised emperors. These are also the essential activities of Apollonius. Philostratus often presents his hero as a sophist, particularly in his philhellenism, antiquarian interests, and relation to the emperor Vespasian.[5] Yet, the true importance of the *VA* lies less in its literary aspects than in the place it holds in the evolution of second-century asceticism. G. W. Bowersock's judgment of

1970), 9. Julia Domna's suicide is dated by Dio LXXIX.23.6. That the *VA* predates the *Lives of the Sophists* (*VS*) by the same Philostratus is proven by a reference to the former work in *VS* 570.

3. Pace M. Dzielska, *Apollonius of Tyana in Legend and History*, trans. P. Pieńkowski, Problemi e Ricerche di Storia Antica 10 (Rome, 1986), 32–39.

4. Philostratus coins the term in *VS* 481; see Bowersock, *Greek Sophists*, 8. Bowersock's book provides an excellent introduction to the Second Sophistic in general; see also *Approaches to the Second Sophistic: Papers Presented at the 105th Annual Meeting of the American Philological Association*, ed. G. W. Bowersock (University Park, Pa., 1974); B. P. Reardon, *Courants littéraires grecs des IIe et IIIe siècles après J.-C.*, Annales littéraires de l'Université de Nantes 3 (Paris, 1971); and E. L. Bowie, "The Greeks and Their Past in the Second Sophistic," *Past and Present* 46 (1970): 3–41. In specific relation to Philostratus, see Anderson, *Philostratus*; R. J. Penella, "Philostratus's Letter to Julia Domna," *Hermes* 107, no. 2 (1979): 161–68; and J. Moles, "The Career and Conversion of Dio Chrysostom," *JHS* 98 (1978): 79–100.

5. "It is in Philostratus's *Lives of the Sophists* . . . that a substitute for a Greek political and cultural history of the recent past is found. Emphasis is laid equally on sophists' contributions to Greek culture and benefactions to Greek cities and on their high rank and acceptability in Roman governmental circles. . . . A similar presentation of Greek cultural history through the biography of a sophist (this time largely fictional) is to be found in his earlier work on Apollonius of Tyana," Bowie, "Greeks and their Past," 17. See also his "Apollonius of Tyana: Tradition and Reality," *ANRW* II.16.2 (1978): 1667–71.

Julia Domna herself was once seen as a major figure in this movement, since Philostratus mentions being a member of a "circle" of intellectuals and literary figures that surrounded the empress (*VA* I.3; cf. Dio LXXV.15.6–7, LXXVII.18.3). Bowersock, *Greek Sophists*, 101–9, has deflated the sweeping claims scholars have made for this salon, characterizing its members as generally "second-rung types" on a par with the pet intellectuals hired on by wealthy houses in Lucian's *On Salaried Posts*.

this literary movement in general applies most especially to the *VA:* "It can be argued without apology that the Second Sophistic has mcre importance in Roman history than it has in Greek literature."[6]

Both the author and the work have been beset with scholarly difficulties and polemic. Prior to the *VA* sources for Apollonius are scarce. The first surviving mention of him is in Lucian, interestingly enough, and dismisses him as a notorious charlatan.[7] A collection of letters purported to be from Apollonius has also come down to us; some of which are glaring fakes, though others may well be genuine.[8] Philostratus himself mentions forged letters circulating in Apollonius's lifetime (*VA* VII.35). In addition to letters, Philostratus names his other sources as local traditions, including temple accounts, a testament of Apollonius, a book by Maximus of Aegeae of Apollonius's *acta* in that city, and the highly problematical memoirs of Apollonius's disciple Damis. In addition Philostratus warns his readers away from an earlier biography by Moiragenes, "a man ignorant of many things about Apollonius" (I.3f. and 19).[9]

Critical studies of the *VA* have essentially focused on questions of historicity, concerning anachronisms and contradictions within the text, and whether Damis and his memoirs existed either in the form claimed by Philostratus or in some other, or whether both the person and the work were simply a creation of Philostratus.[10] R. Reitzenstein consid-

6. *Greek Sophists*, 58.

7. *Alex.* 5: "His [Alexander's] teacher and lover was born in Tyana and was one of the followers of the notorious Apollonius and was versed in all of that one's shenanigans. You can see what kind of 'school of philosophy' the man comes from." See Chapter 3, page 70.

8. C. P. Jones, "A Martyria for Apollonius of Tyana," *Chiron* 12 (1982): 144. The most recent edition of the letters is R. J. Penella, *The Letters of Apollonius of Tyana: A Critical Text with Prolegomena, Translation and Commentary*, Mnemosyne suppl. 56 (Leiden, 1979), complemented by I. Tsavari, "Une Edition récente des Lettres d'Apollonius de Tyane," Δωδώνη 16, no. 2 [Philol.] (1982): 205–25. As with virtually every aspect of the *VA*, scholarly opinion differs. E. Meyer, "Apollonios von Tyana und die Biographie des Philostratos," *Hermes* 52 (1917): 410f., finds the Apollonius of the letters utterly different from the figure in the *VA*, though this is not to say that the letters are genuine. Penella, 26–28, finds the letters to be mostly concordant with the *VA*, and apparent discrepancies readily explicable. Bowie, "Apollonius," 1677 and 1683, argues that the letters were assembled or fabricated at Athens c. 140 and formed part of the work of Moiragenes. Most recently G. Anderson, *Philostratus*, 185–91, has argued the plausibility of their authenticity. Philostratus himself mentions the collection in *VA* VIII.20, and cites letters in V.2, 40, 41; VI.29, 33.

9. On Philostratus's sources see Solmsen, *RE*, 147–53; R. Reitzenstein, *Hellenistische Wundererzählungen* (Leipzig, 1906), 39–54; F. Grosso, "La 'Vita di Apollonio di Tiana' come fonte storica," *Acme* 7, fasc. 3 (1954): 333ff.; and Bowie, "Apollonius," 1686–89.

10. Criticism in this regard began early. Philostratus records that Damis was censured

ered the *VA* an ancient "adventure novel" (*Reiseroman*) imposed upon an earlier Pythagorean polemical work against the Cynics and Stoics.[11] E. Meyer deliberately set out to demonstrate that Damis never existed and that his memoirs could be nothing else than a Philostratan invention, anachronism and contradiction playing a large role in his argument.[12] This opinion held sway until F. Grosso, responding to the *ipercriticismo eccessivo* of previous scholarship, set out to validate the *VA* as a historical source. Arguing directly against Meyer, Grosso offered a possible reconciliation of the chronological difficulties and concluded, rather subjectively, that where we do have control from other sources, Philostratus is not far from the mark.[13]

Within the past twenty years, scholars have generally fallen either into Meyer's or Grosso's camp.[14] Among the most comprehensive and important work is that of E. L. Bowie, who rejects Grosso's method as having no formal validity and vigorously reasserts Meyer's thesis, contending that Damis was an invention of Philostratus. Ultimately, Bowie

---

to his face for being too anecdotal and trivial (*VA* I.19). Eusebius, *C. Hier.* 9, 13–15, 32, 36f., was quick to exploit the logical inconsistencies in the *VA* in his polemic against Hierocles, which is actually a lengthy argument against Philostratus's work. For bibliography, see Grosso, 345–64, including a detailed review of nineteenth-century scholarship; G. Petzke, *Die Traditionen über Apollonius von Tyana und das Neue Testament,* Studia ad corpus Hellenisticum Novi Testamenti 1 (Leiden, 1970), 239–50 (the organization of Petzke's work makes it useful as a "thematic index" to the *VA*); Bowie, "Apollonius," 1692–99; and Anderson, *Philostratus,* 304–9. For bibliography on the Damis question specifically, see Penella, 1 n. 3. Another preoccupation with scholars of the *VA* has been aretalogy; that is, reading the text as a specimen of a genre of "miracle tale" (see below, pages 118–20, 125).

11. Reitzenstein, *Wundererzählungen,* 43–48, but largely ignoring the issue of historicity.

12. Meyer, 371–78, 382ff., 393, 402. On the positive side, Meyer refuted Reitzenstein's suggestion of *Schulpolemik* as a motive or motif in the work.

13. Would Philostratus, Grosso asks, have had the courage to lend authenticity to an invented Damis under the name of such a formidable figure as Julia Domna? He concludes that though Philostratus takes *qualche licenza* in a rhetorical work such as this, the evidence is far from convicting him of deliberate falsehood. See Grosso, 345–90, 511f. (Anderson comes to the same conclusion; see below.) Bowie, "Apollonius," 1654f., argues that simply because the *VA* generally accords with known historical events does not therefore mean that any of the specific details of the Apollonius biography are true.

14. G. Petzke, 67–72, though ignorant of Grosso's work, raised several objections to Meyer's thesis. W. Speyer, "Zum Bild des Apollonios von Tyana bei Heiden und Christen," *Jahrbuch für Antike und Christentum* 17 (1974): 46 n. 1 and 50–52, expresses caution regarding Petzke's work and asserts that the Damis memoirs were a forgery originating in a Neopythagorean circle around Julia Domna, reasserting Reitzenstein's earlier thesis. A notable exception to this trend is G. W. Bowersock, introduction to *Life of Apollonius,* 17–19, who prefers to suspend judgment.

holds the *VA* to be a novel, a well-rounded, entertaining piece of literature with no propagandistic aims or claim to historicity.[15]
   Some new light has finally been shed more recently. T. G. Knoles has
studied the *VA*'s literary qualities in relation to its themes.[16] His analysis of the role of Damis as narrator reveals a degree of complexity
and intractability that bespeaks Philostratus's working with a difficult
source. The use of a double narrator and the interplay between Damis
and Philostratus belies the novelistic, popular work Bowie presents. It
also challenges the thesis that Damis is a simple fabrication; a writer of
Philostratus's caliber would have invented a far less cumbersome and
contradictory character.[17] Finally, G. Anderson's recent study has offered new support for Grosso's arguments on more solid methodologi-
cal grounds—though his audacious identification of the historical Damis as an Epicurean disciple of Apollonius, later disaffected from his
master, is conjectural at best.[18] Anderson's less dogmatic approach and

   15. Bowie, "Apollonius," 1653, 1655–68. Most recently M. Dzielska, *Apollonius,*
largely follows Bowie on controversial questions; see esp. 19–29. Though containing
some useful material, Dzielska's book is fatally flawed by a poor translation from the
Polish original. I hesitate to comment upon her scholarship fearing that her arguments
have been mutilated by the translator.
   16. In a worthy, though unfortunately unpublished, dissertation: "Literary Technique
and Theme in Philostratus' *Life of Apollonius of Tyana,*" Ph.D. diss., Rutgers University,
1981. The work is particularly noteworthy since in all the previous scholarly polemic,
treating the *VA* in its own right and examining its inner dynamics and connection to
issues in its own society had been utterly neglected, Knoles, 15. The same point is made
by P. Cox, *Biography in Late Antiquity: A Quest for the Holy Man* (Berkeley and Los
Angeles, 1983), 4.
   17. See Knoles, 25–62. Knoles does not carry his analysis through to conclusions regarding the historical Damis. Yet his literary arguments carry inescapable weight for the
historical consideration of the *VA*. Knoles, 107f., has also demonstrated that the items
proved to be anachronistic in the *VA* function only to provide color or background, while
sections dealing with material of historical or political significance to the *VA* as a whole
are usually transcribed with attention to details that can be verified as factual. This is not
to say that all the stories in the *VA* are historically accurate, but rather that the circumstances surrounding important stories correspond with what we know. Though illuminat-
ing the problems of anachronism in the text, this point does not advance claims for historicity. Bowie's argument still stands, that Philostratus's attention to the correctness of
historical detail does not ensure that his description of events in Apollonius's life actually
happened. Grosso himself, 391–440, quietly admitted this in speaking of Apollonius's
meeting with Vespasian in *VA* V.27–38. He states that Apollonius may, in fact, have
never met the emperor, but that Philostratus is careful to make sure that the setting and
details of the story correspond to the political, military, and philosophical environment of
the times.
   18. See J. R. Morgan, review of *Philostratus: Biography and Belles Lettres in the Third
Century A.D.,* by G. Anderson, in *CR* 38 (1988): 235f. Morgan's criticism regarding
Damis is well taken, but he is too dismissive of Anderson's other arguments regarding the
VA, a document that Morgan himself admits he has difficulty understanding.

his accounting for the inconsistencies in the text by the difficulties Philostratus would have encountered in dealing with his sources allow him to conclude that "a good many other verdicts of guilty against the biographer should be changed to 'not proven.' "[19]

The obsession with historicity and the existence of Damis has overshadowed the significance of the fact that various well-developed opinions and traditions about Apollonius clearly existed before the VA.[20] Scholars of all opinions concur that Philostratus reworked these source materials, but no one has examined this rehabilitation on its own merits. The true importance of the VA has thus been largely ignored. The portrait Philostratus paints of his hero possesses a historical character independent of whether it is an accurate representation of the first century C.E.[21] Its value, rather, pertains to the second century, the era when the traditions about Apollonius developed after his death and before the writing of the VA, and the third, the social and cultural environment in which Philostratus wrote.[22] It is precisely in this rehabilitation of Apollonius that Philostratus integrated the radical ascetic into the social and cultural mainstream of his society, allowing for the great flowering of asceticism later in his own century.

---

19. Anderson, *Philostratus,* 121–39, 155–85, 191, 227–39. One is struck by the resemblance here to the history of Lucianic scholarship (see Chapter 3, pages 54–55). Lucian was dismissed essentially because the careers of his Alexander and Peregrinus did not fit preconceived notions about the character of imperial society in the period. The same is true of Philostratus's Apollonius. L. Robert's epigraphic research and the scholarship of the past decade have definitively rehabilitated Lucian. I would hazard to predict that once similar prejudices regarding the VA are overcome—an end to which this work contributes—Philostratus will also be seen as giving an accurate portrayal of certain aspects of his own society.

20. See Bowie, "Apollonius," 1663–85; Speyer, 47–63.

21. For the purposes of this work, it cannot be overstressed that I am speaking of the *images* of Apollonius in the various sources. The reader should always keep in mind that, unless stated otherwise, none of the following discussion should be taken to refer to the historical, first-century Apollonius. To do so would be to become embroiled in the less productive polemics just outlined.

22. Meyer, 424, noted this fact but did not perceive its importance: "dieser Apollonios ist ein Produkt und Repräsentant nicht der ersten Jahrhunderts, sondern der ersten Jahrzehnte des dritten." R. MacMullen, *Enemies of the Roman Order: Treason, Unrest, and Alienation in the Empire* (Cambridge, Mass., 1966), 115, correctly remarks: "No one can distinguish for certain between stories current in the lifetime of their subject (not strictly historical, of course) and others added by his biographers, especially Philostratus. Everything hangs suspended, as it were, between the early second and early third century"; pace Bowie, "Apollonius," 1652. On the literary level, Cox, 37, arrived at a similar conclusion: "The biographical process of creating an ideal character out of the historical data of a man's life suggests that it is the philosophical and historical stance of the biographer, rather than the subject himself, that determines the composition of biography."

Earlier Traditions Inimical to Apollonius: *Goeteia*

At the outset Philostratus announces that the purpose of his writing is to defend Apollonius against the calumny that he was a magician (μάγος) or false philosopher (βιαίως σοφός, I.2). The accusation is repeated in various ways throughout the work and persisted into the next century.[23] All traditions outside of Philostratus agree that Apollonius was a prophet and miracle worker and most hold a contemptuous opinion of him.[24] Philostratus's contemporary Dio describes him as "both a *goes* and a skillful magician" (LXXVII.18.4). Even Philostratus is forced to admit his hero's reputation as an astrologer and author of four books *On the Prophecies of the Stars,* an embarrassment he covers with a rhetorical flourish (III.41).[25]

Accusations of magic and *goeteia* abound in this period, but determining the nature and meaning of these accusations is particularly problematic. The term "magic" itself is frequently a red herring in scholarly discussion, and various attempts to reach a definition of it by structuralist and functionalist methods have often sacrificed its historical context in favor of taxonomic purity. The essential point is not how we would classify the phenomenon, but how the Hellenistic world itself defined magic. This poses a second problem, for the definition of magic in antiquity was itself changeable and dependent upon its social context.[26]

23. γόητα, ἀνθρώπῳ μὴ καθαρῷ (IV.18); γόητι ἀνθρώπῳ (VIII.19); γόης, ἱκανὸς τὴν τέχνην (VII.17); see especially the trial before Domitian in VIII.1–5 and Apollonius's *apologia* in VIII.7. On the persistence of these charges into the next century, Eus., *C. Hier.* 40: ὡς μόνον γόητα πάλαι τε καὶ εἰσέτι νῦν νενομίσθαι, also 5, 15, 22, 24, 27, 35, 38, 42.

24. Bowie, "Apollonius," 1686; see also Reitzenstein, *Wundererzählungen,* 42, and Anderson, *Philostratus,* 138f.

25. Philostratus implies that he could not find a copy of this book and states: "I consider astrology and all such divination to be beyond human nature, and I do not know if anyone ever had such power"; see Anderson, *Philostratus,* 142. On astrology as a suspect practice, see MacMullen, *Enemies,* 128–42; in general, F. H. Cramer, *Astrology in Roman Law and Politics,* Memoirs of the American Philosophical Society 37 (Philadelphia, 1954), esp. 252ff.

26. D. E. Aune, "Magic in Early Christianity," *ANRW* II.23.2 (1980): 1557; A. F. Segal, "Hellenistic Magic: Some Questions of Definition," in *Studies in Gnosticism and Hellenistic Religions: Presented to Gilles Quispel on the Occasion of his 65th Birthday,* ed. R. van den Broek and M. J. Vermaseren (Leiden, 1981), 350ff. and 375—an article that brings remarkable clarity to the entire topic. K. F. Smith, "Greek and Roman Magic," in *Encyclopaedia of Religion and Ethics* (New York, 1955) is dated in its interpretation but still provides a useful overview of the topic and conspectus of the chief sources.

The law points to some definition, but is not sufficiently embracing.[27] The *XII Tables* VII.3 merely addresses those who would use incantations or magic to hinder another's crops. The laws of the *Codex Justinianus,* though considerably later than the second century, offer a broader definition.[28] Of the eight laws dealing with magic, four are specifically directed against divination (IX.18.2, 3, 5, 7), two are directed against using magic to plot against another's life (18.4, 6), and two forbid the practice of magic or its study without giving any indication of what magic is (18.8, 9). It appears then that divination, foretelling or influencing the future, was the sort of magic that most concerned the law, but it is just as clear that this was not its only definition. *CJ* IX.18.4 specifies that the practice of magic in pharmacy or for the sake of the crops is legal. Obviously such things as potions, spells, and incantations are included. This law also bespeaks the confusion not only regarding the definition of magic, but also the occasions on which its practice was legal or illegal. Evidence of a similar confusion between philosophy and magic occurs in IX.18.2, which specifies that the study of geometry is laudable, but that of divination is damnable.[29]

The *Sententiae* of Julius Paulus (fl. c. 210 C.E.) come closer to the period under study and manifest the same concern and confusion as the *CJ.* Divination is again a theme, and it is specifically stated that divination regarding the life of the emperor or regarding a master by his slave are punishable by death (*Sent.* V.21.3–4). Taking auspices involving homicide or the use of one's own blood is likewise a capital offense (V.23.16). The use of potions to induce abortion or as love-philters is punishable by exile or the mines, even if no malice is intended (23.14), while death resulting from the administration of a drug is punishable by exile or death (23.19). In an apparent reference to the *S.C. de Bacchanalibus,* the use of impious or nocturnal rites to enchant, bewitch, or bind someone is likewise punishable by death (23.15).[30] Magicians and persons addicted to magic (without further definition) are to pay the

27. For commentary and discussion regarding the laws, see T. Mommsen, *Römisches Strafrecht,* Systematisches Handbuch der Deutschen Rechtwissenschaft I.4 (Leipzig, 1899), 639–43 and 861–65.

28. The earliest law cited is IX.18.2, issued by Diocletian and Maximian; 18.3–7 were issued by Constantine; 18.8 by Valentinian and Valens; 18.9 by Valentinian, Theodosius, and Arcadius.

29. The modern distinction between astronomy and astrology was not nearly so clear-cut in antiquity. The situation is further confused by the inconsistent and blurred usage of such terms as astrologus, mathematicus, *prophetes,* magus / *magos,* and *goes;* see R. Mac-Mullen, *Enemies,* 128, and the chapter he devotes to magicians.

30. *ut quem obcantarent, interficerent, obligarent, fecerint, faciendave curaverint.* On the *S.C.,* see Chapter 5, pages 148–49, esp. notes 57, 58.

capital penalty (23.17); books on the subject are banned (23.18). Ultimately, it was left up to the courts to determine whether an individual was guilty of magic based on the intent and effects of a given act.[31]

The laws give only a very limited definition, but they do point to more important considerations. The first is that magic was clearly viewed as real and efficacious, otherwise it would have been tried and punished under the laws against fraud. Second, it was widely practiced despite the laws, which necessitated the re-issuing of the legislation.[32] Third, magic is often a matter of perception, defying precise definition but palpable nonetheless. In other words, the people of this age "knew magic when they saw it." Magic was not so much legally as socially defined, as seen in the procedures of the courts, which hinged upon intent and effect. In this way, the charge of magic was likely to be brought against those who were viewed as a threat to the social order, but who had, as yet, committed no other prosecutable offense.[33] In her study of the charges of magic made against miracle workers, A. Kolenkow delineates three major types of accusations: (1) subversion, (2) doing harm either in the process or as a result of a miraculous occurrence, and (3) prodigious increase of wealth or power.[34] The first species of accusation has already been encountered in discussing Marcus Aurelius and Lucian. The second is reflected in the laws. The third is exemplified by another literary figure of the period: Apuleius (born c. 123 C.E.).

Man of letters, scholar, cosmopolite, and philosopher, Apuleius found himself in the fortunate position, while traveling in North Africa, of marrying a wealthy older widow, Pudentilla. Fearing the loss of control over Pudentilla's property and their inheritance, her son and brother-in-law hauled Apuleius into court on charges of having seduced the widow by magic. The whole sordid affair and Apuleius's response is recorded in his *Apology*.[35] Obviously, Apuleius "rose too fast" in the

---

31. Mommsen, 641, who further concludes that some acts, in and of themselves, were sufficient to require punishment. These were the performance of rites at night, human sacrifice, summoning the dead or actions using corpses and graves, and actions intended to harm or kill.

32. These two points are taken from Segal, 357f.

33. Segal, 370. Conspicuous among these are sophists, philosophers, political opponents, and of course Christians. Examples occur throughout this work.

34. A. B. Kolenkow, "A Problem of Power: How Miracle Workers Counter Charges of Magic in the Hellenistic World," *Society of Biblical Literature Seminar Papers* 1 (1976): 107.

35. See A. R. Birley, *The African Emperor: Septimius Severus*, 2d ed. (London, 1988), 25–36; J. Tatum, *Apuleius and the Golden Ass* (Ithaca, N.Y., 1979), 105–19, for the

opinion of some, and this very conspicuousness made him a target. The marriage was contracted of Pudentilla's free will in the eyes of the law, so no other recourse was possible against this domestic interloper except a charge of magic.[36] Yet, there is more. In the *Apology,* Apuleius states that he is accustomed to dress as a philosopher, carrying wallet and staff, and that his profession and its accompanying poverty in themselves bring suspicion upon him (18, 22). Philosophers are used to having slanders, particularly of magic, brought against them by the uneducated (3, 27), and Apuleius feels that he must defend philosophy's reputation in addition to his own (1, 3).

Some of the specific accusations are clearly portrayed as comic. Apuleius has great fun with these provincials in stating that his "incantations" are no more than a list of names of marine species (38), and that his quest for a rare fish was scientific, not sinister, in nature (29ff.).[37] More serious are charges of bewitchment in throwing a boy into a seizure (42ff.), practicing nocturnal rites (57), and Apuleius's refusal to name the god of his particular devotion (65). As will be seen below, these charges closely parallel those made against Apollonius.

Apuleius also includes a discussion of the definition of magic in the course of his defense. He acknowledges its reality, but draws a distinction between good and bad magic, citing the law of the *XII Tables* mentioned above (47). As for the term "magus," it derives from the name of Persian priests, men renowned for their learning and sanctity. To be called such is no crime; indeed, it is a compliment (25). Apollonius, faced with the same charge, makes the same argument.[38] The confusion of the law itself and the ambiguities surrounding the operational definition of magic within society can thus be exploited for a defense against the charge of *goeteia.*

In this period, therefore, the person accused of being a magus or *goes* is likely to be someone who is *perceived* to pose some danger to society, against whom no other specific charge can be brought. He will be con-

---

general situation; and H. E. Butler and A. S. Owen, *Apulei Apologia* (Oxford, 1914) for detailed commentary on the text.

36. The situation in this North African town offers a microcosm of how the charge of magic operated in society as a whole. Apuleius's marriage upset the established social order of Pudentilla's family and home town. Her new husband was also an outsider, foreign and strange. Though there is no crime, "there must be something wrong" to account for such a disruption; hence magic is adduced. See Segal, 361f.

37. Note, however, in light of the laws discussed above, that incantations and the mixing of potions (for which the fish was required) form part of the accusation.

38. In *Epp. Apoll.* 16 and 17, discussed below.

spicuous, frequently by his ascetic practices, but also simply for his reputation as a teacher or his ability to attract a following.[39] Most of all, he
will be suspect less on the basis of his specific actions than on perceptions based upon those unwritten codes that define the acceptable limits
of behavior in his society. The defense against such a charge will, therefore, also focus on social perceptions, issues, and functions.[40]

Returning to Apollonius, scholars have considered the chief indictment of magic against him to have been the lost work of Moiragenes in
four books.[41] Philostratus condemns this author as ignorant (I.3), but
not as a perpetrator of the *goes* calumny. The negative characterization
of Moiragenes' work is actually based on a passage from Origen:

> So on the subject of magic (μαγείας) we say that anyone inter-
> ested in examining whether or not even philosophers have some-
> times been taken in by it may read what has been written by
> Moiragenes of the memoirs of Apollonius of Tyana, the magi-
> cian and philosopher (μάγου καὶ φιλοσόφου). In them the au-
> thor, who is not a Christian but a philosopher, observed that
> some not undistinguished philosophers were convinced by the
> magic (μαγείας) of Apollonius, although when they went to him
> they regarded him merely as a charlatan (γόητα). Among such,
> so far as I remember, he included even the well-known Euphrates
> and a certain Epicurean. (*C. Cels.* VI.41)[42]

Bowie, arguing that this passage reflects Origen's opinion rather than
Moiragenes' biography, contends that the latter's work was not hostile
to Apollonius. Rather, it presented him in a different light and in an
anecdotal style à la Xenophon's Socrates, one unacceptable to Philostratus's professed intention to cast Damis's memoirs in a better rhe-

39. M. Smith, *Jesus the Magician* (New York, 1978), 84 and 90f. See Chapter 2, note
82.

40. "In other words, there is no universal definition of magical procedure in Hellenistic
culture. Instead, the charge of magic and its meaning depended on a complicated series of
assumptions. . . . Thus, the charge of "magic" helps distinguish between various groups of
people from the perspective of the speaker but does not necessarily imply any essential
difference in the actions of the participants," Segal, 367.

41. This opinion has held sway throughout the history of scholarship from Meyer, 392
(1917) through Bowersock, introduction to *Life of Apollonius*, 11f. (1970). Anderson,
Philostratus, 299f. (appendix 3), reasserts this view against the alternative thesis of Bowie
and Raynor discussed below.

42. Translation by H. Chadwick, *Contra Celsum*, rev. ed. (Cambridge, 1980); see also
his comment on the passage, 356 n. 3. Anderson, *Philostratus*, 168, identifies the Epicurean mentioned here with Damis. On Euphrates, see below.

torical style (I.3).[43] D. Raynor then endeavored to reconcile this view
with Origen's text, arguing a distinction between *magos* as a positive or
neutral description and *goes* as a pejorative term. The philosophers in
the passage were at first actually attracted to Apollonius as "*magos* and
philosopher"; only after meeting him in person did they brand him a
goes. Philostratus disapproved of Moiragenes because he praised Apollonius for the wrong reasons, as too much the magician and miracle
worker. In contrast, Philostratus was concerned that his hero be portrayed as no common thaumaturge, but as an ascetic Pythagorean philosopher.[44]

Raynor's view is supported by the two brief letters of Apollonius addressed to his Stoic nemesis Euphrates in which he equates *magos* with
divine or "godly" man (*theios aner*).

> You think that you should call philosophers who follow Pythag-
> oras magi, and likewise, I suppose, those who follow Orpheus.
> But I think that even those who follow Zeus should be called
> magi, provided they are godly and just. (*Epp. Apoll.* 16)

> The Persians call godly men magi. Thus a magus is a worshipper
> of the gods or one who is of a godly nature. But you are not a
> magus, you are a godless man. (*Epp. Apoll.* 17)[45]

The letters are clearly responses to accusations. The writer, whether
Apollonius or not, turns the tables on the accuser by turning the intended slander of *magos* into an accolade.[46] In the first letter, the
slander is aimed specifically at Pythagorean philosophers. Pythagoreans
always had the double aspect of *magos* and philosopher, so it is not
surprising to find this in Apollonius.[47] If, at least in some circles, *magos*
was not a pejorative term (unlike *goes*, which was always negative) then
it is not a question of "one or the other" but of "both and."[48] One
proposed reading of an epigram on Apollonius first published in 1978

43. Bowie, "Apollonius," 1673ff.
44. D. H. Raynor, "Moeragenes and Philostratus. Two Views of Apollonius of Tyana,"
CQ, n.s. 34 (1984): 222–26.
45. Translation by Penella; for commentary, see *Letters of Apollonius*, 99f. All subsequent translations of the letters are taken from this edition.
46. In Apuleius, *Apology* 25–27, the same opinions are expressed and the same strategy
is used.
47. Anderson, *Philostratus*, 137, notes that Philostratus did not impose on Apollonius
such elements of the Pythagorean legend as the golden thigh or the arrow of Abaris,
which would serve too easily as proof of *goeteia*.
48. Petzke, 47ff. This double-sided nature is particularly conspicuous in the Arabic
tradition regarding Apollonius; see Petzke, 28–33.

suggests this same double-sided characterization of Apollonius's person and career.[49] Part of another letter, the otherwise mundane content of which would suggest authenticity, addresses the point:

> And if two different accounts of me are circulating and continue to circulate in the future, is there anything surprising in that? For conflicting stories are inevitably told about anyone who seems to have achieved eminence in any respect. Thus, in the cases of Pythagoras, Orpheus, Plato, and Socrates contradictory things were both said and written—not surprisingly, seeing that inconsistent things are said and written about God Himself. (*Epp. Apoll.* 48.2)[50]

Philostratus's own first line of defense against the *goeteia* charge also appeals to the example of ancient philosophers. The *VA* in fact begins with a description of Pythagoras, not of Apollonius (I.1). The salient features of Pythagoras's life are listed: reincarnation, abstention from animals in food, clothing, and sacrifice, special relations with the gods, personal authority, silence, and direct divine approbation, along with a description of the life of Pythagoras's followers. Having so clearly announced his theme, Philostratus then proceeds: "Apollonius's practice was very much like theirs, and he was more divine than Pythagoras in pursuing wisdom and in overcoming tyrants" (I.2). Pythagoras is a precedent that Apollonius superseded. Directly refuting the charge of *mageia*,[51] Philostratus notes that Empedocles, Pythagoras, Democritus, and Plato consorted with *magoi*, exotic prophets, and priests, but were not themselves judged to be *magoi* thereby. Socrates and Anaxagoras possessed foreknowledge by virtue of wisdom, not by practicing magic.

49. N. J. Richardson and P. Burian, "The Epigram on Apollonius of Tyana," *GRBS* 22 (1981): 283–85. This reconstruction of the text offers a parallel between ethical activity and miracle working during Apollonius's life that, in my opinion, reflects the dual role of φιλόσοφος and μάγος. On the inscription, see G. Dagron and J. Marciliet-Joubert, *Türk Tarih Kurumu Belleten* 42 (1978): 402–5; Bowie, "Apollonius," 1687f.; and J. and L. Robert, *Bulletin épigraphique* (1979): 592. For alternative proposed readings, see C. P. Jones, "An Epigram on Apollonius of Tyana," *JHS* 100 (1980): 190–94; and W. Peek, "Epigramm auf Apollonius von Tyana," *Philologus* 2, Band 125 (1981): 297–98. The variants are collected and discussed by Dzielska, *Apollonius,* 64ff. and 160–62.

50. See Penella's commentary, 115.

51. In this chapter of the *VA*, Philostratus always uses the word *mageia* never *goeteia*, though the latter term is used later in the work. Perhaps he did not want to use such a pejorative term at the very start, or it may be that the specific writers he is addressing used the former term rather than the latter. That Philostratus himself considered either *magos*, or its use by his opponents, to be pejorative is clear: "They considered him a *magos* and slandered him as a false philosopher (βιαίως σοφόν), thinking ill of him" (I.2).

Likewise, Apollonius's achievements and wonders were performed "on account of his wisdom" (κατὰ σοφίαν) and not "by magical skill" (μάγῳ τέχνῃ). Philostratus's rehabilitation begins with giving Apollonius an intellectual pedigree, placing him in the succession of the luminaries of classical culture.

Philostratus adduces a religious argument as well to distinguish his hero from a *goes*. Apollonius is a pious worshiper of the traditional beneficent gods. In fact he is a religious virtuoso. *Goetes*, in contrast, do not attribute their works to the gods, but to magical practices and malevolent demons:

> *Goetes* . . . say that they alter fate by resorting to torturing the spirits of the dead, or by barbaric sacrifices, or by certain charms and ointments . . . while Apollonius obeyed the decrees of the Fates and foretold only those things that were destined to happen; and he foreknew these things not by *goeteia*, but from what the gods revealed. (V.12; cf. VIII.7.2, 9)[52]

That such suspicion toward Apollonius could have been founded in fact is evidenced by his performance of private religious rites at sunrise, which only disciples practiced in the four-year Pythagorean silence could share and which Philostratus does not detail (I.16).[53]

Another distinguishing point is that *goetes* are primarily motivated by gain: "They are all money-loving, for they refine their skills so that a reward may come to them and search out after great piles of cash" (VIII.7.3; cf. VII.39). To this, Apollonius can contrast his own voluntary poverty (πενία δὲ αὐθαιρέτως) and contend: "I disdained money even as a boy. Indeed, viewing my inheritance—which was a splendid property—as an ephemeral thing, I gave it over to my brothers and friends, and to my poorer relatives, disciplining (μελετῶν) myself from my very hearth and home, so to speak, to need nothing" (VIII.7.3).[54] Religious conformity and ascetical poverty must therefore also be reckoned as characteristics that distinguish Apollonius from the *goetes*.[55]

52. The mention of fate here would have a certain Stoic appeal about it.
53. Raynor, 225, notes Philostratus's embarrassment at the thaumaturgic traditions concerning Apollonius. As he could not suppress them, he was forced to assimilate them either in passing references or polemic justifications.
54. Cf. I.13 and *Epp. Apoll.* 35, 45. Immediately before this statement, Apollonius quoted a letter from Vespasian commending his poverty (*Epp. Apoll.* 77f.).
55. In light of this discussion, and that of Apollonius's trial before Domitian on charges of *goeteia* at the end of this chapter, it is difficult to comprehend Dzielska's contention, *Apollonius*, 52 and 90, that Apollonius attributed his powers to magic and was proud to

Apollonius's Ascetical Practice

Apollonius is a genuine ascetic and calls himself such. When asked to make a customs declaration on the Mesopotamian border, he lists his "handmaids" as Prudence, Justice, Virtue, Temperance, Courage, and *Askesis* (I.20). These are repeated as the "gifts" he brings to king Vardanes (I.28). *Askesis* now takes its place among a catalogue of intellectual and moral virtues.[56] The same mixture of ascetical and moral virtues is found in *Epp. Apoll.* 43: "If anyone asserts that he is my pupil, let him also assert that he remains inside, completely abstains from bathing, does not kill animals or eat their flesh, is free from envy, maliciousness, hatred, the urge to slander, and hostility, and is called a member of the class of free men."[57] The refusal to bathe and the preference for staying indoors are conspicuously absent from the *VA*. According to Philostratus, Apollonius possesses charm and a fondness for company and cheerfulness, even in the midst of his five-year discipline of silence (I.14). The concern to emphasize the simple social graces recalls Lucian's portrait of Demonax. How much this portrait has been embellished is difficult to determine; the overall impression given by the letters is certainly less fetching. In the *VA*, however, ascetical rigor is always carefully balanced by concern for humanity and society.[58]

Correct motivation is required for taking up an ascetical life. In VI.8 Apollonius criticizes the Gymnosophists of the Egyptian desert for tak-

---

call himself a magician. As seen in the letters cited above, his defense of the term "magus" is actually a rebuttal of the charge of magic. This underscores the importance of defining what is meant by "magic" in each specific case.

56. The handmaids are σωφροσύνην, δικαιοσύνην, ἀρετήν, ἐγκράτειαν, ἀνδρείαν, ἄσκησιν. The list is a pun, for all these virtues are in the feminine gender in Greek, and thus can appear to be the names of women. These companions are, however, far from any harem the customs agent would recognize. Like Oscar Wilde, Apollonius has nothing to declare but his genius. Petzke, 218ff., notes that in the *VA* ἀγαθός (good) = θεῖος (godly) = σοφός (wise), an equation of moral, religious, and philosophical values. Apollonius's pursuit is of "purity" in the physical, religious, and ethical sense: "Diesem Ziel dient die asketische Lebenshaltung, die mit einer tugendhaften Lebensführung zusammengeht." Given this context, *askesis* here begins to take on the definition given by Cox, 25: "The wellspring of the sage's perfect self-knowledge, which enables him never to change, is his asceticism, which in Late Antiquity connotes not mere 'training' but a renunciation of worldly values and bodily deprivation, if not actual abuse"; see *VA* VI.35.

57. Cf. *Epp. Apoll.* 8. Epictetus, *Epict. Diss.* IV.xi.1–35, rails against those who refuse to bathe under the pretext of philosophy, drawing a congenial parallel between physical and ethical purity, between the attraction to beauty and to philosophy.

58. Thus Reitzenstein, *Wundererzählungen*, 43: "Apollonius hat aus allen Philosophien die pythagoreische allein sich erwählt, die an Askese nicht weniger verlangt wie die kynische, aber den Menschen weit über jene heraushebt."

ing pride in their asceticism since their nakedness is due to the necessity of the climate not the strength of their rigor. The familiar motif of condemning ascetical practice for mere display or reputation again appears. "Eating barley bread and wearing a simple cloak are good practices, not if they are flaunted in the manner of one seeking repute, but only if they are seriously observed, when circumstances naturally lead to them" (*Epp. Apoll.* 79; cf. 85).[59] In one case, however, reputation was a valid consideration. When the Indian king Phraotes expressed his desire to become one of Apollonius's disciples, the philosopher dissuaded him: "In a king, a more moderate and demure philosophy makes for an admirable temperament, as is apparent in you. One, however, that is rigorous and severe would appear vulgar, O king, and quite beneath your station, while the envious would think it smacked of conceit" (II.37). Apollonius's asceticism would be excessively rigorous and severe for a king, and might be perceived as vainglorious. This sentiment is certainly appropriate to the second-century C.E. Roman Empire; whether it is appropriate to first-century India need hardly be discussed here. Certainly Marcus Aurelius would have heaved a knowing sigh of agreement with the sentiments of Apollonius.

Aurelius's thought also echoes in Apollonius's views on facing death: "So, too, philosophers must await the right opportunities in which to meet death, so that they may be neither unprepared nor appear suicidal, but comport themselves in a deliberate and careful manner" (VII.31).[60] It is impossible to determine whether Apollonius would have considered Peregrinus's self-immolation to be a case of a philosopher choosing the circumstances of his own death or, to use Aurelius's phrase, a case of stage-heroics. Apollonius is presented as a great admirer of the Brahmans, who were renowned for this very practice, and Lucian specifically states that Peregrinus's death was partially in imitation of them.[61] Yet, in all the lengthy discussion of the Brahmans in the *VA*, and of their life and philosophy, self-immolation is never mentioned (III.10–51). Leaving conjectures about Apollonius's opinion aside, it is evident that Philostratus held a low opinion of Peregrinus's death, viewing it as the ultimate example of his presumptuousness. Here too it appears that the

---

59. See Penella's commentary, 134. In *Epp. Apoll.* 10, Apollonius states that philosophers who lecture publicly, as opposed to those concerned with individual teaching, have been overcome with a desire for recognition (δόξης ἥττων ὤν διαλέγοιτ' ἄν). Recall Lucian's criticism that Peregrinus did everything for the sake of notoriety (δόξης ἕνεκα). See also *Epict. Diss.* IV.viii.6–23.

60. Cf. Marcus Aurelius, *Meditations,* XI.3; see Chapter 2, page 45.

61. *Peregr.,* 25. On a Brahman who immolated himself in the Roman Forum, to general admiration and praise, see Strabo XV.1.73.

ultimate asceticism, martyrdom, has value only if undertaken for the correct motives.[62]

As in the case of the Stoics, Apollonius's attitude to the body largely determines the basic nature of his asceticism. Some passages in the *VA* and the letters appear to reflect a body- or life-hating dualism: "We men are in that prison all the time, which we call life; for our very soul, bound in a perishable body, endures much, a slave to all those things that haunt the human condition" (*VA* VII.26). In other places, Apollonius equates life with punishment and servitude and proclaims life to be worse than death.[63] The context of all these statements, however, is a *consolatio*—to his fellow prisoners in the *VA*, to grieving friends and relatives in the letters. These are *topoi*, and not necessarily doctrines of Apollonius's particular philosophy.[64] The one exception is in *VA* VIII.31, when Apollonius miraculously appears after his death to a disbelieving student, proving the immortality of the soul "snatched from its harsh and arduous servitude." The pronouncement is oracular, the language poetic; again the statement is a commonplace description of death. The most philosophical statement on the matter occurs in another *consolatio*: "There is no death of anything except in appearance only, just as there is no birth of anything except in appearance only" (*Epp. Apoll.* 58.1). Apollonius goes on to say that in all death and birth one's substance (οὔσης) remains. In death, one becomes a god; all is Providence and, therefore, good.

There is no fundamental body or life versus soul dualism in Apollonius.[65] It is clear that the body is an important tool in the pursuit of the ascetical life, unlike Aurelius and the Stoics who considered it essentially unimportant. "The soul that does not consider the question of the body's self-sufficiency cannot make itself self-sufficient" (*Epp. Apoll.* 82). This letter is addressed to Euphrates, a philosophical opponent

---

62. "This Proteus was one of those so rash and presumptuous in their philosophizing that he even threw himself onto a pyre at Olympia" (*VS* 563). W. Wright in the Loeb edition incorrectly translates θαρραλέως φιλοσοφούντων as "those who have the courage of their philosophy." The connotation of θαρραλέως here is negative, as is clear from the context where Philostratus describes Peregrinus as abusive, insulting, and barbaric in speech. A better rendering would be "those so rash and presumptuous in their philosophizing." The similarity between the "last words" of Peregrinus (*Peregr.* 39) and Apollonius (*VA* VIII.30) is of no significance; they are mere commonplaces.

63. Life is punishment: *Epp. Apoll.* 13 and 90 (which is a one-sentence fragment with no context); life is servitude: *VA* VIII.31; life is worse than death: *Epp. Apoll.* 55.1.

64. Penella, 119f.

65. Petzke, 218, arrived at the same conclusion, though his arguments are rather weak. His contention that the body and earthly life are "eine quantité négligeable" for Apollonius is incorrect.

whom Apollonius criticizes elsewhere for his wealth and luxury.[66] Apollonius's point is that Euphrates cannot achieve self-sufficiency of mind (i.e., true philosophy) unless he achieves self-sufficiency of body by divesting himself of his wealth, living simply and diminishing his wants. Thus the way to become self-sufficient, and therefore truly independent and truly free (αὐταρκης), is through the practice of *physical* asceticism.

Apollonius's specific practices include abstention from alcohol, sexual continence, poverty, and a cluster of other observances specifically connected with Pythagoreanism. Apollonius gave up wine in his youth, as part of his first turning to an ascetical life. Though wine is in itself pure, it nevertheless disturbs the mind and muddies the *aether* in the soul (*VA* I.8). He will not accept Damis's casuistic argument to make an exception for date wine, though, curiously, he allows Damis to drink (II.7).[67] The lengthiest discussion of abstinence occurs in II.35–37 as a necessity for keeping the mind clear for the purposes of dream divination. The reasons for abstinence are thus physiological and, in the broad sense, religious in nature, not moral.

Apollonius rejects both marriage and sex: "Pythagoras was esteemed for the words he spoke, that a man must have relations with no other woman except his wife. Apollonius, however, said that Pythagoras ordained this for others and that he himself would never marry nor even as much as approach having intercourse" (I.13).[68] Even in his youth, he so mastered and controlled himself that he was never overcome with passion (I.13). He regarded pederasty as particularly abominable (I.12, VII.42). Sexual asceticism is not only a matter of deprivation. Chastity (*sophrosyne*) is a positive force in and of itself that can overcome the sexual impulse: "For chastity consists in not yielding to sexual desire and drive, and in abstaining from and mastering this madness" (I.33).

66. *Epp. Apoll.* 2, 4, 5, 6, 7, 15, 51; *VA* V.38, VIII.38.
67. In the same passage, Apollonius would also allow his faithful disciple to eat meat. This is in direct contradiction to *Epp. Apoll.* 43, cited above, and *VA* V.21 where it is an essential part of the disciples' philosophic discipline to imitate Apollonius's every word and action. Apollonius may simply be ironic here, for he states that since abstinence has profited Damis nothing so far, he may as well indulge. In another instance, a disciple intends to marry, contrary to Apollonius's own example (IV.25). It appears that Apollonius's full ascetical rigor is unique to himself, a proof of his heroic superiority, and not a manner of life to be preached or propagated. Apollonius did consider his manner of life inappropriate for Phraotes. Neither is Apollonius's practice of poverty meant for all; see below.
68. This passage reiterates the "greater than Pythagoras" theme of the *VA*. More important, it introduces the distinction between Apollonius's practice and that of the mere practitioner or disciple. One philosophical and ethical standard is appropriate to everyone else, but Apollonius operates on a higher plane. This reservation of radical discipline to the heroic few will remove the social threat posed by ascetical values.

This view of sex carries with it a negative estimation of women. The *VA* is a man's world, inhabited by few women and these of a very unsavory character.[69] When one of Apollonius's disciples wishes to marry, his wife turns out to be a vampire (*lamia*), a being whose particular delight in the bodies of young men is both sexual and alimentary (IV.25). In spite of all this, Philostratus mentions false rumors about some sort of sexual impropriety on Apollonius's part (I.13).[70]

Poverty and the use of wealth form another major component of Apollonius's asceticism. Defending himself before Domitian, Apollonius states that he despised money from his youth (VIII.7.3). Yet, his family's wealth allowed him to travel to a number of teachers (I.7).[71] He dispossessed himself of his inheritance gradually, dividing it with his brother, and then sharing his remaining half again with him. In the process of reforming his dissolute brother and winning over his poorer relatives, perhaps from envy over his inheritance, Apollonius finally gave away virtually all his property (I.13).[72] Throughout his career, he declines gifts and offers of money from kings and emperors (I.21, 33, 35, 40; II.40; V.38). He relates to the Gymnosophists the story of his own "choice of Heracles," declining to pursue philosophies that promised him wealth in favor of that which promised virtue, asceticism, and divine power (VI.11).[73] Yet, just as rumors circulated impugning Apollonius's sexual continence, accusations of avarice were also made against him—though these are mentioned in the letters and not the *VA* itself.[74]

There are two sides to Apollonius's view of property and wealth: one moderate, the other harsh. The latter is more pronounced in the letters: "In my opinion virtue and wealth are entirely opposed to one another. For when one decreases it causes the other to increase, and when one

69. Petzke, 224, clearly illustrates the point and concludes: "In der gesamten VA spielt die Frau keine Rolle. . . . Positiv wird in der VA von der Liebe zur Frau nicht gesprochen." This is somewhat curious, given the fact that the *VA* was commissioned by a woman.

70. Charges of immorality against philosophers and holy men have been seen before in Lucian, *Alex.* 5, 41f., and *Peregr.* 9f.

71. The portrait of Apollonius's upbringing is fairly typical of an aspiring sophist; see Bowersock, *Greek Sophists*, 21–25.

72. In *Epp. Apoll.* 4, Apollonius urges Euphrates, a philosopher who had become rich, to redeem himself by giving some of his wealth away to others.

73. See also *Epp. Apoll.* 52. Apollonius's choice is the opposite of that made by Lucian in *The Dream* or *Lucian's Career*, 9–16; see Chapter 3, pages 77–78.

74. The accusation that Apollonius lost interest in his native city later in his career and was himself only interested in making money is addressed in *Epp. Apoll.* 35, 44, 45, 47. That he could still act as benefactor to Tyana, perhaps by interceding with wealthy relatives and friends, is shown in *Epp. Apoll.* 48; see Penella's commentary, 115.

increases it causes the other to decrease. So how could it be possible for a person to have both wealth and virtue, except in the opinion of the ignorant, who equate wealth with virtue?" (*Epp. Apoll.* 35). Apollonius rejects wealth categorically, and contends that he himself despised it even before his conversion to philosophy (*Epp. Apoll.* 45). The issue comes into particular focus in letters to Euphrates, the Stoic who in the *VA* quarrels with and defames Apollonius, eventually denouncing him to Domitian.[75] Apollonius rebukes this Stoic for accepting money for teaching, even from the emperor (*Epp. Apoll.* 2, 5, 51; cf. *VA* VIII.38);[76] for possessing not only more than what is necessary, but even flaunting his wealth (*Epp. Apoll.* 4, 5, 6); and for sycophancy and venality (*Epp. Apoll.* 7, 15; cf. *VA* V.38). As this correspondence is carried on between philosophers, its polemic manifests the "true versus false philosophy" motif seen earlier in both Aurelius and Lucian. Here, however, the distinction is ascetical. The true philosopher is recognized by his voluntary poverty. By the same token a wealthy person, by definition, cannot be a true philosopher.[77] This strident attitude only occasionally surfaces in the *VA* when Apollonius dismisses the wealth of Vardanes as mere chaff (I.38) and when he proclaims that a wise man will generally be forgiven any offense save greed (I.34).

Despite these statements, a more moderate attitude generally prevails in both the *VA* and the letters. The clearest example occurs in *Epp. Apoll.* 84: "We have striven to achieve self-sufficiency not in order to use inexpensive and plain things exclusively, but so that we might not dread such things."[78] Poverty is not an end in itself, but a form of training and mental discipline.[79] The idea echoes Stoic thought on the subject. Another such echo is found in *Epp. Apoll.* 22, that poverty must be borne bravely, wealth humanely. Apollonius prays that the wise may be poor, but that others may be rich, provided they are not fraudulent (*VA*

75. *VA* VII.9. Other instances of Euphrates' spreading slander occur in V.39, VI.7, and VIII.3.

76. Something Apollonius categorically refuses to do in *Epp. Apoll.* 42.

77. That Euphrates was in fact both wealthy and powerful is attested by Pliny, *Ep.* I.10.10, and Dio LXVIII.1.2.; cf. *Epict. Diss.* III.xv, IV.viii, and Marcus Aurelius, *Med.* X.31. See also Grosso, 420f., though there seems to be no need to read an active rivalry between philosophical schools here. The animosity between the two philosophers is always characterized as personal. Euphrates is not denounced for being a Stoic but for being rich. Apollonius's relations with other philosophers are, in fact, depicted as cordial and friendly; see Knoles, 171–81.

78. Cf. the Stoic position discussed in Chapter 1, pages 12–13, 17–18, and Chapter 2, page 36, esp. note 41.

79. *Epp. Apoll.* 97: "Being poor is not shameful in itself, but being poor for a shameful reason is a disgrace."

IV.40, cf. I.33). The same distinction occurs in his conversation with a rich Cilician imprisoned with him under Domitian. Apollonius states that if the man acquired his wealth "either by inheritance or by engaging in trade as a free man and not a huckster, who could be so despotic to deprive you, under the pretense of the law, of that which you have acquired according to the law" (VII.23). The lawful rights of property, and even wealth, are upheld. It is the Cilician who then goes on to list his own "woes of the rich": temptation to revolution; insolence against authority; being surrounded by sycophancy, blackmail, bribery, jealousy; pouring out money in the very effort to secure it. Apollonius responds that as surely as it was wealth that brought him to this pass, its dissipation will free him both from prison and from the yoke wealth imposes. The argument is purely practical, neither deeply philosophical nor ethical.

Philostratus's rehabilitation can surely be seen in the more moderate position in the VA, in which wealth is, of itself, both licit and good. But as the distinction between the letters and the VA is not black and white, the question is a matter of emphasis.[80]

There is an explanation that allows Apollonius to hold both positions simultaneously. In virtually every instance that wealth is decried, the subject is a philosopher. *Epp. Apoll.* 35, proclaiming wealth and virtue to be mutually exclusive, and 45 on despising wealth even before converting to philosophy, were written to Apollonius's brother and reflect the complaint of Tyana that their famous son left to pursue his fortune without any consideration for his home town.[81] Apollonius is speaking here only for himself as a philosopher, and in the face of personal criticism. Recall that Apollonius had no qualms over enriching his relatives from his inheritance or in using his influence to benefit Tyana. The letters to Euphrates do not condemn wealth per se, but a wealthy philosopher. Wealth is unbecoming to and incompatible with Euphrates'

---

80. Bowie, "Apollonius," 1683, also notes the difference in tone between the letters and the VA on this issue, and attributes the moderate position to Philostratus. However, Bowie draws too sharp a distinction between the two sources and thus generalizes that the harsh position reflects the "radical" philosophical culture of the second century while the moderate position originated in the third with Philostratus. In the previous chapter it was shown that Demonax and Nigrinus, whom Bowie cites as examples of radicals, were characterized by Lucian to be just the opposite. Furthermore, Bowie's distinction between the second and third centuries is predicated upon his contention that Damis was a pure invention of Philostratus. If a historical Damis is accepted (or even a pre-Philostratan forgery) the tidy distinction breaks down, for Philostratus explicitly states that the prison story of the rich Cilician came from Damis.

81. Penella, 108.

profession. Greed is unforgivable in a wise man (σοφός, *VA* I.34) which, in this case, may simply be a synonym for "philosopher."

Moderate statements are all directed to laymen. Apollonius's prayer that the wise may be poor but others rich acts as a perfect summary of his position in both the letters and the *VA*. One further point should be made. The rider to the prayer "provided they are not fraudulent," reflects Apollonius's repeated concern for public morality. Greed, strife, luxury, and excess are excoriated, especially in Greek cities. Athens and Sparta are chided to return to their ancient virtues. In all this, Apollonius simply offers the classical commonplaces and common sense of civic government and harmony.[82] There is no divine philosophy in this, merely traditional wisdom.

Radical ascetical poverty is, then, the hallmark of the philosopher— but not a precept for the general population. Apollonius upholds the right to property and wealth for the layman. He is no social radical in this regard; in fact, he is just the opposite. The demand placed upon the wealthy layman is to use his wealth according to the old-time virtues, public morality, and *philotimia* (*VA* I.15, IV.3, 8f.; *Epp. Apoll.* 11).

Apollonius attributes a number of his other ascetical practices to Pythagoras (*VA* I.32). The eating of meat not only necessitates shedding the blood of animals (*Epp. Apoll.* 43) but is also unclean and dulls the mind (*VA* I.8). The wearing of linen clothing is also an abstention from butchered animals or their refuse (I.8, VI.11) and is particularly pure and appropriate for discourse, prayer, and sacrifice (VIII.7.5). Letting one's hair grow and not wearing shoes (I.8) complete the list.

The resemblances between Apollonius and Pythagoras extend beyond ascetical practices as well. This topic has already received extensive study. Briefly, these include abstention from animal sacrifice (V.25), observance of silence (I.14), reincarnation (III.23, VIII.7.4), bilocation (IV.10, VIII.12), understanding the language of animals (I.20), and encounters with a lion (V.42) and with Trophonius of Lebadea (VIII.19).[83]

---

82. *VA* I.7f., 9, 13, 15; IV.2f. (Ephesus), 8f. (Smyrna), 21 (Athens), 27 (Sparta, cf. *Epp. Apoll.* 63); V.23, 26 (Alexandria); VI.34 (Tarsus). See Anderson, *Philostratus*, 137–42. For further discussion of Apollonius's relations to cities, see below.

83. For discussion of parallels between Apollonius and Pythagoras, see F. C. Baur, *Apollonios von Tyana und Christus, oder das Verhältniss des Pythagoreismus zum Christentum* (Tübingen, 1832) = *Drei Abhandlungen zur Geschichte der alten Philosophie und ihres Verhaltnisses zum Christentum*, ed. E. Zeller (Leipzig, 1876), 1–227; I. Lévy, *Recherches sur les sources de la légend de Pythagore*, Bibliothèque de l'Ecole des hautes études, sciences religieuses 42 (Paris, 1926); W. Burkert, *Lore and Science in Ancient Pythagoreanism*, trans. E. L. Minar, Jr. (Cambridge, Mass., 1972); and Knoles, 246–50, 267. A detailed summary with reference to the sources for both Pythagoras and Apol-

That these parallels were entirely too obvious was recognized early; Eusebius contended that Apollonius used Pythagoreanism to mask *goeteia* (*C. Hier. 5*). Philostratus, who shows no great enthusiasm for Pythagoreanism in any of his other writings, is not the source of this aspect of his portrait of Apollonius. This identification with Pythagoras most probably arose in the second century. Once established, it would have taken little for Philostratus to embellish it with what every sophist knew about Pythagoras.[84] Eusebius was partially correct, but it was not Apollonius himself who justified his life by Pythagoreanism, but those who wrote about him.

As is clear from the very beginning of the *VA*, presenting Apollonius as a serious philosopher was the foundation of Philostratus's rehabilitation. The image of Pythagoras was particularly felicitous in this regard. Eusebius, again, got straight to the point: Pythagoras left no writings of any sort, so how could Apollonius claim to have learned from him? (*C. Hier.* 11). Pythagoras, in contrast to his philosophical contemporaries, lived on more as a personality and legend, and as a literary ideal, rather than in written doctrine and teaching.[85] He was the exemplar, living in the literature of the time, of the type of personal, charismatic leader Peregrinus had himself endeavored to become. There is, in fact, very little philosophy in the *VA*. Nothing appears on the particularly Pythagorean theories of mathematics, music, or astronomy. The concern is with the trappings of Pythagoreanism, especially asceticism; the focus is moral and paraenetic, not intellectual.[86] Apollonius's Pythagoreanism, which is most clearly evidenced in his ascetic practice, serves to legiti-

---

lonius is found in B. L. Taggart, "Apollonius of Tyana. His Biographers and Critics," Ph.D. diss., Tufts University, 1972.

84. So Speyer, 50, correctly argued against Meyer, 383f., that Philostratus could not be the source of the Pythagorean identification. Bowie, "Apollonius," 1672f., suggests a date between 117 and 160 C.E. as a *terminus post quem* for Apollonius's association with Pythagoreanism. Anderson, *Philostratus*, 136f. and nn. 8f., notes the stock Pythagorean *topoi*, and discusses the still unresolved issue of whether an alleged *Life of Pythagoras* by Apollonius, mentioned by Porphyry, could have been used as a source.

85. Petzke, 205, and W. Burkert, "Craft Versus Sect: The Problem of Orphics and Pythagoreans," in *Jewish and Christian Self-Definition*, ed. B. F. Meyer and E. P. Sanders (Philadelphia, 1982), 3:22 and n. 105. On the large amount of Pythagorean literature in the first through fourth centuries C.E., see Burkert, *Lore and Science*, 97–107.

86. Knoles, 246–50. It must, however, also be noted that this concern with philosophical praxis rather than theory is a general characteristic of the age. Stoicism had deliberately promoted this emphasis, while the philosophers in Lucian are judged (and usually condemned) by their actions rather than their teaching. See Chapter 3, note 6.

mate his manner of life by appeal to a canonized classical sage while, at the same time, emphasizing its charismatic and superhuman nature.[87]

In his early education (*VA* I.7), Apollonius attended lectures in all the philosophies, but found himself attracted to Pythagoreanism "by some secret wisdom" (ἀρρήτῳ τινὶ σοφίᾳ). His Pythagorean teacher, Euxenus, was not up to the task. Though he mouthed Pythagoras's doctrines, he did not live Pythagoras's life and remained a slave to his appetites. From the beginning, Apollonius's interest in, and definition of, Pythagoreanism was ascetical. He removed himself from the history of the Pythagorean school and its academic doctrine to follow a version that was simple, radical, and evangelical.[88] So it is that Apollonius travels to the Brahmans (III.10–51), the source of true wisdom who passed this on to the Gymnosophists, who in turn taught Pythagoras (VI.11, VIII.7.12). By returning to the source independently, Apollonius outdoes Pythagoras and is established as an independent authority, while still remaining in the tradition of Greek wisdom.[89] All in all, Philostratus's handling of Apollonius's Pythagoreanism is a sophistic tour de force.

The *VA* thus marks several important developments in the character and understanding of asceticism. The first is that rigorous physical *askesis* is portrayed as a positive force, bringing unique benefits to its practitioner such as clairvoyance and nearness to the gods. Equally important is the concomitant development. Such rigor is not recommended for the layman; it is the preserve of the philosopher, who lives by a much more demanding standard of values. What is permissible and even laudable in others, such as the acquisition and right use of wealth, is forbidden to him. By becoming characteristic of the rare heroic individual, such practices as poverty and celibacy lose their social character and, therefore, their social threat. They cease to be an alternative for the many and become the accomplishment of the few. The philosopher is clearly superior to others, but he is also separated from them. This separation is of fundamental importance to the ascetic's use of the authority gained from his superiority.

87. Burkert, *Lore and Science*, 96: "The Pythagorean pseudoepigrapha meet a subconscious religious need of the Hellenistic period. And when, from the first century B.C. on, people once more came forward to declare themselves Pythagoreans, their most noticeable characteristic is that they are seeking (or even, as for example in the case of Apollonius of Tyana, claiming to possess) a superhuman, divine wisdom."

88. Taggart, 128f.

89. See Taggart, 134–40. For bibliography on Apollonius's eastern journey see Anderson, *Philostratus*, 199–226 and n. 1, none of which is satisfactory according to Anderson.

Apollonius's Exercise of Authority

Throughout the *VA*, Apollonius exercises considerable authority in religious, social, and political spheres. These interventions are consistently on the side of tradition, convention, and established norms.

Apollonius is portrayed as an expert on religious matters. The source of his superior religious knowledge is the gods themselves. Again, Philostratus introduces this theme speaking about Pythagoras: "He was a familiar of the gods and learned from them the ways in which men please or displease them. It was on the basis of this knowledge that he spoke about their nature" (I.1). So Apollonius states that it is the duty of the philosopher daily to converse with the gods at dawn, then later about the gods, and only after that about human affairs (I.16). As a youth, immediately after his assuming the ascetic life, he went to live at the temple of Asclepius at Aegeae where the god himself referred a patient to him (I.9). Upon his return from the East, he received recommendations from some of the most renowned oracles of the Greek world: "Reports from the oracle at Colophon proclaimed that the man shared its own wisdom and was perfectly wise and suchlike, and the same from Didyma and from the shrine near Pergamum; for the god bade many of those in need of healing to have recourse to Apollonius, saying that this was his desire and a thing pleasing to the Fates (IV.1)."[90]

On his journey eastward (I.16), he lectured priests in Greek temples and corrected them if they had departed from tradition. If the cult were barbaric, he would learn its history and straightaway suggest improvements. Apollonius's religious knowledge is universal. After his return, he advised Ionian cities on the dedication of altars and images (IV.1) and corrected the rites at Dodona, Delphi, Abae, the shrines of Amphiaraus and Trophonius, and that of the Muses on Mount Helicon (IV.24). Even at Rome Telesinus, who otherwise sought some pretext to

---

90. Just as the temple at Aegeae was devoted to a god of healing, Asclepius, so also was the great shrine outside of Pergamum; while the oracles at Colophon (Klaros) and Didyma were mouthpieces of Apollo, Asclepius's father and a healing god in his own right. The context here is even more specific than Apollonius's receiving divine approbation generally. He is being portrayed as a sharer in divine healing. Indeed, it is in this book that most of his "miraculous" healings and exorcisms occur, though these are far less spectacular than sometimes portrayed. More important than his physical healings are his "social" healings: the ending of civic strife, the return to ancient virtue, the purification of religion, etc., which are also accomplished in book IV. Philostratus seeks to portray Apollonius's divine healing ability less in miraculous cures than in restoring to human society the order and discipline desired by the gods. On the phenomenon of oracles having connections with and recommending philosophical schools, see R. Lane Fox, *Pagans and Christians* (New York, 1987), 185–97, 200, 256–57.

have the sage arrested, allowed Apollonius to visit the temples and instructed the priests to accept his corrections. The result was a religious revival in the city (IV.40f.). Apollonius drove religious quacks from the Hellespont—interestingly called "Egyptians and Chaldeans," not *magoi* and *goetes*—to the physical and financial relief of the inhabitants (VI.41).

The reception was not so warm everywhere. The hierophant of the Eleusinian mysteries refused him initiation, considering him to be a *goes* (IV.18; the initial reaction was the same at Lebadea, VIII.19). Apollonius rejoined that the real reason was the hierophant's jealousy; Apollonius knew the rite better than he did. Thus, in the religious sphere, Apollonius is portrayed as the upholder of tradition, a veritable religious antiquarian. He is neither a radical nor an innovator, neither a philosopher introducing new gods in the manner of Socrates, nor a *goes* cashing in on a new cult like Alexander.

As in the resemblance to Pythagoras, the appearance is too perfect. Nor can the reputation of Apollonius as a pagan puritan be ascribed to the invention of Philostratus. Perhaps this aspect, like the identification with Pythagoras, is a second-century phenomenon.[91] The possibility remains, of course, that Apollonius could have been much like Philostratus describes him, but such devotion to and preoccupation with religion and cult should be reflected in the letters, at least to some extent. It is not at all.

Another possibility may be suggested. Philostratus, citing Damis, reports that while in Athens:

> His first discourse, since he saw that the Athenians were sacrifice-lovers, was on the subject of religion; how one should make sacrifice, libation, or prayer appropriate to each god and at which time of the day or night. One may also find a book of Apollonius in which he gives these instructions in his own words (τῇ ἑαυτοῦ φωνῇ). . . . Who could still think that one who taught philosophically (τὸν φιλοσοφοῦντα) how to worship the gods was impure in religion? (IV.19)

Moreover, Philostratus states that this work, *On Sacrifices* (περὶ θυσιῶν), can be found in many cities, temples, and houses of learned men

91. J. Göttsching, *Apollonius von Tyana* (Leipzig, 1889), 61ff., held that Philostratus was the religious reformer exploiting Apollonius for his own purposes. As with Pythagoreanism, Bowie, "Apollonius," 1688ff., shows that Philostratus displays no such religious interest in any of his other works.

and calls it a stately composition, well reflecting its author (III.41).[92]
One brief fragment purporting to be from this work survives, in Eusebius, *Praep. Evang.* IV.13 (150b). It speaks of one, first God, superior
to all the others, to whom it is improper to offer any sacrifice whatsoever. Such a God may only be approached with the mind.[93]

If this fragment is genuine, then the opinions of Apollonius appear far
more radical than the simple refusal of animal sacrifice in the *VA*. The
fragment does mention other lesser gods; perhaps sacrifice is allowable
to them, especially by the "unphilosophical" common folk. There is no
way of knowing. Similar sentiments are, however, expressed in two letters addressed to the priests at Olympia and Delphi respectively.

> The gods do not need sacrifices. Then what can one do to please
> them? Acquire wisdom, it seems to me, and do good to honor-
> able men as far as one is able. That is what is dear to the gods;
> sacrifice is the occupation of the godless. (*Epp. Apoll.* 26)

> Priests pollute altars with blood. And then some people wonder
> why their cities, whenever they are in serious trouble, suffer mis-
> fortune. What stupidity! Heraclitus was wise, but not even he
> was able to persuade the Ephesians not to try to wash away mud
> with mud. (*Epp. Apoll.* 27)

It is plausible to suggest that the historical Apollonius may have been a
radical, whose interest in religion was genuine but unorthodox.[94] If *On*

92. σεμνῶς ξυντεταγμένον καὶ κατὰ τὴν ἠχὼ τοῦ ἀνδρός. Philostratus also states that
it needs to be interpreted in some fashion: καί τοι, ἄν τις ἑρμηνεύοι αὐτό. The usual
meaning of ἑρμηνεύω as "translate" cannot apply here; the meaning must be "interpret"
or "explain." Conybeare's note in the Loeb edition (1:321 n. 1), which refers the reader
to IV.19 and states that the document was written in "Cappadocian," is an unsupportable
conjecture. Dzielska, *Apollonius,* 145–57, correctly argues that any such native language
had died out by Apollonius's time. She, however, advances the view that the document
was written in Syriac. Both these views stem from τῇ ἑαυτοῦ φωνῇ in IV.19 being translated as "in his own language" rather than the more literal (though unclear) "in his own
voice," or as above "in his own words." The fundamental difficulty is: Why would Apollonius, if his aim were either to seek acceptance by established religious authorities or
even to publish his own more radical beliefs, have written in a language other than universally accessible Greek? This would certainly be a significant departure from Philostratus's
description of his ardent philhellenism and his pride in speaking perfect Attic (I.7). Perhaps the work "written in his own words" was so erudite (σεμνῶς ξυντεταγμένον) that it
baffled the layman and required some expert in religion and philosophy to explain it
(ἑρμηνεύοι αὐτό).
93. This fragment bears a distinct resemblance to the views on the subject expressed by
Porphyry, *de Abst.* II.49f.
94. Recall that the hierophant regarded him as impure and unworthy, while the priests of
Trophonius accused him of coming to test or confute their cult (ἔλεγχον τοῦ ἱεροῦ, VII.19).

Sacrifices was somewhat inaccessible, as a specialist's work in the libraries of temples and scholars, written in highly obscure and / or technical language (III.41), it would be relatively simple to rehabilitate him as an orthodox champion.[95] His known and arcane interest in religion could be transformed into antiquarianism. Odd religious practices that could not be explained away could be justified by Pythagoreanism. (In the *VA*, Apollonius's abstention from animal sacrifice is purely personal and stems from his philosophy, but he does not object to others' sacrificing in their own way, I.31). Established stories about being rebuffed by religious authorities could simply be expanded and given endings favorable to Apollonius.[96] Such a process would result in exactly the portrait of Apollonius as a religious authority given in the *VA*.

What may be termed Apollonius's teaching authority is intimately connected to religion. While still a youth at Aegeae, he turned the temple into a Lyceum and Academy by filling it with philosophical discussions (I.13); he later lamented that Apollo's temple at Antioch was not a home for serious study. When the sage speaks to priests, the verb used is "to philosophize" (φιλοσοφεῖν, I.16). The clearest example of this conflation of religion and philosophy occurs in Apollonius's visit to the oracle of Trophonius at Lebadea (VIII.19). He comes to the shrine in a matter concerning philosophy (ὑπὲρ φιλοσοφίας) and descends to the oracle wearing his philosopher's cloak (τρίβων) as if to engage the god in formal discourse (ἐς διάλεξιν). His question is simple: "Which, O Trophonius, do you consider the purest and most perfect philosophy?" Trophonius answers by giving Apollonius a volume of Pythagorean philosophy and rebuking his priests for their earlier suspicions. Apollonius thus emerges as both the restorer of ancient wisdom and the apostle of the divinely approved philosophy.[97]

The foundation of Apollonius's authority as a moral teacher is also religious, rather than rational or philosophical. The gods will reward the just and punish the wicked and cannot be bribed by offerings. Worshipers should simply pray for what they deserve (I.11).[98] The term for

95. Bowie, 1685, holds that *On Sacrifices* was not written by Apollonius at all, but was a later forgery written precisely to make Apollonius appear traditional and a religious expert.

96. At Eleusis, Apollonius is finally initiated by a succeeding hierophant, just as he "predicted" at his first attempt. His visit to Lebadea ends with Trophonius giving him his personal approval and rebuking the priests who barred Apollonius's entrance to the shrine.

97. See Anderson, *Philostratus*, 142. Regarding the connection between the Platonists and Delphi, and philosophers serving as prophets of oracles in the second and third centuries, see Lane Fox, 187f. and 197.

98. This view of offerings as bribes is perhaps another remnant of the historical Apollonius's more radical teaching against all sacrifices.

moral purity is the same as that used for the physical purity of asceticism, *katharos,* and the two are simply sides of the same coin. It is also noteworthy that Apollonius refers to this homely moral piety as Asclepius's "philosophy."[99] In a legal case that the Indian king Phraotes gives Apollonius to judge, this simple moralism is given practical application (II.39). The verdict is given in favor of the pious man and against his impious opponent. The judgment is neither secular nor civil, or in fact even legal, but solely religious.[100]

Apollonius uses this occasion to expound a moral hierarchy among even the good of this world:

> The gods give attention and care to those who live a philosophical life with virtue first of all, and only secondarily to those who are without fault and have not as yet been deemed unjust. To philosophers they give to discern correctly in matters both divine and human; while to those who are merely good they give enough to live, so that they might never commit injustice through want of the necessities of life. (II.39)

The gods regard philosophers as morally superior even to "good" people, and give the wise the task of teaching and judging the good. More important, the gods also give to the merely good sufficient material possessions so that they do not have to steal or defraud to support themselves—reflecting a view of property as legitimate, in an extremely condescending way.[101] The corollary is that the morally superior philosopher would have no need of property. Thus moral superiority is evidenced by asceticism.[102]

Apollonius's most dramatic exercise of authority is manifested in his relations to cities. Superior though the philosopher might be, he puts his superior knowledge and insight into the service of society and always

---

99. Eusebius, *C. Hier.* 15, is quick to point out the absurdity of this simple contention of divine distributive justice. A similar sentiment is found in *Epp. Apoll.* 95: "You should envy no man. For good men deserve what they have; and if the wicked do fare well, their lives are of poor quality."

100. Knoles, 161.

101. Recall Apollonius's prayer that the wise may be poor, but that others may be rich, provided they are not fraudulent (IV.40, cf. I.33), above, pages 103–5.

102. Apollonius, or perhaps better Philostratus, is seen to be part of a much larger trajectory in cultural history, well described by Lane Fox, 126: "Philosophy added moral depth to an old Homeric form, and by the Christian era, the 'vision' of a god was attached explicitly to pious spiritual effort. By the mid second century, the new art of theurgy aimed to 'summon' the gods by symbols. . . . Its masters distinguished it sharply from magic, because it required spiritual and moral excellence in its practitioners."

for the preservation of public morality and social order.[103] Apollonius makes this quite clear in a letter to the *probouloi* of the Caesareans of Palestine: "In the first place men need gods, for everything and above everything else, and secondly they need cities. Cities should be accorded a place second only to the gods, and every sensible man should give priority to the affairs of his city" (*Epp. Apoll.* 11). In Pamphylia and Cilicia, whenever he came to a city in a state of internal conflict (*stasis*) he would put an end to the disorder, and all would fall into a hush as if attending the mysteries. For Apollonius *stasis* is more bitter than war (*Epp. Apoll.* 76). During a famine at Aspendus, Apollonius intervened both to restore order to a mob that had nearly lynched the governor and to indict the corn merchants for hoarding—all without breaking his vow of silence (*VA* I.15; *Epp. Apoll.* 77a).

Elements of civic political philosophy emerge in his dealings with Ephesus and Smyrna. In the former, emphasis is placed on the classical ideal of *koinonia* (commonweal): "that it is necessary to support and be supported by one another" (IV.3). In a shameful reversal of traditional civic attitudes, the people of Ephesus no longer praised those who still shared their substance with their fellow citizens, but accused them of being extravagant spendthrifts, while the beneficiaries of their generosity were deemed parasites. At Smyrna, Apollonius's theme is *philotimia*, which is defined as a mixture of concord and competition (ὁμονοίας στασιαζούσης)—concord in ideals and purpose, competition on behalf of the commonweal (IV.8). He concludes by drawing an analogy between the ship of state and a ship at sea: "If those sailors vie for honor (φιλοτιμήσονται) with one another and strive (στασιάσουσι) so that one is as good as the other, then this ship will have safe harbor" (IV.9).

In all the rebukes against cities for effeminacy and luxury, the cases of Athens and Sparta deserve particular mention.[104] The Athenians are upbraided for their revelry at the Anthesteria by comparing them to their ancestors of the Persian Wars, whose monuments of victory "would not have been erected to the shame of the Medes and Persians but to your own shame, if you should so degenerate from those who set them up. . . . You are softer than Xerxes' women" (IV.21). Upon meeting the elegant and delicate envoys of Sparta at Olympia, Apollonius

103. Cox, 23, considers this to be a characteristic element in her definition of the holy man, yet the same can be said of any philosopher or sophist; see Bowie, "Apollonius," 1667–70, and Bowersock, *Greek Sophists*, 10f. Eusebius himself remarks that these legends make Apollonius a "true sophist" cadging for alms in the cities (*C. Hier.* 5).

104. Ephesus: *VA* I.7f., 9, 13, 15; IV.2f.; *Epp. Apoll.* 65. Smyrna: *VA* IV.8f. Sardis: *Epp. Apoll.* 38–41, 56, 75, 75a. Alexandria: *VA* V.26. Tarsus: *VA* VI.34. Athens: *VA* IV.21; *Epp. Apoll.* 70. Sparta: *VA* IV.27; *Epp. Apoll.* 42a, 62–64.

dispatched a shocked letter to the ephors that produced immediate results: "They restored everything to the ancient ways . . . and Lac-
edaemon became like her old self" (IV.27). There could be no better
appeals to ancient civic ideals than these.

Another aspect of Apollonius's authority is revealed here: hellenism.
The sage is an expert on what is truly Greek, and any "orientalism"
perceived in his Indian connection fades into insignificance in Philostratus's portrayal. As a child, Apollonius applied himself to perfect-
ing his Attic (VA I.7) and in later life upbraided a boy for his vile dialect
(VI.36). Damis, a Syrian by birth, expresses his hope that by associating
with Apollonius he will himself become a Greek (III.43)—no small feat
to ask of a Cappadocian. A wise man finds Greece everywhere (I.34),
which, in context, means that there is no excuse for not practicing virtue, even among barbarians! Apollonius has direct access to the very
source of Greek culture, conversing with Achilles (who is quite pleased
to meet him) and asking the hero a number of vexing textual questions
about Homer (IV.11f. and 16). In another sophistic display, also clearly
attributable to Philostratus, Apollonius holds forth on the statue of
Milo at Olympia with commanding antiquarian expertise (IV.28).

While in the East, kings and Brahmans speak Greek (I.32, III.12) and
Apollonius defends the interests and reputation of the Hellenes to the
barbarians (I.35; III.31f.). At home, he is found to do the same in the
face of Roman rule.[105] He is shocked to find barbaric names such as
Lucullus and Fabricius in the decree of the pan-Ionian sacrifices, and
even among his own family (VA IV.5; Epp. Apoll. 71, 72). At the end
of his speech on kingship to Vespasian, Apollonius advises that governors who speak Greek be appointed to rule Greeks. His opinion comes
from personal experience:

> At the time I was staying in the Peloponnese, a man governed
> Greece who knew nothing about the Greeks, and the Greeks un-
> derstood nothing of him either. As a result, he did wrong and
> was done wrong for the most part, for his assessors and coun-
> selors in judicial decisions sold his verdicts and treated the gov-
> ernor as a slave. (VA V.36)

The same sentiment occurs in the letters.

> To the Roman quaestors: The first thing you do is hold office. If,
> then, you know how to hold office, why is it that during your

---

105. For a discussion on various scholarly opinions regarding Apollonius's philhellenism and / or antiromanism, see Knoles, 239f.

term our cities are in worse condition than before? But if you do not know how to hold office, you should have first learned how and only then have held it. (*Epp. Apoll. 30*)

Apollonius to the Roman officials: Some of you take care of harbors, buildings, walls, and walkways. But, as for children in the cities or the young people or the women, neither you nor the laws give them any thought. If things were otherwise, it would be good to be governed by you. (*Epp. Apoll. 54*)

Despite their amicable beginnings, Apollonius refused to speak to Vespasian after he revoked the "freedom of the Greeks" granted by Nero (*VA* V.41; *Epp. Apoll.* 42f–h). Apollonius is portrayed as an arbiter and defender of Greek culture. Such a depiction is a response to the sort of fundamental cultural fears that Lucian held regarding another preaching ascetic philosopher, Peregrinus.

Apollonius's attitude toward Rome introduces the final aspect of his authority, its exercise on the imperial level. The letters contain the sharpest criticism of Roman rule; the *VA* is decidedly more moderate. Apollonius does not really blame the governor he knew in Greece, but his subordinates, and the whole issue of Roman rule only occurs within the context of philhellenism. In Philostratus, Apollonius does not love Rome the less, but Greece more.

Philostratus states that Apollonius's words were "like laws ordained by a sceptered king," and Apollonius himself states that, as a philosopher (σοφός), he should speak as a lawgiver (ὡς νομοθέτης, *VA* I.17). To a satrap he declares that all the earth is his and the right to travel through it (I.21). The Indian philosopher-king Phraotes deems Apollonius's wisdom to be "more kingly" than his own (II.27). The authority of the philosopher is in a sense royal, but unlike the Stoic ideal of the philosopher-king, Apollonius's authority is separate from and above kingship. He informs Domitian that it is philosophy's concern that kings govern rightly (VIII.2), yet he rejects offers to become the permanent counselor of Vespasian (V.37) and Nerva (VIII.27). The calling of the philosopher is too broad and exalted to be so confined. Though instructing rulers is part of the role of a philosopher, to do so exclusively would be to neglect other duties. At least this is true for Apollonius; when Titus made the same appeal for a counselor, Apollonius assigned Demetrius the Cynic to the task (VI.31). On behalf of Sparta (IV.33) and Tarsus (VI.34), Apollonius was instrumental in gaining imperial favor. Yet, the political role of philosophers was not universally

accepted. Dio LXV.12.2, for example, castigates Helvidius Priscus's opposition to Vespasian as no business of philosophy.

The *VA* shows Apollonius to be clearly on the side of the established
Roman order and supportive of the regime.[106] The most striking—and
controversial—example occurs in Apollonius's meeting with Vespasian
at Alexandria in *VA* V.27–41.[107] Originally, while still laying siege to
Jerusalem, Vespasian sent for Apollonius seeking his advice on assuming the throne. The sage declined to go where so much blood was being
shed. So the one motive Philostratus gives for Vespasian's presence at
Alexandria is to visit Apollonius. Euphrates and Dio Chrysostom are
also present (V.27).[108] Vespasian's acknowledgment of Apollonius's authority could not be more dramatic: "Make me emperor." To which the
sage responds: "I have made you so" (V.28). The audacity of the ex-
change is immediately tempered as Apollonius explains that he has
prayed for an emperor who would be "just, noble, and moderate" and,
adding an important practical note after the tangled and murderous
Julio-Claudian successions, the father of legitimate sons.

The following day, the philosophers give their counsel to the emperor. Euphrates delivers an address urging democracy and the restora-
tion of the republic (V.33). Chrysostom doubts whether the Romans,
after years of tyranny, are capable of self-government, but advises that
Vespasian simply leave the decision to the Roman people and abide by
their choice (V.34). Apollonius considers it unwise to change a monar-
chical principle now so firmly established and argues:

---

106. Bowie, "Apollonius," 1681f.

107. As with so many other aspects of the *VA,* Apollonius's decisive role in Vespasian's
assuming power appears too exaggerated to be true. Grosso, 391–430, was the first to
systematically defend the likelihood of its historicity. The details of the story correspond
with known historical data; ultimately, Grosso's argument is simply, "Why not?" Vespasian, with his power base in the East, would have appealed to the Greeks for support and
could have sought the approval of their intellectual leaders—presuming, of course, that
the historical Apollonius was such a leader. See Grosso, 396 n. 11, for prior bibliography.
Bowie, "Apollonius," 1660–62 and 1690, refuting Grosso, focuses on the historical contradictions in the text and offers a likely scenario for Philostratus's invention of the entire
scene. Anderson, *Philostratus,* 182, contends that though Apollonius's relations with emperors could not be what the *VA* claims, this does not preclude any relation whatsoever,
and that some sort of relationship to Vespasian is well within the realm of possibility. In
an important article not known to Anderson, S. Jackson, "Apollonius and the Emperors,"
Hermathena 137 (Winter 1984): 25–32, has forcefully argued in favor of Philostratus's
historicity. The issue remains unresolved. On Alexandria and the emperors in general in
the period, see C. P. Jones, *The Roman World of Dio Chrysostom* (Cambridge, Mass.,
1978), 36–44.

108. Grosso, 396: "Questi, secondo Filostrato, saluterà in nome della cultura il nuovo
imperatore."

> For myself, I care nothing about constitutions, since I live as a subject of the gods. I do not, however, think it right that the flock of humanity perish for lack of a just and temperate shepherd. For just as one man outstanding in virtue changes democracy to appear as the rule of the one man who is best, so the rule of one man who seeks the advantage of the community in everything is democratic. (V.35)

To call this argument "sophistic" is both to describe its tone and content and to name its author: Philostratus.[109] It would be hard to find a more monarchist tautology, or one that would be more congenial to Philostratus's imperial circles.[110] At the same time it must be admitted that Apollonius, in refuting the radical and utopian proposals of Euphrates and Chrysostom, gives Vespasian the only sensible, practical, and realistic advice possible.

The speech also reiterates other familiar themes. Apollonius is indifferent to constitutions, because his life is governed by the gods. The philosopher is actually superior to political authority, and this superiority is based on religious grounds. The philosopher is ruled by gods not by emperors; on the practical level, however, he rules himself, for the philosopher is also the ultimate authority on the gods and the interpreter of their will. The tone toward the rest of humanity is condescending; it is they who need the shepherd, not Apollonius. Out of pity for them he will urge the just man to assume his duty to rule. As for the virtuous man turning democracy into monarchy and the virtuous king turning monarchy into democracy, the paradox is a long-established commonplace in classical political thought. When Apollonius actually gives advice as to how Vespasian should rule, his speech is filled with uninspired platitudes (V.36).

As a warning to Vespasian, which Philostratus expressly states was a retort against Apollonius and the opinion he expressed, Euphrates asserts: "Sanction and embrace that philosophy, O emperor, as henceforth you will be called, which accords with nature; but eschew that which pretends to be divinely inspired (θεοκλυτεῖν), for such people lie about the gods and persuade us to do many foolish things" (V.37).

---

109. A. Calderini, "Teoria e pratica politica nella 'Vita di Apollonio di Tiana,'" *Rendiconti dell'Istituto Lombardo* 74 (1940–41), 213–41, holds the political thought of the *VA* to be largely that of Philostratus.

110. The contradiction with *VA* VII.4, where Apollonius states that the Roman Republic was established as a response to tyranny, is only apparent. This statement occurs in the context of Apollonius's struggle against Domitian, and the case of a tyrant was always separate from that of simple monarchs.

These words of a Stoic express ideas encountered in Aurelius. Philosophy must accord with nature; philosophers who claim a special relation to the divine are suspect.[111] It is exactly to counter such sentiments that Philostratus rehabilitated his hero, as is most clearly seen in the manner in which Apollonius exercises his religious, moral, social, and political authority. His idiosyncratic character, superhuman abilities, and charismatic leadership (all perhaps remnants of the historical Apollonius, hinted at in the *VA* and more pronounced in the letters) are put to the service of traditional religion, normative values, received culture, and the established social and political order.

Miracles and the Holy Man

The *VA* has always played a large role in discussions of "divine men" (*theoi andres*) in literature and history. The varieties of opinion on the *VA*, formidable as they are, pale in comparison to the volume and controversy of work done on the history and character of the divine or holy man in antiquity. This scholarship requires critical assessment. Previous studies have largely been flawed by chronological limitation, simple *Tendenz*, or circularity of argument—establishing the characteristics of the holy man from a set of documents only to conclude that the documents fit the definition. This is especially true in works seeking to establish the existence of a genre of miracle stories, termed aretalogy. By treating the *VA* on its own merits, a clearer light can be shed both on Apollonius as *theios* and on the concept of the holy man in general.

Apollonius's miracles would appear, at first glance, to be the most "divine" element in the *VA*. Recent scholarship has, however, placed these prodigies in their proper perspective, as a relatively minor and unspectacular element of the work. Philostratus is no miracle-monger; if anything, he has downplayed the miraculous element in Apollonius's career.[112] Most of the sage's miracles have to do with prophecy, and he was arraigned before Domitian partly on the charge of having proph-

111. The opposition here between the natural, rational, classical tradition in philosophy advocated by the Stoic and the religious, mystical, personal form of Apollonius's Pythagoreanism is thoroughly described by Grosso, 423, 429, and 521–24.

112. Anderson, 138f.: "By the normal standards of late antique hagiography, the *Life of Apollonius* is either very flat or heavily toned down. Apollonius refuses to perform spectacular magic; his miracles, apart from his own birth, turn out rather tame, and the most spectacular of them tend to involve synchronisms of a kind impossible to prove or disprove." See also above, note 90.

esied Nerva's accession.[113] Apollonius asserts that he is no soothsayer (μάντις), and that his predictions of the future come not from divination (μαντική) but from the wisdom (σοφίᾳ) given by the gods to the wise (IV.44). Prophecy comes from both moral purity and physical purity; that is, asceticism, which increases the *aether* in the soul (III.42).[114]

Of the three cures Apollonius performs, that of a youth for dropsy involves merely the prescription of a lighter diet (I.9); while after raising a girl from the dead, Apollonius himself admits that she may have been simply unconscious (IV.45). The ending of the plague at Ephesus by perceiving its demonic cause remains the only unambiguously miraculous cure (IV.10). Of the four "exorcisms" performed, driving away a satyr was accomplished through antiquarian knowledge of a myth about Midas (VI.27).[115] Apollonius performs one bilocation, in admitted imitation of Pythagoras (IV.10), and one miraculous disappearance and transport, to save himself from Domitian's clutches (VIII.5, 8, 10). Apollonius's miracles usually involve common sense or the application of lessons learned from divination. Philostratus's approach to miracles is quite conservative and rational.[116]

Given the actual nature of the miracles in the *VA*, it is difficult to understand why so much attention has been paid to them, and why the work's own integrity and its connections to issues in its own society have been largely neglected in an attempt to reconstruct the putative literary genre of aretalogy.[117] Nothing survives from antiquity with this

113. Prophesying the death of an individual: I.12, IV.18, VI.32; the year of the four emperors: V.11, 13; the length of his stay with Vardanes: I.22; the lechery of a eunuch: I.33; perceiving the innocence of a condemned man: V.24. On the charge before Domitian: VII.11, VIII.5; on his actually seeing, while in Ephesus, the emperor's assassination at Rome: VIII.26, cf. Dio LXVII.18.1f.

114. Thus Photius, *Bibliotheca* 44, states explicitly that Philostratus wrote that Apollonius was no mere miracle worker, but that the wonders he performed were attributable to his philosophy and purity of life. An intriguing study of phenomena of precognition in antiquity, including various "rational" explanations for prophecy, is found in E. R. Dodds, "Supernormal Phenomena in Classical Antiquity," in his *The Ancient Concept of Progress and Other Essays on Greek Literature and Belief* (Oxford, 1973), 156–210.

115. The others are of the demon that caused the plague at Ephesus, a possessed boy (IV.20), and the *lamia* (IV.25).

116. J. M. van Cangh, "Santé et salut dans les miracles d'Epidaure, d'Apollonius de Tyane et du Nouveau Testament," in *Gnosticisme et le monde hellénistique: Actes du Colloque de Louvain-la-Neuve, 11–14 mars 1980*, ed. J. Reis et al., Publications de l'Institut Oriental de Louvain 27 (Louvain, 1982), 270–73. See also Bowie, 1690.

117. See Cox, 4. For a superb history of divine man and aretalogy scholarship from 1832 to 1972, see M. Smith, "Prolegomena to a Discussion of Aretalogies, Divine Men, the Gospels, and Jesus," *JBL* 90 (1971): 188–95; for more recent works up to 1983, see

literary label, and the argument for its existence presumes that a vast
amount of material was created and then subsequently lost without a
trace. Recent defenders of aretalogy can maintain its existence only in
a formal, conceptual sense, while others have rightly abandoned the
thesis.[118] Literary studies have independently concluded that the *VA* is a
mixture of several different genres, none of which should be used to
characterize the entire work.[119]

In literary studies, the search for aretalogy has been connected to
defining the character of the divine or holy man (*theios aner*), under the
assumption that the holy man would be chiefly defined by his miracles.
Since, however, miracle working does not play a large or important role
in the *VA*, Philostratus must use other means if he is to characterize
Apollonius as *theios*.

The birth of the sage has been seen as the incarnation of a god. Proteus appears to Apollonius's mother and announces that she will give
birth to himself (I.4). What has been neglected, however, is the fact that
Philostratus, by his own admission, is speaking in a poetic metaphor:
"Why should I describe to the readers of the poets how great Proteus
was in wisdom, how versatile, changeable in form, masterful at escape,
and how he was reputed to know and foreknow everything" (I.4). Wisdom, knowledge, prophecy, and eluding capture—an obvious reference
to Nero, Domitian, and Euphrates' attempts to put him out of the
way—are the hallmarks of Apollonius's career. The sage is, in fact, not
to be Proteus, but actually greater than Proteus in prophecy and a more
accomplished master in overcoming the difficulties and dangers that

Cox, 3. Many of the major works in this area are listed in the discussion of scholarship on
the *VA* at the beginning of this chapter.

118. A summary defense was offered by M. Smith and M. Hadas, *Heroes and Gods:
Spiritual Biographies in Antiquity*, Religious Perspectives 13 (New York, 1965). Later,
Smith, "Prolegomena" (1971), 196, reduced his position to the "conceptual" sense. H. C.
Kee, "Aretalogy and Gospel," *JBL* 92 (1973): 402–22, offered a thorough critique of
Smith's position. This provoked a vehement reaction by Smith, "On the History of the
Divine Man," in *Paganisme, Judaïsme, Christianisme: Influences et affrontements dans le
monde antique. Mélanges offerts à Marcel Simon* (Paris, 1978), 345, which only served to
clarify the minimalism of his position. D. Tiede, *The Charismatic Figure as Miracle
Worker*, SBL Dissertation Series 1 (Missoula, 1972), 1, begins his study with the statement that there is no justification for speaking of aretalogy as a literary genre. On this
controversy, see D. E. Aune, "Magic in Early Christianity," *ANRW* II.23.2 (1980): 1544
with notes, especially on the conflicting opinions of Smith and Tiede; also M. P. Nilsson,
Geschichte der griechischen Religion, vol. 2, *Die hellenistische und römische Zeit*, 2d ed.,
Handbuch der Altertumswissenschaft, Abt. 5, Teil 2, Band 2 (Munich, 1961), 228.

119. Petzke, 51, 58–60; Speyer, 48. For bibliography on genre studies of the *VA*, see
Petzke, 51 nn. 1–4.

confronted him (I.4).[120] In the same way, neither is he Pythagoras, nor Pythagoras reincarnate, but greater than Pythagoras (I.2). A thunderbolt marks his birth, as a sign of how he would *approach* unto the gods (ἀγχοῦ θεῶν, I.5). Some of his countrymen *say* (φασι) that he is a son of Zeus, but the sage called himself the son of Apollonius (I.6). Philostratus, while clearly portraying Apollonius to be extraordinary, is careful not to make him a god, or a son of a god, but an unusually gifted *man*.

It is Damis who consistently views Apollonius as godlike. His response to Apollonius's "gift of tongues" is one of wonder and reverence: "He worshipped him . . . and regarded him as a *daimon*" (I.19). The sage's prodigious memory and love of learning also strike him as "godlike" (δαιμόνιον, III.43). When Apollonius effortlessly removed his prison chains and slipped them on again, "it was then Damis says that he first clearly understood Apollonius's nature, that it was divine (θεία) and more than human" (VII.38; cf. VIII.13).[121] The Brahmans prophesy that he will be esteemed a god not only after death, but while he is still alive (III.50), a fact Apollonius himself confirms in *Epp. Apoll.* 44. The Alexandrians regard him as such (V.24) while the Lacedaemonians planned to celebrate him as a god (θεοφάνια αὐτῷ ἄξουσι), an honor Apollonius declined lest he arouse envy (IV.31). Upon his vindication and escape from Domitian, "Greece came close to worshipping him (προσκυνεῖν), and they considered him a divine man (θεῖον ἄνδρα) most especially because he never made a show over what had happened" (VIII.15).

Damis twice calls Apollonius a "divine man" as a result of some miraculous event. In all the other cases, this judgment stems either from his character or some more mundane act, such as restoring Sparta's ancient virtues. In none of the other miracle stories is Apollonius proclaimed divine.[122] When Domitian, upon first seeing the sage, exclaims

120. ὅστις μὲν δὴ τὴν σοφίαν ὁ Πρωτεὺς ἐγένετο, τί ἂν ἐξηγοίμην τοῖς γε ἀκούουσι τῶν ποιητῶν, ὡς ποικίλος τε ἦν καὶ ἄλλοτε ἄλλος καὶ κρείττων τοῦ ἁλῶναι, γιγνώσκειν τε ὡς ἐδόκει καὶ προγιγνώσκειν πάντα; καὶ μεμνῆσθαι χρὴ τοῦ Πρωτέως, μάλιστα ἐπειδὰν προϊὼν ὁ λόγος δεικνύῃ τὸν ἄνδρα πλείω μὲν ἢ ὁ Πρωτεὺς προγνόντα, πολλῶν δὲ ἀπόρων τε καὶ ἀμηχάνων κρείττω γενόμενον ἐν αὐτῷ μάλιστα τῷ ἀπειλῆφθαι.

121. Kee, 407 n. 49, contends that this feat was meant to show that the wise man is truly free everywhere and not to be an epiphany. The meaning of the symbolism involved is certainly correct, but to say that nothing else was intended ignores the force of Damis's reaction. Kee rightly observes, however, that Damis's response contradicts Apollonius's refusal of divinity.

122. It is worth noting that Hierocles accuses the Christians of doing exactly this: "Whereas we consider Apollonius who performed such wonders not a god, but only a

that he is a *daimon,* Apollonius responds that he is a mere man
(VII.32). On being accused of receiving divine honors in his trial before
Domitian, he is adamant:

> He says that men consider me a god and proclaim this publicly
> having been thunderstruck by me. Before making the accusation,
> however, he should have set forth these things: by what manner
> of speaking, by what wonders of word or deed, I induced men to
> pray to me (προσεύχεσθαι). Never did I announce among the
> Greeks what my soul had changed from or what it will change
> into, even though I know this. Never have I put forth such re-
> ports about myself. Never have I come out with predictions or
> oracles, those specious productions of prophets. Never have I
> heard of any city in which an assembly was decreed to sacrifice
> to Apollonius. (VIII.7.7)

Apollonius complains that even Socrates was accused merely of teaching novelties about *daimones,* not of being one himself (VIII.7.1).

Of the various attempts made in scholarship to define and characterize the holy man, the first remains the most satisfying—that of L. Bieler
derived from his survey of the use of the term *theios aner* from Homer
through the third century C.E.[123] It is also the description that most suits
Philostratus's portrayal of Apollonius.[124] The holy man is an extraordinary *man,* with a special relationship to the gods and a practical function is his society based upon his perceived authority. The definition is
general and flexible and, therefore, does justice to the variety of holy
men found in antiquity and to the narrow line between the human and
divine common in Greek thought.[125] Rather than reading the charac-

---

man pleasing to the gods; they, on account of a few tricks, proclaim this Jesus a god"
(Eus., *C. Hier.* 2).

123. ΘΕΙΟΣ ΑΝΗΡ: *Das Bild des "Göttlichen Menschen" in Spätantike und Frühchristentum,* 2 vols. (Vienna, 1935–36). An excellent and thorough critical review of the scholarship is given by E. V. Gallagher, *Divine Man or Magician? Celsus and Origen on Jesus,*
SBL Dissertation Series 64 (Chico, Calif., 1982), 1–26.

124. Bieler, 1:20, "Wir haben so in großen Umrissen ein Bild dessen gewonnen, was
der Begriff θεῖος ἀνήρ umfaßt: er ist ein Mensch mit Menschenmaß überragenden
Eigenschaften und Fähigkeiten, Liebling der Götter und eine Art Mittler zwischen der
Gottheit und den Menschen, zugleich ihr Rategeber und κατορθωτής, zu dem sie von
fehrner gezogen kommen. Daß seine Tätigkeit, vor allem, wo das Volk sein Bild zeichnet,
viel konkreter ist und den Nöten des täglichen Lebens näher steht als Platons und Aris-
toteles' Worte verraten, dürfen wir von Anfang vermuten und wird sich im Laufe unserer
Untersuchung bestätigen."

125. Gallagher, 10–22, is quite correct in expressing the opinion that Bieler's work has
generally been misunderstood and underappreciated. The following discussion regarding
Apollonius offers further independent support to Gallagher's conclusions (which he bases

teristics of the Late Antique holy man back into the classical period, it is obviously a more correct perspective to view the various elements of the *theios aner* as a continuum in Greek culture stretching from the archaic period through to Byzantine hagiography.[126] In many respects, the nature and function of holy men actually changed very little from the archaic period on.[127] As for the conflation of philosophers, miracle workers, and holy men, this phenomenon was not a new product of the second century C.E., but a theme that can be traced back to the fourth century B.C.E. and earlier.[128]

Attempts to define the unique character of the Late Antique holy man, and thus establish when the image of the holy man changed, have foundered. D. Tiede's description of a slow change from the first through third centuries C.E., from Lucian fighting against the growth of cult figures such as Alexander and Peregrinus to Philostratus and Porphyry finally accepting them, is refuted historically by P. Cox.[129] Furthermore, Philostratus carefully and deliberately describes Apollonius as

on his analysis of Origen's *Contra Celsum*) on the correctness of Bieler's approach and on the history of holy-man scholarship in general; see Gallagher, esp. 173–80.

126. Anderson, 146, notes that a number of traits assembled by P. R. L. Brown, "The Rise and Function of the Holy Man in Late Antiquity," *JRS* 61 (1971): 80–101 = *Society and the Holy in Late Antiquity* (Berkeley and Los Angeles, 1982), 103–52, apply much earlier to Apollonius. Surely this is no surprise since the culture described by Brown inherited centuries of accumulated tradition about holy men in both their literary portrayal and their social function. It is not Apollonius who resembles Brown's Syrian holy men; it is the Syrians who resemble Apollonius.

127. For the archaic period, see E. R. Dodds, *The Greeks and the Irrational*, Sather Classical Lectures 25 (Berkeley and Los Angeles, 1951), chap. 5: "The Greek Shamans and the Origin of Puritanism," 135–78.

128. Tiede, 30–56, is correct in pointing to the conflation of the characters of philosophers with miracle workers in all the various philosophical schools. His work is valuable for its rich collection of evidence. However, his central thesis that these two representations were originally separate and distinct traditions, only later conflated, has been refuted by M. Smith, review of *The Charismatic Figure as Miracle Worker*, by D. Tiede, in *Interpretation* 28 (1974): 235–40, and "History of Divine Men," 335–38 and 345. Smith correctly points out that in the earliest Greek literary traditions the thaumaturge and sage are found together, and that this is certainly true in the representations of Socrates. This offers a literary parallel to the historical argument made throughout this work that the ascetic, wonderworker, and philosopher are seldom separate historical figures, but are most often aspects of one individual. This double-sided nature of holy man and philosopher is certainly found in Apollonius. It is, therefore, not any innovation of Philostratus, but a traditional mode of representation.

129. Tiede, 99; refuted by Cox, 30–34. Clearly Plato's Socrates and other fourth-century B.C.E. testimonies regarding Empedocles and Pythagoras conflate the two images as well. On Socrates, see also Bieler, 82–95. In addition, Tiede's related contention that the "complete, aggregate portrait" of the divine man was achieved only in Philostratus and Porphyry is unacceptable for the same reasons. Though he denies its existence, Tiede is still influenced by aretalogy in looking for some sort of "complete type" of the holy man.

opposing any such deification and as a champion of traditional religion. He is portrayed as the exact opposite of Alexander and Peregrinus for the very reason that such figures remained unacceptable in Philostratus's time. L. Belloni sees in the VA a change from rational to "thaumaturgic" accounts of phenomena.[130] Yet, many of the "miracles" in the VA have rational explanations attached to them, and an apologetic was already at hand in the first century that explained that prodigies were really not contrary to reason, if the nature of the gods were properly understood.[131]

Some of Cox's own distinctions between the "earlier" characterizations of the holy man (a category in which she includes Apollonius) and those of Late Antiquity are also found not to apply to the VA. According to Cox, the earlier divine philosophers are proselytizers not teachers.[132] Apollonius, however, is conspicuous for *not* preaching his Pythagoreanism, but rather for teaching traditional values. He starts no movement, nor are any of his disciples in the VA of any repute. Cox also contends that to call Apollonius divine is to suggest that he was a son of God, possessed of miracles and prophetic and intellectual powers far beyond human capacity, as opposed to the Late Antique description in which such figures are merely extraordinary mortals.[133] Yet, Philostratus took pains to show that his hero was not a son of God, but precisely an extraordinary mortal. Miracles are a minor aspect of the VA, and as for prophetic and intellectual powers, Cox herself has shown that these were an established feature of earlier lives of philosophers. The overall impression Philostratus conveys of Apollonius is not one of superhuman power, as Cox would have it, but of supernatural insight.[134] The majority of Apollonius's miracles are works of prophecy, resulting from the purity of his ascetic life and his intimacy with the gods. Indeed, Cox's description of the distinguishing characteristics of Late Antique biographies of holy men fits Apollonius precisely.[135] Thus all attempts to distinguish the character and characterization of "later" from "earlier" holy men have proven unsuccessful.

---

130. L. Belloni, "Aspetti dell'antica σοφία in Apollonio di Tiana," *Aevum* 54 (1980): 145.

131. Plut., *Coriol.* 32 and 38; see Cangh, 270–73.

132. *Biography*, 24, a point Cox herself appears to contradict on 41, where she speaks of the vagueness of Apollonius's preaching.

133. *Biography*, 44.

134. Cox, 38f.; refuted by Kee, 406.

135. Cox, 44: "To call Origen or Plotinus divine was to suggest that he was an especially gifted man, blessed by God, whose status was achieved by the purity and steadfastness of his devotion to philosophical tradition and to the reasoning faculty."

In sum, it seems wise not to search for the holy man, for—as in Bieler's definition—he is everywhere and in many forms, a constant rather than a developing figure in classical culture. The attributes and character of the "divine man" were not a fixed type, but a collection of traits that could be drawn on in different combinations and emphases. Indeed, these traits actually run a continuum from *theos* to *theios aner* to *magos / goes*.[136] As in the case of Apollonius, the same behaviors and characteristics could be used to demonstrate that the sage was either a philosopher or a sorcerer. What ultimately decides the issue are social considerations: Does the individual help or hinder his society? Does he support traditional values and beliefs? Does he defend the established order? It seems plausible, therefore, that if a difference exists between the holy man of the second century and his later counterparts, it does not lie in the holy man himself but in his relation to the society around him.

This establishes several important conclusions regarding the *VA* and its place in cultural history. Parallels clearly exist between Lucian and the *VA*. One view of their connection holds that these works of Lucian represent parodies or "anti-aretalogies" of a type of literature later perfected by Philostratus.[137] Yet, there is no evidence of these earlier aretalogies. It appears, therefore, that "anti-aretalogy" came first. The first examples we have of holy-man biographies in sophisticated literature are negative because the opinion of sophisticated people in the second century toward ascetics and self-styled holy men was negative. This is evident both in Lucian and Marcus Aurelius. Holy men and traditions about them certainly existed, but as Lucian makes clear, their appeal was generally limited to the lower classes.[138] Exactly these sort of traditions existed locally about Apollonius, most especially in miracle tales.[139]

It would appear that Moiragenes, whether he viewed *mageia* positively or not, included them in his work. Philostratus was then confronted with a significant and intractable source that contained useful historical information (such as in what cities Apollonius was partic-

---

136. Gallagher, 70–73.

137. J. Bompaire, *Lucien écrivain* (Paris, 1958), 617 n. 4: "Le *Pérégrinos* et l'*Alexandre* seraient deux parodies de ces 'Propheten-Aretalogien' dont le type achevé sera la *Vie d'Apollonios de Tyane*"; see also 614–21, and Cox, 20.

138. For example, *The Fugitives,* hence also Lucian's alarm at Rutilianus's embrace of Alexander's cult.

139. Bowie, 1686–1689. On the appeal of miracles to the masses, see E. S. Fiorenza, "Miracles, Mission, and Apologetics: An Introduction," in *Aspects of Religious Propaganda in Judaism and Early Christianity*, ed. E. S. Fiorenza (Notre Dame, 1976), esp. 7, 12, and R. MacMullen, *Paganism in the Roman Empire* (New Haven, 1981), 96.

ularly active), but that couched this information in the unacceptable terms of *goeteia* and equally unacceptable style and language. Then there was Damis, an invaluable source whose memoirs Philostratus admits needed sophistic polish, and who consistently views Apollonius as *theios* and *daimonios*. To turn all this into a successful piece of serious, artistic literature,[140] Philostratus exploited the double-sided nature of a canonical sage, Pythagoras, incorporating elements of a holy-man tradition that had existed for centuries.[141] Philostratus did not create something new; rather, he elaborated in great detail something quite old. Apollonius does not look forward to Byzantine saints as much as he recapitulates classical philosophers and heroes, a point reinforced by his consistent action on behalf of established norms and values.[142] The result was not a new genre of literature, but rather the baptism of themes of miracle working and apotheosis into serious literature, muted and masked by social conservatism, traditional philosophy, and rigorous asceticism.[143]

The Socially Acceptable Ascetic

Apollonius's trial before Domitian (*VA* VIII.1–5) serves as a reprise of the entire work, and Philostratus's *apologia* (VIII.7), cast in the form of a defense speech Apollonius never delivered, is its peroration. The charges leveled against Apollonius summarize the suspicion in which an ascetic philosopher / *goes* was held and also, therefore, the elements of Philostratus's rehabilitation of Apollonius as a socially acceptable fig-

140. Philostratus's only aim according to Bowie, 1666.

141. So it is that Philostratus did not invent a new genre, but merely took up all the various strands of the existing holy-man tradition and wove them into one work. Anderson, 136: "He was able to write not just a *Life of Apollonius* but an encyclopedia of hagiography, by making his sage outdo every philosopher or holy man in every known genre: Apollonius was to be a superman's superman."

142. Belloni, 149: "Apollonio di Tiana è ancora l'antico σοφός, ma aperto ad un rinnovamento che è per lui garanzia di sopravvivenza nel crepuscolo degli dei."

143. This conclusion regarding the "muting and masking" themes is further confirmed by Knoles's literary analysis of the *VA*, conducted solely on the internal structure and dynamics of the work, independent of the historical and social contexts considered here. Knoles, 297 with 228 and 254, concludes that if Philostratus's work is regarded as a biography of a wonderworking holy man written not to define or explain his philosophy, but simply to portray him in a positive way *as* a philosopher, the relationship between literary technique and philosophical theme that exists in the *VA* is completely understandable.

ure. At the same time, this episode offers an extraordinarily clear example of the nature and operation of the accusation of magic in the period.[144]

At the trial itself, the charges against Apollonius are four in number: (1) his manner of dress, (2) being called a god, (3) forecasting a plague in Ephesus, and (4) sacrificing a boy to divine Nerva's chances for the throne. These reduce themselves into the familiar themes of asceticism, apotheosis, prophecy, and politics. The same themes emerge in the longer list of accusations in the *apologia*. Earlier in VII.33, Domitian accused Apollonius of being a *goes,* and in addition impudent, an impostor (or perhaps vagabond philosopher: ἀλαζών), money-loving, and contemptuous of the law. All these accusations, and a few more, are found in *Epp. Apoll.* 8 as slanders leveled against Apollonius by Euphrates. Given their repetition (they occur previously in *VA* VII.11 and 20) and their lengthy rebuttal, they appear to be either the actual allegations made against Apollonius or the suspicion persisting about him in Philostratus's time. The effect is the same.

In the *apologia* (VIII.7.1–16) a detailed defense is given to each charge. Apollonius refutes the *goeteia* slander by demonstrating his devotion to the traditional gods and his ascetic poverty (2–3). Abstention from meat and the wearing of linen are justified by invoking Pythagoras and physical purity (4–5). His long, unkempt hair hearkens to the ancient practice of Sparta. Defense is made through appeal to antiquarianism and philhellenism (6).

At the accusation of being worshiped, Apollonius first asks for proof, then notes the common practice among Greeks of describing outstanding men as *theioi*. No reference is made to the incidents in the *VA* where this does, in fact, occur. Given the fact that Apollonius was apotheosized after his death, Philostratus could not deny him any divine character, but neither could Apollonius be seen to arrogate divinity to himself while alive. The topic is actually avoided (7).

The charge of predicting the plague in Ephesus engenders a lengthy explanation of prophecy. Apollonius does not deny the charge, but asks if he can be blamed for saving a city of such pure Greek pedigree, or for predicting the future when Socrates, Thales, and Anaxagoras had done the same. Appeal is again made to philhellenism and to the canonical sages of Greece. The ability to prophesy itself is due to the sage's ascetic diet, producing a clarity and lightness of soul. Prophecy is not magic; it

144. Kolenkow, 1473 n. 5, notes that to arrive at a historically accurate definition of magic "one must look not only in places such as Roman laws, but in accusations and defenses of philosophers and rhetors who are so assumed to be associated with the divine-demonic arts. There is a regular spectrum used between philosophers and *goetes;* rhetors may rightly be accused of magic."

is a simple physical process. The argument is both ascetical and rational (8–10).

The charge of divination by human sacrifice to determine the succession to the throne provokes an equally long discussion of that art. But Apollonius's well-known aversion to shedding even animal blood should be sufficient to show the absurdity of the accusation. As for Nerva and his companions, they are all "honorable men" (11–15).[145]

As for speaking against the emperor, Apollonius contends he was merely delivering an address on fate. The context is clearly that Apollonius predicted Domitian's fall, which was treason (16). Regarding fate, Philostratus had already argued that Apollonius did not try to alter the future by *goeteia*, but merely predicted what fate had already decreed (V.12).

Apollonius is arraigned because of his ascetical practice, his prophetic ability, the divine honors he appears to be accorded, and his political connections. Over all hangs the suspicion of *goeteia*. Philostratus defends him by invoking asceticism, Pythagoreanism, antiquarianism, and philhellenism—the exact qualities that characterize the portrait given in the *VA* as a whole. Apollonius gives his own summary of his career as part of his defense against claiming divinity: "And yet I have been much esteemed by the several cities that had need of me, and their needs were such as these: cures for the sick, greater holiness in their mysteries and sacrifices, the extirpation of insolence, and the strengthening of the laws" (VIII.7.7). His own description of himself is that of a healer of the physical, religious, moral, and social health of his civilization. Rather than offering a Pythagorean alternative to the life of the polis,[146] Apollonius is the most stalwart supporter of the classical social order.

In writing the *VA* in the manner he did, Philostratus made the ascetic miracle worker into an acceptable literary figure. But more than that, he demonstrated how such a figure could be shorn of his suspicious nature and turned into a pillar and exemplar of classical pagan ideals. By the time of Hierocles in the late third century, Philostratus's Apollonius was exactly that.[147] As a work of literature, the *VA* looks backward to tradi-

---

145. Besides, the sage had an alibi for the night in question, and boys' livers are not any good for the purpose (13–15).

146. Burkert, "Craft Versus Sect," 2. See M. Detienne, "Les Chemins de la déviance: Orphisme, Dionysisme, et Pythagorisme," in *Orfismo in Magna Grecia: Atti del Quattrodicesimo Convegno di Studi sulla Magna Grecia, Taranto, 6–10 Ottobre 1974* (Naples, 1975), 49–78, and *Dionysos mis à mort* (Paris, 1977), 163–207.

147. The nature of this rehabilitation of Apollonius offers further refinement to the hypothesis that Philostratus may have been influenced in some way by the new and growing respectability of Christianity in presenting Apollonius in the manner he did (see note 1

tional depictions of *theioi andres* and philosophers. In its historical importance, it opens a door forward to the ascetic flowering to follow.[148] The ascetic holy man had to overcome a great deal of opposition to become what he was in Late Antiquity. Little changed in the holy man himself in the course of this evolution; what did change, however, was his perception by his surrounding society. By raising the "wondrous" Apollonius from local legend to artistic literature, Philostratus raised the ascetic from being a threat to culture and society to being its paragon and exemplar.

---

above). The virtues he stresses in Apollonius are those he would find absent in the followers of Jesus. By making Apollonius a paragon of Greek culture and Roman order, Philostratus would imply that the Christians were a threat to both; that is, the new religion was barbaric and subversive. Philostratus's view would then be identical to that of Celsus, as discussed in the following chapter. Celsus sought to demolish the new religion on the basis of the *nomos* and *palaios logos* of classical culture. Philostratus offered both a reassertion and a renovation of that *nomos* and *logos* in Apollonius, and an alternative to the attraction some found in Jesus. If Philostratus was alarmed at Christianity's gains among the upper classes in this period, his Apollonius served as a call to that class to return to their rightful spiritual inheritance. This also creates a deeper resemblance between Philostratus and Lucian, who was so irked at the defection of people like Rutilianus to holy men like Alexander and Peregrinus. The hypothesis that the *VA* is, in part, an anti-Christian work would reveal greater unanimity and creative vigor among pagan intellectuals in this period.

148. Belloni, 141: "Tutto questo mi pare suggerisca come Apollonio non sia solamente il taumaturgo di Tiana; questa sua identità appare piuttosto secondaria, è la veste esteriore di una 'figura-tipo' che accoglie in sé l'antico e il nuovo, a testimonianza del'evolversi di una cultura."

C h a p t e r   F i v e

CELSUS

Christians, Ascetics, and Rebels

CELSUS BRINGS ISSUES BETWEEN ASCETICISM and authority to bear against the person of Jesus and the Christians in his *True Doctrine (Alethes Logos).*[1] Written c. 180, the only attested work of this otherwise unknown author, *True Doctrine* offers what is arguably the most complete defense of the entire "inherited conglomerate" of classical civilization ever conceived.[2] The work clearly and directly articulates the

1. Throughout this chapter these words, in Greek and English, will be used both in common syntax and as the title of Celsus's work. To avoid confusion, the words will be capitalized to denote the title. There is a debate over whether the title should be rendered *True Doctrine* or *True Discourse.* M. Borret in the Sources chrétiennes edition of Origen's *Contra Celsum,* 5:24–28, prefers "discourse." The question remains unsettled; see T. Hägg, "Hierocles the Lover of Truth and Eusebius the Sophist," *Symbolae Osloenses* 67 (1992): 141 and n. 13, for citation of relevant opinions. I myself prefer "doctrine" for reasons that will become obvious in the development of this chapter.
   An introductory annotated bibliography to the study of Christianity and the classical world is provided by E. A. Judge, "'Antike and Christentum': Towards a Definition of the Field. A Bibliographical Survey," *ANRW* II.23.1 (1979): 3–58; see esp. 47–58 for topics on asceticism and the Early Church relevant to the material covered in this chapter.
2. The dating of *True Doctrine* is not without a certain amount of conjecture, but there is a consensus for c. 180; see Borret, 5:128f. Pace H.-U. Rosenbaum, "Zur Datierung von Celsus 'ΑΛΗΘΗΣ ΛΟΓΟΣ," *Vig. Chr.* 26 (1972): 102–11, who argues for a date c. 160.

ideals and norms that motivated Aurelius, Lucian, and Philostratus. For
the first time, these ideals and norms are used to give a careful and
detailed judgment of the most important ascetical holy man of antiquity: Jesus Christ.[3] More important, Celsus's social objections to the
Christians of his day appear to address a particularly ascetical form of
Christianity. Ironically, these Christian ascetics were also judged by
their own more conservative coreligionists in the same way pagans
judged both their own ascetical deviants and the Christian Church as a
whole.

Regrettably *True Doctrine* survives only in the excerpts quoted by
Origen in the *Contra Celsum,* written in 249.[4] How much of the original work is represented by Origen's transcriptions remains a matter of
debate. Although several attempts have been made to reconstruct Celsus's text, none has so far been considered definitive.[5]

Even in its fragmentary form and set in a detailed refutation, Celsus's
work stands out as brilliant. The contention of L. Rougier that *True
Doctrine* was ignored in Celsus's lifetime is without foundation.[6] That
no Christian response to Celsus's work survives before Origen proves
nothing. Any number of possibilities could account for this. The fact

---

3. It should be noted in passing that Origen's defense of Jesus in the *Contra Celsum*
bears similarity to Philostratus's defense of Apollonius precisely in the *social* role of these
holy men. A detailed discussion of Origen on this point would exceed the limits of this
work.

4. Dated precisely by P. Nautin, *Origène: Sa vie et son oeuvre,* Christianisme antique
1 (Paris, 1977), 381, with 375–84. The most recent and complete edition of the *Contra
Celsum* is M. Borret, *Contre Celse,* 5 vols., Sources chrétiennes 132, 136, 147, 150, and
227 (Paris, 1967–76). English translation by H. Chadwick, *Contra Celsum,* rev. ed.
(Cambridge, 1980), with invaluable notes; all translations of the *Contra Celsum* below
are taken from this edition.

5. It had been generally assumed that virtually all of Celsus's work had been preserved
in Origen. The first to raise objection to this was M. Miura-Stange, *Celsus und Origenes:
Das Gemeinsame ihrer Weltanschauung,* Zeitschrift für die neutestamentliche Wissenschaft und die Kunde der Älteren Kirche, Beiheft 4 (Giessen, 1926), 26, 162. For a
summary of the debate, see Chadwick, *Contra Celsum,* xxii ff., and Borret, 5:15ff. Twen-
tieth-century attempts at reconstructing *True Doctrine* include O. Glöckner, *Celsi AΛ-
HΘHΣ ΛΟΓΟΣ,* Kleine Texte für Vorlesungen und Übungen 151 (Bonn, 1924); L.
Rougier, *Celse ou le conflit de la civilisation antique et du Christianisme primitif* (Paris,
1925); R. Bader, *Der ᾿Αληθὴς Λόγος des Kelsos,* Tübinger Beiträge zur Alter-
tumswissenschaft, Heft 33 (Stuttgart, 1940); A. Wifstrand, "Die wahre Lehre des Kelsos,"
*Société Royale de Lettres de Lund Bulletin / Kungliga Humanistika vetenskapssamfundet i
Lund Aarsberättelse* 5 (1941–42): 391–431; C. Andresen, *Logos und Nomos: Die Pole-
mik des Kelsos wider das Christentum,* Arbeiten zur Kirchengeschichte 30 (Berlin, 1955);
Borret, 5:30–121; and R. J. Hoffmann, *On the True Doctrine: A Discourse against the
Christians* (New York, 1987). On the textual difficulties, see Andresen, 8–43.

6. Rougier, *Celse contre,* 57f.

that Origen had not deemed it necessary to write a response until his friend Ambrose requested it (*C. Cels.* Praef.1) neither proves that Origen was previously ignorant of the work nor, if he had known it, that he did not take it seriously. The undertaking of such a vehement and protracted rebuttal demonstrates that the Alexandrian Father took Celsus as a dangerous threat. All the issues raised by Rougier speak more to the nature of the pagan / Christian conflict up to the time of Origen, and to the audience of Christian (and for that matter pagan) apologetics, than to the dissemination of Celsus's work. That it took seventy years from Celsus's writing for this response to appear again proves nothing about the popularity or provenance of *True Doctrine*. Theodoret was still writing against Porphyry in 423, more than a century after his *Against the Christians*!

Before Celsus, the Christians went largely unnoticed by pagan writers. The few references to them are curt, dismissive, and insulting. It was the Christians themselves, in the writings of the second-century Apologists, who first demanded to be taken seriously. A convincing case has been made that Celsus was motivated to write his attack by the claims and arguments of Justin for the new religion.[7] Previously, pagans and Christians talked past each other, and it has long been a question whether Christian Apologies were ever really intended for readership outside of the Church. It is only with Celsus that the opposing sides finally join battle directly and strategically.

An intriguing question is whether the author of *True Doctrine* is identical with a Celsus Lucian mentions as an admired friend in *Alex.* 1, 21, and 61. From Lucian's statements that his Celsus was familiar with the writings of Epicurus (47) and that the defense of Epicurus in the *Alexander* would have given his friend particular pleasure (61), it has been assumed that Lucian's Celsus must have been an Epicurean himself. Since the writer of *True Doctrine* is clearly not an Epicurean, and is generally agreed to be a Platonist,[8] it is argued that he cannot be identified with Lucian's friend. Origen himself complicates the problem by referring to Celsus at one time as an Epicurean (*C. Cels.* I.8) and at

---

7. Andresen, 308ff. Comparisons and parallels between Celsus and Justin were first suggested by E. Pélagaud, *Un conservateur au second siècle: Etude sur Celse et la première escarmouche entre la Philosophie et le Christianisme naissant* (Lyon, 1878).

8. As will be seen below in detail, the author of *True Doctrine* holds a number of views antithetical to Epicureanism; for example, the denigration of the body, the immortality of the soul, the possibility of its ascent to the divine, the active involvement of the divine in the administration of the world, and the necessity of active involvement in political and civic life. See Chadwick, *Contra Celsum*, xxiv ff., who argues against an Epicurean identification on these grounds and classifies the author as a middle-Platonist. For bibliography, see below, note 21.

another as a Platonist (IV. 83).[9] Scholars have been equally divided on
the matter.[10] Lucian, however, nowhere calls his friend an Epicurean
outright; this has been assumed solely on Lucian's praise of Epicurus in
a work dedicated to Celsus. It is just as plausible to argue, on the basis
of these references, that Lucian himself was an Epicurean. Although
turn-of-the-century scholars endeavored to do this, it is now clear that
Lucian was not a follower of this philosophical school.[11] The strong
possibility remains that Lucian's friend was also not a professed Epicurean, but merely an admirer of the philosopher, as was Lucian himself.

What then did Lucian so admire in the teachings of Epicurus that he
could ignore the doctrinaire attitude of the Epicureans themselves and
portray them as heroes in the struggle against Alexander? The answer
to this question introduces a consideration, overlooked in scholarship
thus far, that speaks in favor of the identification of Lucian's friend
with the author of *True Doctrine*.

It is curious that Lucian, who elsewhere shows himself to be an enemy of philosophical dogmatism, should show veneration for the most
dogmatic school in antiquity, one that habitually invoked *ipse dixit*.
Lucian himself gives the reason for his esteem in describing the benefits
to be derived from Epicurus's *Principal Doctrines* (κύριαι δόξαι): liberation from terrors, apparitions, and portents, from "vain hopes and
extravagant cravings," and the development of the intellect with
straight thinking (*logos orthos*), truthfulness (*aletheia*), and frankness
(*parrhesia, Alex.* 47).[12] Alexander feared Epicurus as "an opponent and
critic of his trickery" (43). Some of the false prophet's deceptions were
quite accomplished and required a Democritus, an Epicurus, a Metrodorus, "or someone else with a mind adamant against such things, so as
to disbelieve and determine what they really were" (17).

This is an interesting triad. Democritus (born sometime 460–457
B.C.E.)[13] lived a century before Epicurus. The great commonality of their
respective doctrines is atomic theory, with its emphasis on unclouded
rationalism and its consequent beliefs in the mortality of the soul and

9. On this discrepancy see J. C. M. van Winden, "Notes on Origen, Contra Celsum,"
Vig. Chr. 20 (1966): 204ff.

10. A convenient summary of opinions may be found in Borret, 5:134ff. T. Keim,
Celsus' Wahres Wort (Zürich, 1873), was the first to suggest that Lucian's statements do
not necessarily imply that his friend was an Epicurean. Chadwick, *Contra Celsum*,
xxiv ff., objects unconvincingly, and is refuted in turn by Hoffmann, 30–33.

11. See Chapter 3, pages 54–55, esp. note 4.

12. See Chapter 3, pages 72–73.

13. Diogenes Laertius 9.41.

the necessity of removing from it any emotional perturbation, especially the fear of death. The Metrodorus mentioned is probably that of Lampascus, Epicurus's devoted friend and pupil, or possibly that of Chios, the pupil of Democritus. What is important to note here is the contribution these men make to Lucian's case: their adamant rationality gives them the necessary predisposition of disbelief toward an Alexander and, thus, the ability to discern the truth (17). Lucian's high opinion of Epicurus is not due to belief in the specifics of Epicurean doctrine, but to Epicurus's demand for rationality and his refusal to allow emotional appeals or inward fears and terrors to cloud his judgment. Epicurus's glory lies in his method, which he shares with other thinkers like Democritus and Metrodorus.

I suggest, therefore, that the essence of "Epicurus" for Lucian lies in opposition to credulity, superstition, and base appeal to the emotions by the application of *alethes logos*. This is the common thread that binds together Lucian, his friend Celsus, Epicurus, and the author of *True Doctrine;* indeed, it serves as an excellent synopsis of the polemical stance against the Christians in the work. This understanding of the true significance of Epicurus's doctrine, in Lucian's eyes, allows the author of *True Doctrine* to be identified with Lucian's friend, who was noted for writing a book *Against the Magicians* (κατὰ μάγων).[14] Given the social nature of the accusations of *goes* and *magos,* it would be quite likely that such an author would also write against that growing group of social deviants and followers of a crucified magician: the Christians. If the term "Epicurean" was used in a very loose sense as a term of opprobrium,[15] it would suit Lucian's sense of irony and love of outrage to turn the issue on its head and make Epicurus his model of rectitude. After all, it was Alexander who first labeled his enemies "Epicureans." So Lucian, turning the intended insult into a compliment, holds Epicurus up as a friend and exemplar to anyone with the sound reasoning to perceive the fraud of an Alexander or, it may be assumed, a Jesus.

The identification of Lucian's friend Celsus with the author of *True Doctrine* can, at this point, neither be proved nor disproved. Obviously, for the purposes of this work, identification would be desirable. In either case, Lucian, his friend, and our Celsus share an identical set of norms and values, and this is the significant point.

---

14. ". . . in the book you wrote against the magicians, a very fine and at the same time useful work, capable of instilling common sense in those who happen to come upon it" (*Alex.* 21).

15. W. R. Inge, "Origen," *Proceedings of the British Academy* 32 (1946): 125.

Scholarship has long noted the prominence of tradition and authority in Celsus's arguments against Christianity.[16] For A. von Harnack, Celsus was an agnostic whose sole interest was the preservation of the empire and whose concern with religion was predicated solely on the fact that the empire required it. For him, *True Doctrine* was nothing more than a political pamphlet. A. Miura-Stange, a student of Harnack, held that Celsus's attack was primarily political and emphasized social conservatism as a primary motive. Taking a different emphasis, A. Wifstrand and H. Dörrie developed the theme of religious and cultural tradition and authority, which culminated in C. Andresen's masterful analysis of *nomos* in Celsus.[17]

It is incorrect, however, to draw distinctions too sharply and either to dismiss Celsus's religious beliefs as an adjunct to an almost Machiavellian political creed[18] or to subsume his political concerns completely under the umbrella of a religious ethos.[19] To do either denies the genius of paganism—the practical unity of religion, politics, culture, and society. As R. Wilken observes:

> He [Celsus] approaches the institutions and mores of society as an intellectual prepared to offer philosophical and religious arguments in support of the traditional political and social order. His philosophical and religious ideas are not simply theoretical convictions; they are interwoven with the institutions, social conventions, and political structures of the Graeco-Roman world.[20]

In opposition to those who seek examples of decadence or ossification in the religious and philosophical thought of the second century, *True Doctrine* offers a clear sign of the intellectual vigor of imperial society

16. Andresen, 8–107, provides an exhaustive review of scholarship; see also Borret, 5:145–198 (Bibliographie Critique, which strangely ignores the work of Miura-Stange). General bibliography in Andresen, 401–10. Brief, useful introductions to Celsus are found in S. Benko, "Pagan Criticism of Christianity During the First Two Centuries, A.D." *ANRW* II.23.2 (1980): 1101–8, with a select bibliography on the entire topic, 1110–18; R. Wilken, *The Christians as the Romans Saw Them* (New Haven, 1984), 94–125; and Hoffmann, 5–45.

17. A. von Harnack, *The Mission and Expansion of Christianity in the First Three Centuries*, trans. J. Moffat (New York, 1908), 1:501ff.; Miura-Stange, esp. 2, 22; Wifstrand, "Die wahre Lehre"; H. Dörrie, "Die platonische Theologie des Kelsos in ihrer Auseinandersetzung mit der christliche Theologie: auf Grund von Origenes c. Celsum 7.42ff.," *Nachrichten der Akademie der Wissenschaften in Göttingen*, Philologisch-historische Klasse 1 (1967): 23–55; Andresen, esp. 189–238.

18. Contra Miura-Stange, 17.

19. Contra Andresen, 359.

20. *Christians*, 95.

in the period. It is itself an example of the great work of cultural synthesis that challenged some of the finest pagan minds of the age—the reconciliation of philosophical and popular religion ("high and low church" paganism would be an apt if mixed metaphor) and the systematic, reasoned articulation of the beliefs and norms upon which both the culture of Greece and the empire of Rome were based.

Celsus is a synthetic thinker. Much work has been done to identify the precise nature of his philosophical beliefs, a task complicated by Origen's contradictory statements. Earlier arguments that Celsus was a thoroughgoing Platonist have now been nuanced by more complete understandings of the eclectic nature of Middle Platonism and by evidence of his having received formal training in Stoicism.[21] Celsus is fundamentally a Platonist, especially in his view of the body, which, as will be seen, has a surprising bearing on his attitudes toward asceticism. Celsus is, however, not philosophically dogmatic, nor is intellectual purity his highest value. If at times he appears to contradict Platonic doctrine, it is not because he is a shoddy thinker or has fallen under the spell of the "creeping superstition" of his age. Rather, philosophy serves a higher value: that of the *alethes logos* of which philosophy is only a partial expression. It is this universal truth, expressed in the traditional values and norms of classical civilization (*nomos*, to use Andresen's terminology) that must at all costs be preserved against the Christians who would overthrow it.[22]

The Person of Jesus

Celsus was the first critic of Christianity to give careful attention to the figure of Jesus himself, making the founder of the sect as important an issue as the beliefs and behavior of his followers.[23] Jesus is portrayed as

21. On Celsus's complete Platonism, O. Glöckner, "Die Gottes- und Weltanschauung des Kelsos," *Philologus* 82 (1926–27): 329–52; corrected and refined views: H. Chadwick, "Origen, Celsus, and the Stoa," *JTS* 48 (1947): 34–49; Andresen, 292–307; and J. M. Rist, "The Importance of Stoic Logic in the Contra Celsum," in *Neoplatonism and Early Christian Thought: Essays in Honor of A. H. Armstrong*, ed. H. J. Blumenthal and R. A. Markus (London, 1981), 64–78.

22. Andresen, 77: "Der Verfasser des Alethes Logos läßt ungeachtet der schulphilosophischen Gegensätze seiner Tage die Stoa in der großen Phalanx mit aufmarschieren, die er gegen das Christentum errichtet. Er betrachtet sie als einen Zweig einer für alle verpflichtenden geistesgeschichtlichen Tradition." Wifstrand, 398f., defines the *alethes logos* as the intellectual and cultural tradition which made up the common treasury of hellenism.

23. Wilken, *Christians*, 108.

an uncouth, conniving magician and prophet (*goes*, *C. Cels.* I.71) of dubious ancestry, preying on the gullible and uneducated for purposes of self-glorification. The parallels to Peregrinus, Alexander, and the negative traditions concerning Apollonius are obvious.[24] Both Celsus and Origen agree that such figures are commonplace, especially in Palestine.[25] It remains, however, to examine the parallels in attitudes, norms, and values that lay behind the similarity of depiction.[26]

Through the mouthpiece of his Jewish narrator, Celsus provides Jesus with a scurrilous biography reminiscent of Lucian's treatment of Peregrinus and Alexander. Born in disgrace as the product of adultery (I.28, 32), Jesus flees with his mother to Egypt where he apprenticed himself in magic (I.38; cf. 68). Celsus capitalizes on his familiarity with the infancy narratives of the gospels to develop the sort of unsavory connection with Egypt seen earlier. Peregrinus visited the place twice and there learned to perform his Cynic outrages. Philostratus, in Apollonius's ungracious meeting with the Gymnosophists, distanced his hero from Egyptian lore both in the persons of its unworthy practitioners and in its doctrine, which is shown to be a pale derivation of the true philosophy Apollonius learned in venerable India.

The next episode of Celsus's portrait presents Jesus collecting an infamous band of disciples of the lowest class and character who, Celsus is careful to point out, lacked even the rudiments of education. Together they go about begging, huckstering, and performing commonplace sorcery in market-squares (I.62–68; cf. II.46, III.50). In characterizing the beginnings of Christianity as a religion of the lower classes and of slaves inspired (or aroused) at the words of an itinerant preacher, Celsus invites a comparison with Lucian's *Fugitives* in which the same sort were stirred up by the preaching of Cynics.[27] Jesus is shown to be an agitator of a very familiar type, one that Dio Chrysostom excoriated as a clear and present danger to social order in Alexandria. Jesus is but another street preacher, vaunting his indigence as ascetical poverty, appealing to the ignorant, and inciting the crowd against their social betters. In the same way Lucian pronounced his verdict on Peregrinus,

24. For a detailed outline of the parallels in depiction, see E. V. Gallagher, *Divine Man or Magician? Celsus and Origen on Jesus*, SBL Dissertation Series 64 (Chico, Calif., 1982), 151–65.

25. *C. Cels.* II.8, VI.11; cf. Lucian, *Lover of Lies* 16, for his description of a Syrian exorcist from Palestine.

26. Note the contemporaneity involved: 180 is the approximate year assigned to *True Doctrine*, the year of M. Aurelius's death, and the *terminus post quem* for the death of Lucian. As for the "next generation," Philostratus was born c. 170, Origen c. 185; fewer than thirty years separate the *Life of Apollonius* from *Contra Celsum*.

27. See Andresen, 174–78, 233; cf. *C. Cels.* III.44, 50, 59, 65.

Jesus is revelaed as an enemy of society and culture alike. When Celsus describes him as the author of sedition or *stasis* (τῆς στάσεως ἀρ-χηγέτης) he means it literally (VIII. 14).

Although *True Doctrine,* at least in the fragments we have, makes no mention of the accusations of murder, cannibalism, and incest that appear to have been leveled earlier against the Christians,[28] it is incorrect to say that with Celsus the grounds of the polemic have moved from the moral to the intellectual.[29] Jesus' character is described as morally reprehensible, in the same way as that of Peregrinus and Alexander. While not possessing the shock value of the earlier accusations, the depiction of Jesus and his immediate disciples is no less repugnant to an educated Roman than the wild slanders spread against their followers. It is simply a truism that classical moral theory accounts for evil as the product of an evil personal character. The threat posed by Christianity had to have its roots in some maleficent individual or individuals. Celsus's genius was to transfer the malevolent source of Christianity's threat from the Christians themselves to the person of the historical Jesus. His manner of doing so was to reduce Jesus to a known character type unacceptable to the norms and values of his age. What Lucian does in the context of satire colored by invective, Celsus does in polemic colored by philosophy. In both cases, the issues, norms, and values involved are the same.

For Celsus, Jesus is clearly a *goes,* specifically a charlatan who dabbled in magic: "These were the actions of one hated by God and of a wicked sorcerer (γόητος, I.71)."[30] Again displaying his ability to turn a

---

28. The reality of these accusations is debated. Among pagan writers before Celsus, Tac., *Ann.* XV.44, mentions the outrageous crimes (*flagitia*) of the Christians, but is no more specific. Pliny, *Ep.* X.96, mentions the "outrageous crimes attached to the name," and goes on to state that, upon investigation, the Christians were discovered to eat only "a commonplace and harmless food." This would appear to be a reference to the infanticide and cannibalism slanders. The specific charges of cannibalism and incest occur first only in Christian writers of the second century: Athen., *Legat.* 3, 31–32, and Justin, *1 Apol.* 26, who suggests that such behavior may occur among "fringe groups," but does not characterize Christians in general. A convenient summary of the evidence is found in Wilken, *Christians,* 15–25, with a more detailed discussion in S. Benko, *Pagan Rome and the Early Christians* (Bloomington, Ind., 1984), 1–29 and 54–102. A broader treatment is that of R. M. Grant, "Charges of 'Immorality' against Various Religious Groups in Antiquity," in *Studies in Gnosticism and Hellenistic Religions: Presented to Gilles Quispel on the Occasion of His 65th Birthday,* ed. R. van Den Broek and M. J. Vermaseren (Leiden, 1981), 161–70. See also below, pages 152–53, 155–60, 166–72.

29. Contra Hoffmann, 25.

30. Recent research on Jesus as a magician is reviewed by D. E. Aune, "Magic in Early Christianity," *ANRW* II.23.2 (1980): 1507–57, with bibliography in the notes. In connection with the subject at hand, see Gallagher, 41–73; M. Smith, *Jesus the Magician*

gospel passage against itself, Celsus states that Jesus even admitted that
"evil men and charlatans" (κακοὶ καὶ γόητες) would perform the
same signs and miracles as himself and that, in *those* cases, such
wonders were signs of cheats and wicked men (II.49ff., I.6; cf. Matt.
24.23–27, 7.22f.). The logical question follows: If these are signs of a
goes for any who would come after Jesus, why are they not so for him?
As their founder, so his followers. Celsus is the first pagan critic to
explicitly accuse the Christians (as opposed to Jesus himself) of practicing magic, deriving their power from pronouncing the names of demons
and by incantations (I.6). Origen offers what may appear to modern
eyes a very feeble response: Christians perform miracles not by invoking
demons but by the name of Jesus.[31]

Origen is not begging the question. The issue here, for both Celsus
and Origen regarding Jesus and the Christians alike, is what constitutes
the practice of magic. Both Celsus and Origen admit the reality of miracles and miraculous power. The difficulty, and therefore the point of
contention, is when and how an individual or group crosses the line
from the prodigious to the magical. As seen in the previous chapter, the
determination, either in antiquity or in modern scholarship, is difficult
to make. "Magic" was always suspect and generally illegal, but what
exactly constituted magic varied among individuals, groups, and historical periods.[32]

Little of the legal definition of magic applies to Celsus's criticism of
Christianity. The implied illegality of incantations in general and the
banning of "impious and nocturnal rites" (on the example of the Bacchanalia) would be the only possibilities. Two passages from Paulus,
however, are specifically useful. *Sent.* V.21.1 states that soothsayers
who feign being infused with divinity (*qui se deo plenos adsimulant*)
shall be expelled from cities to prevent the corruption of public morals
through credulity and the perturbation of the minds of the common

(New York, 1978), esp. 21–67; and H. Remus, *Pagan-Christian Conflict over Miracle in
the Second Century,* Philadelphia Patristic Monograph Series 10 (Cambridge, Mass.,
1983), esp. 104–58. Also worth noting on the subject of magic and Christianity is M.
Smith, *Clement of Alexandria and a Secret Gospel of Mark* (Cambridge, Mass., 1973),
220–37.

    31. On the magical use of the name of Jesus, see Aune, 1545–49. Benko, *Pagan Rome,*
115f., notes that the Christian contention that miracles performed in Jesus' name were not
magic is found well before Origen in Justin and Ireneus.

    32. On Origen, see G. Bardy, "Origène et la magie," *Recherches de science religieuse* 18
(1928): 126–42; on Celsus, see Remus, 109ff. Smith, *Jesus,* 143, rightly notes that magic
did not always simply equal miracle working. See the detailed discussion of magic in
Chapter 4, pages 90–94.

people.[33] Similarly, V.21.2 states that those who introduce new religious doctrines unknown to traditional usage or reason, by which the minds of men are influenced, are to be punished by exile or death. This reintroduces the themes of charismatic authority, credulity, and disruption of the social fabric. The common definition of magic, then, lies not so much in specific practices condemned by the law, but in the perception of the negative effects certain persons (labelled *goetes* by their enemies) had on other individuals and on the assumptions and structures of society as a whole. As has been argued throughout the course of this investigation, deviance is perceived first. The accusation of magic is an explanation for, and condemnation of, this deviant behavior.[34]

In his discussion of magic and early Christianity in the context of Graeco-Roman religion, D. Aune advances his preference for a structural-functionalist approach and specifies two criteria for a definition of magic: (1) religious deviance whereby individual or social goals are sought by means alternate to those normally sanctioned by the dominant religious institution, and (2) the attainment of those goals by the management of supernatural powers in such a way that the results are virtually assured.[35] Seen in this way, all of Christianity could be condemned as magic by the first criterion. Origen's defense against the charge that the Christians practiced magic has to do with the second. Christians do not "force" supernatural powers to do their will, much less do they force Jesus. Rather, the mere name of Jesus is sufficiently powerful to work miracles.[36] This is proof not of magical power but of Jesus' true stature as Son of God.

---

33. Paulus's statements on magic throughout the *Sententiae* closely parallel the accusations made against Apollonius in *VA* VIII.7.1–16. Philostratus and Paulus were contemporaries, and the charges in the *VA* may themselves be an illustration of the definition of magic in the late second and early third centuries. See Chapter 4, pages 126–28.

34. See Chapter 2, pages 48–50, esp. note 82; and Chapter 4, notes 26, 34, and 40.

35. Aune, 1514–16, but also see A. F. Segal, "Hellenistic Magic: Some Questions of Definition," in *Studies in Gnosticism and Hellenistic Religions: Presented to Gilles Quispel on the Occasion of His 65th Birthday*, ed. R. van Den Broek and M. J. Vermaseren (Leiden, 1981), 350f. and 375, for the limitations of this approach. Given the evidence from Lucian on Alexander and Peregrinus, I would suggest that Aune's first criterion could be expanded beyond the specifically religious sphere to include the pursuit of any individual or social goals by means that are *perceived* to be a perversion of those normally sanctioned. This then approaches Segal's "functional-practical" definition. Lucian calls both Alexander and Peregrinus *goetes* because they abused traditional religious belief and practice and a traditionally accepted school of philosophy, respectively, by using them purely as a means to attain personal power.

36. See the note on the passage (I.6) in Chadwick, 10 n. 1. Apuleius, *Apol.* 26, states that his accusers charged him with coercing divine beings as well.

The issue is framed in terms identical to the accusations of *goeteia* brought against Apollonius. His strict Pythagorean life brought him under suspicion as deviating from religious and social norms. His powers of prophecy and healing were attributed to daemonic influence and "the torturing of spirits," while the alleged sacrifice of the Arcadian boy was a divinatory rite to ascertain the name of Domitian's successor.[37] His defense was not to deny his powers—the sacrifice of the boy was nothing more than a malicious lie—but to attribute them to his ascetical manner of life and intimacy with the gods, that is, to his practice of true philosophy.[38] Apollonius's miracles, though greatly muted in comparison to the gospels, prove not that he is a *goes*, but that he is favored of the gods. Celsus's attack was typical of his age, as was Origen's response.[39]

Aune's first criterion also serves to explain the connection observed in all the cases studied here between asceticism and *goeteia*. Both are manifestations of social deviance whereby individual or social goals are pursued by means not sanctioned by society. The Cynic's pursuit of personal freedom involved both physical austerity and the flaunting of all social conventions. In Peregrinus's case, according to Lucian, this traditional deviance was exacerbated by his pursuit of personal power—the development of a charismatic authority unchecked even by the broad limits of his philosophical sect. Apollonius, too, stepped outside the boundaries of his school to become "greater than Pythagoras" by going directly to the source of true philosophy in the Brahmans. Rejecting most of the religious conventions of his society (though not, most im-

---

37. Prophecy is another issue on which Celsus criticizes Jesus and the Christians (II.13ff., VII.1ff.), though not pertinent to the matter at hand. The subject has been thoroughly discussed by R. J. Hauck in his Duke University dissertation published as *The More Divine Proof: Prophecy and Inspiration in Celsus and Origen*, AAR Academy Series 69 (Atlanta, 1989).

38. Apuleius found himself in a similar position, accused by his wealthy wife's family of using magic to win her affections. His opponents' case was aided by Apuleius's wearing the philosopher's habit, another instance of the fine line that existed between philosophy and *goeteia*, and the suspicion under which both were held. An essential part of Apuleius's defense was the insistence that he was merely a learned, curious man interested in philosophy, wrongly presumed on this account to be a *goes* (*Apol.* 3ff., 25ᵀ. See also Chapter 2, note 83, and Chapter 4, pages 92–94.

39. "Because of the dominant perception of the magicians, such accusations were most often vehicles for social, moral, and intellectual invective. Terms like *magia* and γοητεία were used to create, strengthen, and reassert social, moral, and intellectual boundaries, such as those between in- and out-groups, higher and lower social classes, and true practitioners and charlatans. Celsus uses similar language to try to separate the magicians (Jesus and the Christians) from the philosophers (himself and those he favors). Origen responds in a similar fashion," Gallagher, 47.

portant, belief in the gods themselves) he pursued his own path to the gods by means of individual asceticism. The very success of his religious quest nearly cost him his life on a trial for sorcery. When Celsus relates the opinion of the Egyptian musician Dionysius, "that magical arts were effective with uneducated people and with men of depraved moral character, but that with people who had studied philosophy they were not able to have any effect, because they were careful to lead a healthy way of life" (VI.41), Origen adduces Apollonius himself as a counterexample.[40] Philostratus had defended his hero precisely by demonstrating that he conformed to and upheld the values of his society, contrary to the appearances of his deviant life as a wonderworker and ascetic.

In much the same way, E. V. Gallagher has shown how Origen constantly invokes the idea of "philanthropy," the continuing effect of Jesus' life and teaching for moral reform and the bettering of others, as the true test of the legitimacy of his prophecy and miracle working (see I.68). It is incorrect, however, to conclude with Gallagher that philanthropy formed part of Celsus's and Origen's *definitions* of *theioi andres*.[41] As in the *VA*, benefaction to humanity is, rather, an apologetic *justification* for wonderworkers and ascetics who were already considered "divine" by those writing about them. For Celsus, such figures included Heracles and Pythagoras; for Origen there is, of course, only one: Jesus.[42]

Merely doing good is not sufficient to establish a good—much less divine—character. Celsus can even entertain Jesus' performing philanthropic miracles (I.68, II.28). The holy man must be worthy of his role, and this determination is made by the degree of his social and cultural conformity. To contradict one of Gallagher's own examples, Lucian's portrait of Alexander was not a "parody of a civic benefactor" who "did not deliver according to expectations."[43] On the contrary, Alexander brought influence and notoriety to his city, petitioning the emperor to have it given a more prestigious name and bringing influential men in the imperial administration to it. What galled Lucian and provoked him to stinging satire was not that Alexander was a disappointment, but that he was totally unworthy and unfit for the amazing suc-

40. If the results of magic are not "virtually assured" when directed against educated and philosophical persons, the question may be asked whether Celsus really believed in magic at all. There is no contradiction if it is remembered that such persons are few and far between and that, as has been seen in Aurelius and Philostratus, the philosopher has risen above forces, both interior and exterior, that affect other mortals. See also Chadwick, *Contra Celsum*, 356 n. 1.
41. Gallagher, 75–116 and 140–50.
42. For further discussion, see below, pages 147–49, and Remus, 106ff.
43. Gallagher, 157.

cess he did in fact achieve. Recall the Stoic insistence on motivation as the determiner of the morality of an act—good actions can only be performed by good people. In portraying Jesus as a *goes,* a base man of no education and sinister intent collecting a similar rabble about him, Celsus precludes any attempt to justify him on the basis of philanthropy.

Celsus's Concept of Religion

Concomitant with Celsus's estimation of the person of Jesus are his criticisms of the Christians of his own day. The foundation of Celsus's judgments is both religious and social in nature, but it is of the utmost importance to realize that such distinctions would have appeared quite arbitrary to Celsus himself. It is quite wrong to emphasize one of these aspects at the expense of the other. As regards religion, the *alethes logos* is much more than simply "die gemeinsame alte Tradition von Gott und den Göttern,"[44] though it certainly includes the collective theological beliefs (and assumptions) of classical antiquity. Celsus's thought—and that of his culture, the norms and values of which he articulates—has as its hallmark the unity of the religious, social, political, and cultural aspects of human endeavor in one organism of civilization. The *alethes logos,* that ancient doctrine that has existed from the very beginning (I.14), is the term used to denominate this unity, and it is both the constituent elements of this unity and the unity *itself* that Celsus defends against the Christians.

It was once fashionable to speak of second-century paganism as a bankrupt religious system that had ceased to command the attention, much less the conviction, of the citizens of the empire. The explanation of the eventual triumph of Christianity was sought in a decrepit paganism riddled with contradictions and plagued with rising "superstition" and "oriental syncretism."[45] The intellectual landscape of the age was painted as rife with conflict and confusion between unity and diversity, polytheism and monotheism, rationalism and irrationalism, East and West.[46] Even a scholar as sympathetic to paganism as E. R. Dodds could state that while Christian intellectuals endeavored to *supplement* au-

---

44. Wifstrand, 401.

45. A good example is E. Renan, *Marc-Aurèle et le fin du monde antique,* Histoire des origines du christianisme 7 (Paris, 1899), in which "le fin" is blamed squarely on rising credulity, superstition, and the wholesale abandonment of the "rational" element in pagan religious thought both in religion proper and in philosophy. As for oriental syncretism, F. Cumont ranks as its chief proponent.

46. J. Beaujeu, *La Religion romaine à l'apogée de l'empire,* vol. 1, *La politique religieuse des Antonins (96–192)* (Paris, 1955), 30–36.

thority with reason, contemporary pagan philosophers tended to *re-place* reason with authority.[47] Such views have now been shown to be in clear contradiction to the evidence.[48]

Opinions on Celsus's conception of religion are, of course, colored by these opinions on the religion of his age.[49] Both Miura-Stange and Andresen have spoken of the "tension and contradiction" between Celsus's rationalism and his unashamed belief in divination, oracles, miracles, and the cult of Asclepius (VIII.45; IV.88; III.3, 22, 24, 43; VII.53). The former would resolve this contradiction by asserting that Celsus was no believer himself and that his opinions on religion are merely those required to support the political order. The latter holds that Celsus only grudgingly accepted and was forced to defend these "superstitions" because of their antiquity and integration into the inherited conglomerate of the *nomos*.[50] Such studies have, however, neither attempted to determine whether Celsus himself ever perceived such tension and contradiction, nor questioned whether the modern, post-Christian distinction between "rationalism and superstition" is applicable to ancient Greek religious expression. There is ample evidence and argumentation to support the contention that these modern distinctions are neither helpful nor applicable to an understanding of Celsus.[51]

Andresen is surely correct in stating that these so-called superstitious elements of classical paganism were accepted by Celsus as part and parcel of the *alethes logos,* but there is no need to characterize this as grudging or under duress. Andresen underestimates the scope and power of the *nomos* he himself so meticulously describes. That certain religious rites have been hallowed from antiquity is not a grudging but

---

47. E. R. Dodds, *Pagan and Christian in an Age of Anxiety: Some Aspects of Religious Experience from Marcus Aurelius to Constantine* (Cambridge, 1965), 122.

48. See R. MacMullen, *Paganism in the Roman Empire* (New Haven, 1981) and R. Lane Fox, *Pagans and Christians* (New York, 1987), 27–168, both with notes and bibliography; R. L. Gordon, "Mithraism and Roman Society: Social Factors in the Explanation of Religious Change in the Roman Empire," *Religion* 2 (1972): 92–121, also containing very sane and sound comments on the study of ancient religion in general; and D. Georgi, "Socioeconomic Reasons for the 'Divine Men' as a Propagandistic Pattern," in *Aspects of Religious Propaganda in Judaism and Early Christianity,* ed. E. S. Fiorenza (Notre Dame, 1976), 27–42. Even Beaujeu, *La Religion romaine*, admits that the reaction of the traditional religion to the conflicts he describes was "très vive"; this would, it appears, speak more to the diversity and vigor of paganism rather than to crisis and anxiety.

49. Hauck, 7–12, offers a brief review of the scholarship.

50. Miura-Stange, 16, 105, 136; refuted by Wifstrand, 404. Andresen, 60; refuted by Hauck, 103f., who offers his own less satisfactory explanation.

51. Hauck, 12, 77–81, 85 n. 24. In support of which see Remus, 73–82, and H. W. Attridge, "The Philosophical Critique of Religion Under the Early Empire," *ANRW* II.16.1 (1978): 45–78, both with numerous references to the ancient sources.

an extremely powerful reason for their continued observance.[52] Their
apparent efficacy offers a very rational support for this argument, for
what could be more irrational than to deny empirical evidence? As an
example, Celsus himself states that the ancient oracles, always consulted
before the founding of a colony, were responsible for the growth and
dissemination of the very culture of which he is so rightly proud
(VIII.45). Since they are efficacious, they support the continuance of
society and thus form an integral part of the *nomos*. Celsus, then, does
not seek to reduce traditional religious phenomena and expression to
rational explanation, but to provide a rational justification for their vital role in civilized society. Beneath Celsus's criticism of the Christians
as irrational is that they are *incomprehensible* within the boundaries of
the universally received and accepted body of religious knowledge and
wisdom.

This incomprehensibility becomes clear in Celsus's objections to certain pagan religious cults of his time.

> And he compares those who believe without rational thought to
> the begging priests of Cybele and soothsayers, and to worship-
> pers of Mithras and Sabazius, and whatever else one might meet,
> apparitions of Hecate or of some other daemon or daemons. For
> just as among them scoundrels frequently take advantage of the
> lack of education of gullible people and lead them wherever they
> wish, so also, he says, this happens among the Christians. He
> says that some do not even want to give or to receive a reason
> for what they believe, and use such expressions as "Do not ask
> questions; just believe," and "Thy faith will save thee." (I.9)

> Let anyone who likes show what sort of miscellaneous ideas we
> use to persuade men to follow us, or what terrors we invent, as
> Celsus writes, though he gives no proof. . . . Furthermore he says
> that with these we combine misunderstandings of the ancient tra-
> dition, and we overwhelm men beforehand by playing flutes and
> music like the priests of Cybele who with their clamour stupefy
> the people whom they wish to excite into a frenzy. (III.16)

> For this reason he compares us to those in the Bacchic mysteries
> who introduce phantoms and terrors. (IV.10)

Just as Celsus intimated unfavorable parallels between Jesus and men
like Peregrinus, Alexander, and Apollonius, so here he openly draws

52. See, for example, Cicero's treatise on traditional religion in *de Leg.* II.18–57.

comparisons between Christianity and unrespectable and arcane religious movements that offended the sensibilities of most Romans.[53]

There is significance in those Celsus chooses to mention. He objects not to the cult of Cybele itself, but to its priests, itinerant ascetics and wandering prophets earning a living by begging.[54] Soothsayers are classic *goetes*, prophesying on streetcorners. Images of Peregrinus and Jesus, of Cynic preachers and Christian apostles, come to mind. Origen himself objects that since Cynics are not compared to marketplace magicians and beggars on account of their streetcorner preaching, neither should Christians (III.50). Apparently, Origen did not have either Lucian or Dio Chrysostom in mind at the time.

Here again arises the recurrent negative estimation of the self-styled holy man among educated pagans of the second century. E. V. Gallagher has already given this subject an exemplary treatment with regard to Celsus,[55] so that a few brief comments will suffice. Though Celsus refers to the great sages of the past as *theioi andres* (VII.42; cf. 45), he is adamant that neither philosophers, nor heroes, nor other benefactors of humanity were deemed gods (III.22, VI.1). His essential criticism of the Christians in this regard is that they do just the opposite and exalt the man Jesus, not only to the level of a god, but even as a rival to the Most High God himself (VIII.12). What the Christians (and, for that matter, most holy-man scholars who deal with Celsus) fail to understand is that humanity and divinity for Celsus are not absolute categories, but a continuum. There is no single established type of divine man, identifiable and intermediate between mortals and gods. Rather, there is an entire spectrum of "degrees" of divinity running from humanity, through intermediate beings (such as *daimones* and the "governors" of nations) through to the Most High God who, by his very nature, is one and unique. Exemplary and "holy" men do exist, but must not be honored above their rightful station. It is the mark of the *goes* that he seeks this sort of exaltation from his followers.

How then can an exemplary mortal's rightful station be established? Consistent with Celsus's valuation of history and the received tradition of classical culture, only time can tell. The accumulated judgment of generations of the learned and devout defines the status of a Heracles, Plato, or Asclepius. "Holy men," by definition, can only exist in the remote past or, possibly, in the more recent past—provided that their

53. Wilken, *Christians*, 96; Miura-Stange, 17–20.

54. See A. D. Nock, *Conversion: The Old and the New in Religion from Alexander the Great to Augustine of Hippo* (Oxford, 1933), 82f.; cf. Cic., *de Leg.* II.40 and Apuleius, *Met.* VIII.24ff.

55. See Gallagher, esp. 151–80, on which the following analysis is based.

characters and actions conform to ancient and approved norms in an exemplary way. Since this judgment can only come from history, social consensus, and the *nomos* of traditional values, any living contemporary purported to be or, most especially, claiming himself to be a *theios aner* must be treated with the utmost suspicion.[56]

Mithras, Sabazius, the priests of Cybele, the Bacchic mysteries, and Christianity are associated with "phantoms and terrors," instilling fear and exciting the mob to frenzy. Alexander did the same, and it is precisely as an antidote to phantoms and terrors that Lucian recommends the reading of Epicurus. Those susceptible to frenzy and terror are the uneducated and gullible—precisely the kind of audience Alexander sought in Paphlagonia. Celsus attacks not only fanatic religiosity but also its root cause, credulity: "Do not ask questions; just believe" (I.9). This opinion Celsus shares with Marcus Aurelius and Galen as well as Lucian.

The purpose of such an emotional appeal is clear: "to persuade people to follow the cult leader(s) who will lead them wherever they wish" (III.16 and I.9). Frenzy and terror are thus instruments of social control, and therefore dangerous. This is especially so when they are wielded by self-styled holy men who use them to arrogate a personal, charismatic authority to themselves independent of the social restraints and controls imposed by the received religious tradition. Peregrinus, Alexander, and Jesus all operated in this way. Danger, therefore, comes not only from fanatical leaders but also from their followers. Celsus's mention of the Bacchic mysteries undoubtedly refers to this. The shocking revelations concerning the devotees of Bacchus in Rome in 186 B.C.E. and their tumultuous aftermath were enshrined both in a decree of the senate, still preserved, suppressing secret rites and meetings, and in Livy's lurid account of the events that fixed suspicion of such activities firmly in the Roman mind.[57] The suspicion of secret associations particularly of a religious nature endured, and it is this sentiment that Celsus invokes.

---

56. In VII.9 Celsus speaks of the prophets of his day wandering about cities and military camps, laying some claim to divinity, and threatening dire retribution to those who refuse to believe. Chadwick's notes on this passage are particularly helpful.

57. *CIL* I².581; Livy XXXIX.8–18. So Origen reports Celsus's opinion that the Christians' refusal to erect altars, images, and temples is a sure sign of an obscure and secret society (ἀφανοῦς καὶ ἀπορρήτου κοινωνίας, VIII.17). On the *S.C. de Bacchanalibus* as a model for established Roman attitudes toward religious and other organized groups perceived as deviant, see the important study by J. North, "Religious Toleration in Republican Rome," *Proceedings of the Cambridge Philological Society* 205 (1979): 85–103. More recently on the Bacchanalia, R. A. Bauman, "The Suppression of the Bacchanals: Five Questions," *Historia* 39 (1990): 334–48.

Indeed, the first charge that Origen answers is that the Christians form a secret association contrary to the law.[58]

Celsus's mention of "phantoms and terrors" also recalls a law of Marcus Aurelius: "If anyone should do anything through which weak-minded persons become terrified by superstition, the Divine Marcus stated in a rescript that men of this kind should be relegated to an island" (*Dig.* XLVIII.XIX.30).[59] Christianity had been described as a *superstitio* from its earliest mention among pagan authors (Tac., *Ann.* XV.44.2–8; Suet., *Nero* 16; Pliny, *Ep.* X.96.1–10), but so also were Isiasm, Judaism, and the cults of Cybele and Bellona (Suet., *Domit.* 1; Juv. VI.511ff.). The use of the term in antiquity is notoriously slippery. Simply speaking, *superstitio* seems to be operationally defined as "a religious expression of which one disapproves." To be more elegant, it gains its definition only from its opposition to *religio,* that is, any belief or practice foreign to, or exceeding the bounds of, traditional religion, which, by implication, is also seen as inimical to or destructive of religion.[60] Of course, the definition of religion can be just as nebulous as

---

58. I.1; cf. VIII.17. The relationship to the Bacchanalia here is on the issue of secrecy and secret rites. The specific law in question in I.1 is not the *S.C. de Bacchanalibus* but the *Lex Julia de collegiis,* probably 22 B.C.E., which required that all associations (*collegia*) be sanctioned by the state. See *CIL* VI.4416 = *ILS* 4966, and Suet. *Aug.* 32.2.

59. "*si quis aliquid fecerit quo leves hominum animi superstitione numinis terr[er]entur, Divus Marcus huiusmodi homines in insulam relegari rescripsit.*" A more precise rendering of *superstitione numinis* would be "excessive fear of supernatural power." There is no evidence, however, that Christians suffered under the provisions of this particular law; see G. E. M. de Ste. Croix, "Why Were the Early Christians Persecuted?" *Past and Present* 26 (1963): 14. The issue here is one of attitude rather than action. Superstition, though vaguely defined, was perceived as a threat to be addressed in laws and penalties. Compare this law of Aurelius with Paulus, *Sent..* V.21.1: "*vaticinatores, qui se deo plenos adsimulant, idcirco civitate expelli placuit, ne humana credulitate publici mores ad spem alicuius rei corrumperentur, vel certe ex eo populares animi turbarentur,*" and V.21.2: "*Qui novas, et usu, vel ratione incognitas religiones inducunt, ex quibus animi hominum moveantur, honestiores deportantur, humiliores capite puniuntur.*" See pages 140–41 above.

60. In the case of Christianity, the threat of a foreign superstition to overthrow the traditional religion is clear. Plutarch, *de Superstitione* (*Moralia* 164E–171F), explains how excessive fear of the gods is also impious, for it sees the gods as rash, vengeful, and cruel, and leads ultimately to atheism, for such a rude picture of the gods leads mortals to disbelieve in them entirely. So, too, foreign cults can be inimical to religion not because they seek to overthrow the traditional gods, but because they tend to extremes of fear, devotion, and behavior. See also Theophrastus, *Char.* XVI, for his description of the superstitious man, a portrait reminiscent of Lucian's representation of Alexander's most renowned disciple, Rutilianus.

that of superstition: "*Religio* is the worship of the true God, *superstitio* of the false" (Lactantius, *Div. Inst..* IV.28.11).[61]

The definition of *religio* holds, at least, no mystery for Celsus. True religion is the religion of one's ancestors or nation:

> Now the Jews became an individual nation, and made laws according to the custom of their country; and they maintain these laws among themselves at the present day, and observe a worship that may be very peculiar but is at least traditional. In this respect they behave like the rest of mankind, because each nation follows its traditional customs, whatever kind may happen to be established. This situation seems to have come to pass not only because it came into the head of different people to think differently and because it is necessary to preserve the established social conventions, but also because it is probable that from the beginning the different parts of the earth were allotted to different overseers, and are governed in this way by having been divided between certain authorities. In fact, the practices done by each nation are right when they are done in a way that pleases the overseers; and it is impious to abandon the customs which have existed in each locality from the beginning. (V.25)

Religio is socially defined. This is not, however, to say that religion is merely a subordinate department of the social establishment. For along with the necessity of preserving established social conventions (δεῖ φυλάττειν τά ἐς κοινὸν κεκυρωμένα) there is the theological reality that different nations are ruled by particular deities subordinate to the Most High God (see also VIII.35). Religion is defined by social norms, customs, and values that, in turn, receive their sanction from a religious principle. This is an excellent example of the unity of religion, society, and culture that is the genius of paganism. It is this unity that Christianity threatens. .

The issue is one of a religion that sets itself up as an authority independent of and superior to the knowledge, customs, and culture of its surrounding society. In attacking the pretensions to truth of the Christian revelation with the accumulated wisdom of his culture, and by insisting that Christianity conform to the traditionally understood role religion played in holding the fabric of civilization together, Celsus disputed not only a novel doctrine but a new and potentially dangerous

---

61. On the difficulties of the word *superstitio*, see also Beaujeu, *Religion romaine*, 351; MacMullen, *Paganism*, 74; and L. F. Janssen, "'Superstitio' and the Persecution of the Christians," *Vig. Chr.* 33 (1979): 131–59.

concept of religion altogether. By refusing integration into the *nomos* of its society, Christianity represented a "privatization" of religion, the transferal of values from the public sphere to either a private association or to the individual.[62] This is concomitant with the figure of the holy man himself, who played such a central role in these religious movements, both Christian and pagan. Religious figures such as Alexander, Peregrinus, Jesus, and Apollonius had proprietary rights over their respective revelations and personal power to employ their mysterious forces at their own discretion.[63] Taken together these phenomena threatened to transform the entire structure, and even the very concept, of religious authority in Roman society.

True Doctrine offers eloquent evidence of the vigor of second-century paganism. Far from experiencing a "failure of nerve,"[64] the old religion displays a growth and vitality in its ability to organize its various expressions into a coherent whole, to perceive the nature of the threat against it in such clear terms, and to launch such a thoroughgoing attack against its enemy.[65]

Social Values and Social Order

The profound integration of religious and social thought provides the basis of Celsus's critique of Christianity, and it is on social issues that he presses his attack most vehemently. In the passage cited above (V.25), the preservation of established social conventions is clearly

62. Wilken, *Christians*, 125; see also D. Letocha, "L'affrontement entre le christianisme et le paganisme dans le Contre Celse d'Origène," *Dialogue* 19 (1980): 381f. Hoffmann, 20, notes that the precondition of the growing viciousness of attacks on Christian morality during the second century (to judge from the writings of the Apologists) "was the common preconception among Roman intellectuals that the Christians, in despising the rituals and conventions of imperial civilization, possessed no basis or standard by which to measure the morality of their actions."

63. See Chapter 3, note 68.

64. G. Murray, *Five Stages of Greek Religion*, 3d ed. (Garden City, N.Y., 1951), 119–65.

65. "Die Welt der Frömmigkeit ist darin für ihn zu einer Einheit geworden, daß ihre beiden Pole (rationale Gotteserkenntnis und kultische Dämonenverehrung) von dem gleichen Strom einer altehrwürdigen Tradition leben," Andresen, 77. So also the arguments advanced by the pagan interlocutor in Minucius Felix, *Octavius*, written c. 200 C.E., parallel those of Celsus regarding the antiquity of pagan religion, the secrecy of the Christians, and—as will be seen below—the absurdity of the resurrection and the social and intellectual inferiority of the followers of the new religion; see Benko, *Pagan Rome*, 54ff. and G. W. Clarke, *The Octavius of Marcus Minucius Felix*, Ancient Christian Writers 39 (New York, 1974).

meant as an imperative of natural, human, and divine law. Just as Aurelius's Stoicism gave a philosophical justification for the social status
quo, so Celsus's concept of religion gives it a theological explanation.
By suggesting, in the same passage, the principle that different parts and
peoples of the earth are assigned to specific divine "governors," Celsus
allows for the sacralization of all social custom. There is a direct link
between piety and society, with "custom as king of all" (V.34).[66] The
denial of this imperative is the "original sin" of the Christians. Historically and socially, the Christians are Jews who have abandoned the law
of their ancestors (II.1, 3, 4), just as the Jews themselves, who were
historically ethnic Egyptians, revolted from their ancestors' nation and
religion (III.5). In effect, the Christians are guilty of a double apostacy.
Furthermore, while Jewish worship is at least traditional and specific to
a distinct and identifiable society, the Christian novelty creeps in among
peoples who already have their appropriate deities.[67] So it is that Christians, by refusing to honor the deities of the nations and the other pa-
tron *daimones* that watch over human life, turn themselves into social
outcasts:

> Reason demands one of two alternatives. If they refuse to wor-
> ship in the proper way the lords in charge of the following activ-
> ities, then they ought not to come to marriageable age, nor to
> marry a wife, nor to beget children, nor do anything else in life.
> But they should depart from this world leaving no descendants at
> all behind them, so that such a race would entirely cease to exist
> on earth. But if they are going to marry wives, and beget chil-
> dren, and taste of the fruits, and partake of the joys of this life,
> and endure the appointed evils (by nature's law all men must
> have experience of evils; evil is necessary and has nowhere else to
> exist), then they ought to render the due honors to the beings
> who have been entrusted with these things. And they ought to

66. νόμον πάντων βασιλέα φήσας εἶναι. Celsus is quoting Pindar, frag. 152 Bowra.
See the pertinent discussion in Borret, 3:74ff., 104ff.: "La citation ne peut que résumer ce
qui vient d'être dit sur l'obligation pour chaque peuple de se conformer à l'ordre établi."

67. Lane Fox, 428f., makes a relevant point. Given prevailing anti-Semitism, the strange
rites and "atheism" of the Jews, and their even waging three wars with Rome itself, why
were the Jews not persecuted in the manner of the Christians? The answer lies in the fact
that Jewish religious practice was more familiar to pagan eyes, with a temple and animal
sacrifice—at least before the destruction of Jerusalem. At the same time, Judaism's sheer
antiquity, a quality that provoked veneration among Romans, could excuse many of its
idiosyncrasies. On the social level, Judaism supported values of family life and social
stability similar to those of surrounding pagan society. This last point stands in particular
contrast to the Christian ascetic radicals discussed below.

offer the due rites of worship in this life until they are set free from their bonds, lest they appear ungrateful to them. It is wrong for people who partake of what is their property to offer them nothing in return. (VIII.55)

Like attracts like. So it is that the Christian outcasts can only make their appeal to and convert the very dregs of society:

the vulgar (οἱ ἰδιῶται)[68] and illiterate . . . it is successful only among the uneducated because of its vulgarity and utter illiteracy. (I.27)

[Celsus says] we are unable to convert anyone really good and righteous, and that this is the reason we open our doors to the most impious and abominable men. (III.65)

Whosoever is a sinner, they say, whosoever is unwise, whosoever is a child, and, in a word, whosoever is a wretch, the kingdom of God will receive him. Do you not say that a sinner is he who is dishonest, a thief, a burglar, a poisoner, a sacrilegious fellow, and a grave-robber? What others would a robber invite and call? (III.59)

As their appeal is based upon credulity, the Christians actually drive away the intelligent should they come to them, proclaiming "Let the stupid draw near!" (III.44). Their accustomed prey are therefore slaves, women, and little children (III.18, 44, 50, 59; VI.14; VII.49). The very social status of the Christians, or at least those with whom Celsus is familiar, makes them suspect.[69]

68. The same Greek word, *idiotai*, is used by Lucian to describe Christians, the admirers of Peregrinus, and the ignorant masses in *The Fugitives*. See Chapter 3, note 9.

69. Gallagher, 86, argues that Celsus exploits this suspicion to turn opinion against the Christians who, contrary to what was expected of their class, generally led quite moral lives. Gallagher offers no evidence for this assumption. In effect, he is saying that Celsus knew the Christians to be virtuous and law-abiding and deliberately lied. As will be seen below, pages 162–78, in discussing the Montanists, Gnostics, and other so-called extremist groups, the Christians with whom Celsus was familiar might well have carried on disreputable activities. The assumption that the vast majority of Christians were blameless and harmless, in effect uncritically accepting the bald statements of the Apologists, still pervades scholarship. Though it is extremely difficult to challenge this prejudice after nearly 2,000 years, it should at least be recognized for what it is: an assumption. On the varying social status of Christians in this period, see F. Blanchetière, *Le Christianisme Asiate aux IIème et IIIème siècles* (Lille, 1981), 458ff., and W. Meeks's discussion of the

Celsus, quite obviously, had very clear and distinct perceptions regarding class, and from the fact that these considerations form such a large part of his social polemic, it can be assumed that his ideas had a receptive audience. Celsus is an intellectual aristocrat. Like Lucian, he is a man with a profound belief in the superior accomplishments of the culture of *paideia,* and in the "natural right" of persons of education to lead, admonish, and judge their fellows.[70] The gulf between the classes, between the educated and uneducated, was both sharp and wide, as MacMullen observes:

> We may note in passing the categories that are held up for derision: in cities, petty artisans and people of no fixed place of business, the unpropertied; in the countryside, peasants; also, everywhere, slaves, children, and women. What we do not find in anyone is a sense of distance from some particular ethnic enclave, nor even from life in the backcountry. The line of cleavage that counts is a matter not of place, then, but of cultivation, or, we may say, of culture. That line would correspond very considerably with one of class; but among those managing to attain higher education, there were always some not born to it. Whatever their origin, the educated were exposed to ideas beyond the horizon of the unschooled. Thus they sometimes grew away from the most broadly held beliefs. It is common to find specific distinction made between a theology or a point of creed proper for the masses and another reserved for the learned, for initiates, or for believers specially capable of understanding.[71]

In addition to offering a social explanation for Celsus's allegiance to both philosophical and popular aspects of pagan religion, MacMullen points to the depth of a class distinction that is, at once, cultural, intellectual, social, and economic.

The Christian exaltation of the "poor in spirit" (Matt. 5:3) always carried with it some connotation of economic deprivation, to the point that voluntary ascetical poverty became both a spiritual value in itself

---

first century in *The First Urban Christians: The Social World of the Apostle Paul* (New Haven, 1983), 51–73.

70. I.2: "The Greeks are better able to judge the value of what the barbarians have discovered, and to establish the doctrines and put them into practice by virtue"; cf. VI.1.

71. MacMullen, *Paganism,* 8–9. So also Letocha, 386, speaking specifically of Celsus: "La religion est la sagesse du pauvre. Elle doit être régie par les sages." Origen himself can be just as aristocratic, agreeing that the majority of the poor are persons of bad character (VI.16) and, although praising the life of simple believers (VII.44), agreeing with Celsus that Christians who despise intellectual endeavor should be condemned (III.44).

and a means of attaining poverty of spirit. (The connection with itinerant begging prophets and wonderworkers is apparent.) For Celsus, however, just the opposite is true; being poor in spirit is the equivalent of being inspired by a malevolent spirit.[72] That is to say, the lower classes—unless redeemed by education—can be counted upon to be of the worst character. Any who pander to them, much less exalt them, are giving license for the expression of their inherent vices. To use an analogy from modern European history: the poor are the mob, the Christians are the Jacobins or Bolsheviks who organize them.[73]

This concept generates a number of themes. One already encountered is the repeated accusation of magic and *goeteia*, practices that had a particular appeal to the lower class, including, of course, those members of it who followed Jesus.[74] Another is the characterization of Jesus and the apostles as a band of bandit ruffians.[75] Furthermore, as a Platonist, Celsus can describe the lower classes as those particularly bound to the flesh, unable to see reason and spiritual reality, mired in their own bodily wants (VIII.49). The most pronounced theme to emerge, however, is what Andresen has termed the *Depravationstheorie*, that Christian doctrine is merely borrowed from classical religious tradition and philosophy (VI.1; cf. VI.16 and 19, IV.41, VII.59).[76] The Christians teach nothing new (I.4, II.5), but only a pale corruption of the *alethes logos*. While this theme is certainly intended as an argument for Christians to return to their cultural and intellectual home, it is also a demonstration of how the true doctrine could be mutilated when heedlessly expropriated by the vulgar and semiliterate.[77] Celsus is brutally frank as to who is capable of understanding his exposition of the truth:

72. W. den Boer, "La Polémique anti-chrétienne du IIe siècle. La Doctrine de vérité de Celse," *Athenaeum* 54 (1976): 311f.

73. The latter analogy was coined by Rougier, *Celse contre,* 187.

74. See N. Brox, "Der einfache Glaube und die Theologie: zur altkirchlichen Geschichte eines Dauerproblems," *Kairos* 14 (1972): 161–87.

75. III.59 and II.12, 44; cf. I.62 and II.46. This tradition grew with time until Lactantius, *Div. Inst.* V.3f., could report Hierocles' assertion that Jesus led an association of 900 robbers. See Andresen, 233f.

76. Andresen, 146–66; see also P. de Labriolle, *La Réaction païenne: Etude sur la polémique antichrétienne du Ier au IVe siècle* (Paris, 1934), 118ff. Celsus also accuses Moses of the same sort of plagiarism of the true doctrine (I.21–23).

77. This also sheds light on why Celsus allows allegorical interpretations of mythology and popular cult practices while denying such interpretation to the Christian Scriptures (VI.42; cf. I.27; IV.38, 50–52; VI.30). Allegory is an appropriate tool to demonstrate how the popular religious beliefs of the common folk are expressions of the *alethes logos;* its purpose is merely to expound the true and ancient doctrine to those who embrace it— even in a vulgarized form. It cannot be used as a justification for a doctrine that is in itself a depraved and degenerate twisting of the truth. In intellectual terms, truth (*alethes logos*) has a right to allegory as a vehicle for its dissemination; falsehood does not.

These doctrines I have set forth for men of intelligence. If you
understand any of them, you are doing well. And if you think
that some spirit came down from God to foretell the divine
truths, this may be the spirit which declares these doctrines. Indeed, it was because men of ancient times were touched by this
spirit that they proclaimed many excellent doctrines. If you are
unable to understand them, keep quiet and conceal your own
lack of education, and do not say that those who see are blind
and those who run are lame, when you yourselves are entirely
lamed and mutilated in your souls and live for the body which is
a dead thing. (VII.45)

The Christians prey on the most vulnerable elements of society. These
are not only the gullible, but particularly slaves, women, and children
(III.44). The followers of the new religion, therefore, mount an attack
on the very foundation of society itself: the family.[78] Celsus paints a
lurid portrait of how this happens:

In private houses also we see wool-workers, cobblers, laundry-
workers, and the most illiterate and bucolic yokels, who would
not dare to say anything at all in front of their elders and more
intelligent masters. But whenever they get hold of children in
private and some stupid women with them, they let out some
astounding statements as, for example, that they must not pay
any attention to their father and school-teachers, but must obey
them; they say that these talk nonsense and have no understanding, and that in reality they neither know nor are able to do
anything good, but are taken up with mere empty chatter. But
they alone, they say, know the right way to live, and if the children would believe them, they would become happy and make
their home happy as well. And if just as they are speaking they
see one of the school-teachers coming, or some intelligent person, or even the father himself, the more cautious of them flee in
all directions; but the more reckless urge the children on to rebel.
They whisper to them that in the presence of their father and
their schoolmasters they do not feel able to explain anything to
the children, since they do not want to have anything to do with
the silly and obtuse teachers who are totally corrupted and far
gone in wickedness and who inflict punishment on the children.

78. Historically, of course, the accusation of destroying the family by teaching novel
doctrines to the young was not the sole possession of the uneducated and socially marginal. Socrates was condemned for similar reasons, a point Celsus conveniently forgets.

But, if they like, they should leave their father and their school-masters, and go along with the women and little children who are their playfellows to the wooldresser's shop, or to the cob-bler's or the washerwoman's shop, that they may learn perfec-tion. And by saying this they persuade them. (III.55)

This infiltration of family life is framed in terms of a challenge to the traditional authority of the *paterfamilias,* teachers, and social superiors in general by representatives of the lowest elements of society. The spread of Christianity is described as a rebellion (ἀφηνιάζειν) within the fundamental unit of the social structure. Origen's feeble response, that Christians do not, at least, draw youths from better things and incite them toward the worse as their pagan teachers do, must have only confirmed suspicions that Christianity was disruptive and destruc-tive of fundamental values and "harmful to the life of mankind" (I.26; cf. III.75).[79]

The mention of wool- and laundry-workers seducing women and teaching them novel doctrines recalls the slaves and hirelings in Lucian, who stormed about under the guise of Cynic philosophy (*Fugit.* 28). Alexander, too, was said to be guilty of seduction, under the pretense of religion (*Alex.* 41f.).[80] This scenario has a distinguished pedigree. In 57 C.E., A. Plautius gathered a family *consilium* and sat as *paterfamilias* in judgment on his wife, Pomponia Graecina, for the capital crime of adhering to a "foreign superstition" (*superstitio externa;* Tac., *Ann.* XIII.32).[81] In a less-cited passage regarding another cult described as a *superstitio,* the Roman matron Paulina, a devoted worshiper of Isis, was seduced with the connivance of one of her priests. Tiberius's justice was murderous and thorough, and resulted in the banning of the cult from Rome (Joseph., *Antiq. Jud.* XVIII.65ff.). Celsus's accusations were based on both experience and precedent in his own pagan society.

The proselytizing of youth, in addition to being an attack on the fam-ily, carried even graver implications. In turning children away from their fathers and teachers, the Christians attack *paideia* itself—the pro-

79. The Roman family has been the subject of much recent scholarly interest, see Chap-ter 1, note 31. On the phenomenon Celsus describes here, see W. den Boer, "Gynae-conitis: A Centre of Christian Propaganda," *Vig. Chr.* 4 (1950): 61–64.

80. Such accusations cannot be dismissed as mere *topoi* or the fabrications of invective on the part of Lucian or Celsus, as Robert has shown in the case of Alexander. See Chapter 3, note 7.

81. Cf. the words of the consul from the rostra describing a "prava et externa religio" in Livy's account of the Bacchanalia (XXXIX.8–18).

cess of inculcating the traditional *logos* and *nomos* of society.[82] The new religion is not only the enemy of society; it is the enemy of culture. This is only to be expected, given the baseness of its origin, founder, and membership. Celsus declares plainly that the Christians are foes to learning, intelligence, and wisdom (III.49, 59, 72, 75; VI.12).

Civil discord or disaffection (στάσις, στασιάζειν) is the term Celsus uses repeatedly to characterize the social ethos of Christianity. It is important to note that, for Celsus, the spirit of disaffection with society comes first, and only then produces novelties of doctrine and behavior: "a revolt (στάσις) against the community (τὸ κοινόν) led to the introduction of new ideas" (III.5).[83] Such was the case of the Jews against Egypt and the Christians against the Jews, movements that were both led, it should be added, by sinister self-seeking and self-styled holy men: Moses and Jesus (Moses is also called a *goes*, I.26). The spirit of disaffection, once born, provides the glue that holds the Christians together, even in the face of their bitter internecine conflicts: "However, they have a trustworthy foundation for their unity in revolt and the advantage which it brings and in the fear of outsiders" (III.14). The Christians are guilty of deliberate xenophobia and separatism and seek to create their own society in opposition to that which surrounds them, a new society that can only be created by recruiting (or creating) apostates from *logos* and *nomos*. They are traitors and rebels. According to Celsus, religious innovation stems from social causes—a perhaps surprisingly "modern" and rationalist view, but quite common in classical religious, philosophical, and political thought.

All this social disorder is, of course, predicated upon a religious principle: the Christians worship their new god to the exclusion of all others. In a stunning exegesis of "no man can serve two masters" (Matt. 6:24 and Luke 16:13), Celsus takes this text to refer not only to the rejection of the pagan gods, but of the entire structure of imperial society. It is "the rebellious utterance of people who wall themselves off and break away from mankind" (VIII.2; cf. VII.68).[84] Celsus depicts the

---

82. "Paideia und Palaios Logos hängen aufs engste miteinander zusammen." Andresen, 173.

83. Although Andresen, 216f., would limit the meaning of στάσις and κοινόν strictly to the religious sphere, Borret, 2:22f., correctly argues that Celsus's stated concerns are much broader and are characterized by "un sectarisme conservateur et par l'agressivité contre toute infraction à l'ordre établi—social, racial, religieux et politique."

84. The sentiment is akin to the "hatred of the human race" (*odium humani generis*), which Tacitus attributes both to the Christians (*Ann.* XV.44) and to the Jews (*Hist.* V.5). Euphrates makes the same comment about the Jews to Vespasian in *VA* V.33. Aelius Aristides describes "the impious in Palestine" in just the same way: "For the proof of the impiety of those people is that they do not believe in the higher powers. And these men in

Christians as genuine enemies of humanity, a conscious conspiracy (at least on the part of its leaders) of the intellectually doltish, the socially inferior, and the morally bankrupt.[85] The success of such a movement would spell the end of his civilization.

Of this, Celsus was fearfully aware, and he is the first writer to expound on the clear and present danger the Christians posed to the political survival of the Roman Empire itself. Christians "suffer from the disease of sedition" (τῇ στάσει συννοσοῦντες, VIII.49).[86] Two specific accusations are that Christians refuse to accept public office (VIII.75) and refuse military service (VIII.68, 73). Origen refers to this second accusation in asserting that the Christians are not in "revolt." If the Christians' aim were political revolution, Origen argues, they would not refrain from shedding blood. Yet they absolutely refuse to do this, and so do not join the army and even allow themselves to be slaughtered rather than violently resist persecution (III.8). It is clear that Celsus is speaking of political revolution, so much so that Origen can attempt to deflect the charge by maintaining that the Christians would not engage in armed insurrection. The sort of political revolution Celsus is speaking of, however, is far more subtle and sinister that a coup d'état.

This seditious threat on the part of the Christians also has a religious basis, offering yet another example of the intimate connection between religion and society in the pagan mind. On the one hand, by their fanatical monotheism (VIII.12), the Christians refuse to honor the divine "governors" appointed over various regions of the earth and human affairs (V.25, VII.68). Celsus, drawing an analogy between the divine and human social order, suggests that if human governors, procurators, and other agents of the one emperor could do great harm if offended, surely the *daimones* subordinate to the one Highest God could do greater harm if neglected (VIII.35). On the other hand, by setting up Jesus as a rival to the one Highest God who watched over the empire (VIII.15), the Christians overthrow the Homeric teaching "Let there be one king" (*Iliad* II.205). In so doing "there will be nothing to prevent

---

a certain fashion have defected from the Greek race, or rather from all that is higher" (*Or.* 3.671 in Behr = *Or.* 46 in Dindorf, 2:402). Translation by C. A. Behr, *P. Aelius Aristides. The Complete Works* (Leiden, 1981–86). See Benko, "Pagan Criticisms" for a discussion with citations of all references.

85. To paraphrase Andresen's summary description of Christianity "als Welt ohne Logos," 167, 183.

86. The description of rebellion and sedition as a plague (νόσος) has a long history in classical political vocabulary. It is not new here, but it does make clear that Celsus is speaking of an actual political threat to the state; see Labriolle, 24, 168.

the emperor from being abandoned, alone and deserted," for it is to him that the Highest God has given all earthly power (VIII.67f.).[87]

Celsus focuses on the person of the emperor in his accusations of political sedition. Against the Christians' scruples, he argues that it is only right to propitiate both the governing *daimones* and rulers and emperors (VIII.63) since, according to the hierarchy of authority that extends from the divine to the human realm, the *daimones* receive their authority from the Highest God, and human rulers from that God through the *daimones*. The same is true for swearing by the emperor. Such an oath is actually sworn by God, from whom the emperor's authority comes (VIII.67). In neglecting the emperor in both his human and divine authority, Celsus predicts the very fall of Rome:

> If everyone were to do the same as you, there would be nothing to prevent him from being abandoned, alone and deserted, while earthly things would come into the power of the most lawless and savage barbarians, and nothing more would be heard among men either of your worship or of the true wisdom. (τῆς ἀληθινῆς σοφίας, VIII.68)

In his own view of the imperial social contract, it is the duty of all who share the benefits of the empire and imperial civilization to "help, cooperate, and fight for the emperor" (VIII.73).

In emphasizing the person of the emperor, Celsus raises the level of polemic from specific antisocial acts and attitudes on the part of Christians to those elements of the Christian teaching and association that contradicted the very conception of the state. For Celsus, the Christians' deliberate xenophobia and separatism were the symptoms of their desire to create a society distinct from that which surrounded them. His charges of "an obscure and secret association contrary to the laws" speak to this very point. The Christians possess an unbearable arrogance, believing that all the earth was created solely for them.

> They say: "God shows and proclaims everything to us beforehand, and He has even deserted the whole world and the motion of the heavens, and disregarded the vast earth to give attention to us alone; and He sends messengers to us alone and never stops sending them and seeking that we may be with Him for ever. . . .

---

87. For further discussion, see E. Peterson, *Der Monotheismus als politisches Problem: Ein Beitrag zur Geschichte der politischen Theologie in Imperium romanum* (Leipzig, 1935), and Chadwick, *Contra Celsum*, 503 n. 5, with bibliography.

There is God first, and we are next after Him in rank since He has made us entirely like God, and all things have been put under us, earth, water, air, and stars; and all things exist for our benefit, and have been appointed to serve us. . . ." These assertions would be more tolerable coming from worms and frogs than from Jews and Christians disagreeing with one another. (IV.23)[88]

The Church was a body that existed above any state, and allegiance to Christ took clear precedence over loyalty to any emperor. The Christians set themselves not only apart from but above state and society in a way incomprehensible and inadmissible to pagan thought. E. A. Judge outlines the broader context:

> The philosophical critique of Christianity tells us how the movement was viewed within a limited circle of intellectuals. But their ongoing preoccupation with its illogicality and vulgarity, I believe, correctly identifies the mainspring: the beliefs of the Christians contradicted both the accepted ways of understanding the world and its hierarchy of social values. Beliefs and social action, moreover, were coupled together in a unique manner, with effects unknown before in classical antiquity. An alternative form of community life was being created, and had begun seriously to disorient those who valued the old city-based culture. The persecutions demonstrate the fact that this threat not only arose in the conceit of philosophers, but was taken to heart by government and public as well. The reasons are also clear. The concern was for national security, a fully traditional reaction.[89]

Viewed in pagan terms, the prospect of a Christian Empire was equivalent to extinction. The Christian God had a dismal track-record in looking after those who revered him: the Jews and Christians (VIII.69). Still Celsus is confident that even if a succession of emperors would embrace the new faith, one would come who would succeed in exterminating the Christians before they were able to convert him (VIII.71).

88. Celsus's own opinion in this regard is very Stoic: humanity is but one part of nature and the cosmos, with no reason to consider itself superior, and several reasons to consider itself inferior, to other parts (IV.74–99, passim). On this and Origen's response, see P. R. L. Brown, *The Body and Society: Men, Women, and Sexual Renunciation in Early Christianity* (New York, 1988), 175–77.

89. E. A. Judge, "Christian Innovation and Its Contemporary Observers," in *History and Historians in Late Antiquity,* ed. B. Croke and A. Emmett (Sydney, 1983), 22f.

Fears such as these would not diminish quickly, nor did Origen's response to these assertions give much reassurance to the pagans of his own time. In a pun on the specifically Christian and the broader meanings of the word *ecclesia,* Origen notes that the "church" of contemporary Athens was at peace while the "assembly" of that city was riotous (III.29f.). The pun clearly paints the Church as a superior alternative to political society. Although Origen can admit that the empire prepared the way for the Church, coining an apologetical motif that would become so important in the next century and beyond (II.30), and can envision a Christian Empire (VIII.72), his interest in political and civic matters is mediocre at best. True and lasting value was to be found only in the spiritual realm and the kingdom of his Christ: "En donnant des fondements distincts au religieux (qu'il a redéfini) et au politique, Origène pose les conditions de possibilité de la séparation de l'Eglise et de l'Etat. . . . Hereusement pour son équilibre nerveux, Celse est mort depuis longtemps!"[90]

Asceticism, Heresy, and Second-Century Christianity

Asceticism is linked to the social and religious grounds of Celsus's opposition to Christianity. Although Celsus directly says precious little about ascetical practices, ascetical figures appear throughout *True Doctrine* in the persons of Jesus, the apostles, and other itinerant Christian missionaries, all in the pattern of the figures seen in Lucian and of Apollonius of Tyana. All the elements that cluster about ascetical figures of the period: social deviance and dissent, miracles, prophecy, assertion of personal charismatic authority, accusations of magic, and suspicions of intent to overthrow the social order, are present in Celsus's description of Christianity in the clearest and most dramatic way. On the level of social theory, the separatism and xenophobia that, Celsus contends, characterize the Christian community provide a seedbed for the growth of ascetical practice:

> A group which seeks to seal itself off from external incursion will
> tend to symbolize the desire for absolute community isolation
> through strict control of sexual and dining behavior. In other
> words, a group determined to form a tight "island" community
> in the sea of a larger society will often tend strictly to regulate

90. Letocha, 388.

the exercise of bodily functions, a tendency which has been called "Encratism."[91]

As with the Stoics and Cynics, Celsus's Platonist opinions concerning the body and soul color his perceptions and judgments of ascetic behavior. The soul is the work of the Highest God who can fashion only immortal being; the human body is no different from that of bats or worms (IV.54). The body is inherently corruptible and mortal (IV.59), composed of matter that is inherently the origin of all evil.

> It is not easy for one who has not read philosophy to know what is the origin of evils; however, it is enough for the masses to be told that evils are not caused by God, but inhere in matter and dwell among mortals; and the period of mortal life is similar from beginning to end, and it is inevitable that according to the determined cycles the same things always have happened, are now happening, and will happen. (IV.65)

This is so because matter is the intractable limitation of soul or spirit: "In the existing world there is no decrease or increase of evils either in the past or in the present or in the future. For the nature of the universe is one and the same, and the origin of evils is always the same" (IV.62). It is impious to posit an evil power equal and opposite to the Highest God. For Celsus, there can be no devil or Satan:

> That they make some quite blasphemous errors is also shown by this example of their utter ignorance, which has similarly led them to depart from the true meaning of the divine enigmas, when they make a being opposed to God; devil, and in the Hebrew tongue, Satanas are the names which they give to this same being. At all events these notions are entirely of mortal origin, and it is blasphemy to say that when the greatest God indeed wishes to confer some benefit upon men, He has a power which is opposed to Him, and so is unable to do it. (VI.42; cf. VIII.11)

Souls may be "imprisoned" in bodies due to necessity, sin, or purification (VIII.53); Celsus can only speculate on this particular point. The

---

91. S. L. Davies, *The Revolt of the Widows: The Social World of the Apocryphal Acts* (Carbondale, Ill., 1980), 118, citing M. Douglas, *Natural Symbols: Explorations in Cosmology*, 2d ed. (London, 1973), 92–112. The principle that Davies here applies only to the communities of women he believes to be responsible for the Apocryphal Acts is applicable to Christianity as whole.

body is a dead thing (τῷ σώματι ζῶντες, τουτέστι τῷ νεκρῷ, VII.45).
God may be perceived only by rising above the flesh (VII.36). Hence the
Christian doctrine of the Incarnation is a disgusting blasphemy (VI.73),
while that of the resurrection of the body is repulsive and contrary to
nature, for it is right and natural for the body to perish at death (V.14).

It might be expected that Origen, who proclaims in refutation of
Celsus the clear superiority of the virginal life over marriage (VIII.55),
would be in agreement with his opponent in denigrating the flesh. In
fact, he is not. Origen adopts the Stoic position that the body is morally
neutral and not, by its nature, involved in the cause of evil: "For what is
properly speaking abominable is of the nature of evil. But the nature of
the body is not abominable; for in itself bodily nature is not involved in
evil which is the originating cause of what is abominable" (III.42; cf.
IV.66). It is because of this that Christian doctrine can allow the body
to be brought along in the salvation of the whole human being. Since
the body is a morally neutral instrument, it can be used through the
practice of physical asceticism as a vehicle for salvation.[92] To run a continuum of ascetical theory: for Platonists, the body is evil and useless;
for Stoics it is neutral and useless; for Christians it is neutral and useful.

What then can be said of Celsus's attitude toward asceticism specifically? Some hint is given in VIII.28:

> If they follow a custom of their fathers when they abstain from
> particular sacrificial victims, surely they ought also to abstain
> from the food of all animals—such is the view taken by Pythag-
> oras with the intention of honoring thereby the soul and its or-
> gans. But if, as they say, they abstain to avoid feasting with
> daemons, I congratulate them on their wisdom, because they are
> slowly coming to understand that they are always associating
> with daemons. They take pains to avoid this only at the time
> when they see a victim being sacrificed. But whenever they eat
> food, and drink wine, and taste fruits, and drink even water it-
> self, and breathe even the very air, are they not receiving each of
> these from certain daemons, among whom the administration of
> each has been divided?

Pythagorean abstinence is approved in the first place because it is traditional (πάτριον), but also because its intention is "to honor the soul
and its organs." As in Stoic moral theory, intention is the determiner of
the value of an act, not the act itself. If purity of soul is the intent (and

92. See Nock, *Conversion*, 247ff.

the result), abstinence is praiseworthy.[93] Mention of the governing *daimones* again occurs. This too bears upon the issue of asceticism. These beings have charge of the physical domain of the cosmos, thus *excessive* attention to them and to their functions hold the individual down in the flesh.[94] Christians (and Jews) are in the grip of these *daimones*, partially through the *goeteia* of their founders and leaders and partially through their own stupidity and credulity (VII.35f., 45; VIII.60). Standing on its head the Christian contention that the pagan gods were deceptive demons, Celsus argues that it is the Christians who are actually deceived by demons. Christians are entrapped by an inordinate love of the body—insisting that the Highest God became flesh, an insane blasphemy; so that they may perceive him with their senses, a foolish impossibility since God is pure spirit; and expecting their bodies to live forever with their God, a loathsome prospect (VII.35ff., 45).[95]

It therefore seems reasonable to contend that Celsus would approve, as he clearly does of Pythagorean vegetarianism, of a physical asceticism that had as its aim the purification of the soul from the restraints of matter. Later forms of Neoplatonic asceticism, and even of Iamblichan theurgy, he would have probably considered valid manifestations of the *alethes logos*. Any form of Christian asceticism, on the other hand, that sought to redeem the body physically on the model of Jesus' resurrected flesh, would be a repulsive inanity (V.14).[96] Flawed in the very religious premise from which it had sprung, Christian asceticism was unacceptable simply because it was Christian—regardless of how closely it approximated true virtue.[97]

93. As with Apollonius, asceticism and purity of soul prove that his prophetic powers are those of a wise man (σοφός) not a soothsayer (μάντις). His ascetic diet "lightens" his soul, improves its vision, and brings him closer to the gods; this is what gives him prophetic power.

94. The ambivalent nature of the *daimones* as both good and evil, and their position in Celsus's complex "divine bureaucracy," is explained in clear detail by Hauck, 87–94.

95. J. Perkins, "The 'Self' as Sufferer," *Harvard Theological Review* 85 (1992): 245–72, discusses this new focus on the body in the second century. Like Aurelius, Celsus upholds the older and traditional view, which rejects this preoccupation with the physical in the pursuit of virtue. Perkins demonstrates that this new emphasis was not confined to Christians, and that it constituted "part of a far-reaching cultural discourse that constructed new locations for social control and power" (247).

96. For the sake of clarity, it should be noted that Origen is as harsh as Celsus in his independent, speculative thought on the nature of bodies. In *On First Principles* III.5–6, he states that the initial creation was nonphysical and purely spiritual, and that physical bodies came about only after the Fall and as a result of sin. The discipline of asceticism is, therefore, simply "making the best of a bad situation."

97. See Chapter 2, page 34 and note 35 for Galen expressing this very point. I would contend that this line of reasoning offers further proof that Galen's statement is not so

Origen, for his part, in refuting the charge that Christians do not contribute to the public good or the maintenance of the state by public and military service, holds asceticism to be one of the positive contributions Christians make to society and to the cause of the emperor.

> We who offer prayers with righteousness, together with ascetic practices (ἀσκήσεσι) and exercises (μελέταις) which teach us to despise pleasures and not to be led by them, are cooperating in the tasks of the community. Even more do we fight on behalf of the emperor. And though we do not become fellow-soldiers with him, even if he presses for this, yet we are fighting for him and composing a special army of piety through our intercessions to God. (VIII.73)

Celsus would have, no doubt, been unimpressed by Origen's "army of piety" at least on practical grounds.[98] He would, however, certainly agree that piety and virtue make a contribution, but only if they are expressions of the true doctrine and conform to established norms.[99]

A yet deeper link between asceticism and Celsus's critique of Christianity can be forged by specifying the form of Christianity that best lent itself to Celsus's criticisms. For it is, in fact, a particularly ascetical form of the new religion—found among radical Christian groups and in the religious milieu behind the Apocryphal Acts of the Apostles—that either prompted Celsus's attack or was used by him to show all of Christianity in the worst possible light to a pagan audience. These groups drew Celsus's attention and wrath, offering egregious examples of the most shameful and dangerous violations of established social norms. That Celsus was himself familiar with the various contending sects of the second-century Church is clear; he says so explicitly (III.10, 12). These various factions have but one thing in common—the infamous "name."[100] Celsus hits upon a point vital to the understanding of

---

complimentary to the Christians as it seems. Rather, his point too is that Christian virtue is inherently flawed since it stems from a false premise. It is, in fact, all the more frightening since it mimics true virtue and may lead people to believe that the Christians pose no threat.

98. In the words of Stalin: "How many divisions did you say the Pope had?"

99. As in VIII.75, where Celsus states that public office should be accepted "if it is necessary to do this for the sake of the preservation of the laws and of piety." The conjunction here of law and piety echoes what has been said above regarding the place of religion in the state and the interconnectedness of social norms.

100. Benko, Pagan Rome, 1–29, offers a helpful discussion on the "crime" of the Christian name and its meanings and implications.

second-century Christianity. Christian communities were scattered all over the Roman world and beyond, often unaware of each other's existence and formed as social groups by particular local circumstances. Doctrine could vary, discipline—particularly ascetical discipline—even more so.[101] The scholar of the period must always ask the question: What exactly is lying before the eyes or minds of pagan observers when they speak of "Christians"? Origen is himself aware of the problem, and warns that it is incorrect to generalize about all Christians from the behavior and beliefs of one group (III.44).[102]

Excellent recent studies have illuminated the social history of the early Church.[103] What has emerged is the clear conflict between radical interpretations of the gospel and the idea of accommodating the new religion to its surrounding society. Among the radicals lies a constellation of related themes: poverty or the rejection of property; belief in personal, charismatic authority; the personification of this authority in itinerant prophets; the elevation of women to positions of responsibility and leadership within the group; and, frequently, sexual continence or rejection of marriage. What has not been sufficiently emphasized, however, is that this constellation of deviant social values was manifested and focused in the leading of an ascetical life. The radicals are most often ascetics, and the ascetics frequently held radical beliefs that later would come to smack of heresy. Thus, to pagan observers, Christian ascetic radicals manifested the same dangerous attitudes and behaviors seen in their own deviant ascetics. At the same time and within the Christian Church itself, there were those of the same educated outlook as Aurelius, Lucian, and Celsus who regarded the Christian radicals in much the same way. These more conservative Christians, however, had

---

101. Brown, *Body*, 64. Second-century Christianity was a continuum of beliefs and practices in which categories of "orthodox" and "heretic," themselves applied later by the orthodox and especially by Eusebius's rendering of Church history, do not really apply. This was established by W. Bauer, *Rechtgläubigkeit und Ketzerei im ältesten Christentum* (Tübingen, 1934).

102. See also Benko, *Pagan Rome*, 63f.

103. For example: G. Theissen, *Sociology of Early Palestinian Christianity*, trans. J. Bowden (Philadelphia, 1978); W. Meeks, *The First Urban Christians: The Social World of the Apostle Paul* (New Haven, 1983); and E. S. Fiorenza, *In Memory of Her: A Feminist Theological Reconstruction of Christian Origins* (New York, 1984). See also works cited in the notes below and in the Bibliography. To attempt a complete portrait of second-century Christianity would take several volumes. Even a discussion of the varieties and meanings of Christian ascetical practice in the period would require a separate work. Here it must suffice to summarize certain salient points relevant to this discussion of Celsus.

a way of dealing with their social deviants that their pagan counterparts did not possess; they could label them heretics.[104]

"Heresy" is a loaded word and a misleading one to use when describing second-century Christianity. It presumes an established, normative form of the religion at a time when none existed. Adjectives such as "heretical and orthodox," and even "radical and conservative" (used here for lack of alternatives) necessarily reflect the realities of later historical development; namely, that the conservative segment of the Christian Church eventually prevailed and crowned itself with the epithet "orthodox." In the second century, the situation was much more fluid. If some 1,500 years of "Great Church" historical and theological interpretation is laid aside, it is obvious that what constituted normative Christianity varied depending on which group predominated in any given time and place. There is really nothing to prevent Valentinus or the Apocryphal Acts of the Apostles from being considered representative of normative Christianity within the confines of second-century evidence, and of reading the subsequent history as the triumph of the conservative, anti-ascetical faction over the normative radicals and ascetics.

Put simply, the issue should not be how radical and ascetical interpretations of the gospel came about, but rather how these interpretations—which, it can be easily argued, took the Scriptures at face value—came to be supplanted by the conservative view. In the absence of a commonly recognized authority of either scriptural canon or episcopal magisterium, as would develop later, who was to judge the norm and how could it be defined? In viewing, then, this phase of Church history as a conflict to determine authority, the place of asceticism becomes clear and parallel to the conflict seen in pagan sources. The rigorous life of the ascetic conferred upon him or her a personal authority, often associated with charism, prophecy, and opposition to the competing claims of those in ecclesiastical office.[105] This conflict is evident both in Celsus's attack and Origen's rebuttal.

---

104. Lane Fox, 427, notes that the moral accusations made by pagans against Christians are mirrored in the accusations the "orthodox" make against the "heretics." The fact that Christians themselves spread vicious stories about their coreligionists, corroborating pagan opinion, no doubt aided in the spread of anti-Christian sentiment. See also Benko, "Pagan Criticism," 1081–89, with notes and bibliography.

105. Fiorenza, In Memory, 68–92 and 285–315, is particularly persuasive and eloquent in identifying the nature and development of the conservative faction's interpretation of Church history and theology, and the myth it engendered of the "inevitable" triumph of orthodoxy.

Celsus shows himself fairly conversant with several brands of Gnosticism. He condemns the immoral revels of one group, apparently the Carpocratians (V.63; cf. Clement, *Strom.* II.5). Both Irenaeus and Eusebius hold that it is such libertine Gnostic groups that give other Christians their bad reputation.[106] At another point, Celsus quotes an as yet unidentified Gnostic document to prove that the Christians do not worship the Most High God as they claim to do (VIII.15).[107] In a lengthy passage (VI.24–39) Origen refutes what must have been an equally lengthy and detailed explanation of a Gnostic system, given by Celsus as an exposition of Christian theology. Throughout, Origen repeatedly states that this has nothing to do with Christianity, yet he continues to argue against and deride the system point by point. Why does Origen go on at such length? One suspects that competition for dominance between Origen's brand of Christianity and the Gnostics was still alive, and that Origen availed himself of the opportunity to deride the beliefs of a group he himself knew in Egypt. It is clear that the Gnostics must have continued to pose a threat to the Christianity Origen represented at the time he wrote, for he is repeatedly incensed at Celsus's confusion of "Christianity" and Gnosticism (V.61–65, VI.24ff., VII.25, VIII.15). It is doubtful whether such vehemence could be generated over a decided and dead issue.

Celsus specifies the names of five different Gnostic sects; all with the exception of the followers of Simon Magus are associated with the names of women. Origen claims that, despite diligent research, he has never heard of the sects of Marcellina, Salome, Mariamme, and Martha (V.62).[108] Women continued to play a role in Gnostic belief and practice after such roles had been curtailed, precisely in this period, among more conservative Christians.[109] On the basis of Celsus's direct statements, we can go no further regarding Gnosticism. That Celsus views, or wishes his audience to view, Gnostics as typical Christians is clear—despite protests such as those from Justin.[110] The ascetic character of many

---

106. Iren. *Adv. Haer.* I.20.2; Eus., *HE* IV.vii.9–11.

107. On this document, see H. M. Jackson, "The Setting and Sectarian Provenance of the Fragment of the 'Celestial Dialogue' Preserved by Origen from Celsus' Ἀληθὴς Λόγος," *Harvard Theological Review* 85 (1992): 273–305.

108. See Chadwick's notes on the passage for the known references to these names.

109. For a general introduction to the role of women in Gnostic belief and practice, see E. H. Pagels, *The Gnostic Gospels* (New York, 1979), 48–69. Explaining the process by which women came to be excluded in conservative circles is the purpose of Fiorenza's *In Memory of Her.*

110. Contemporary with Celsus, the orthodox apologist Justin strenuously objected to Gnostics being called Christians, *1 Apol.* 26.

Gnostic groups and texts[111] suggests that it was Gnostic ascetics that, in part, stirred Celsus's ire against Christians as a whole. If, as VI.24–39 implies, he was familiar with a group who sought the laudable goal of escape from the constraints of the flesh by bizarre passwords and foolish rituals, we would have a set of Christians who manifested exactly that sort of depraved plagiarism of the *alethes logos* that so repelled him.

Celsus is also familiar with Marcion (II.27, V.62), so much so that there appears to be a definite connection between their respective attacks on the Old Testament.[112] Origen again is forced to clarify that some of Celsus's objections to Christianity are, in fact, objections to the teaching of Marcion (VI.53).[113] While Celsus may have found some of Marcion's exegesis useful, he was appalled at his impious concept of a second, evil god in opposition to the one Highest Divinity (VI.53 and 42). Depraved religious concepts and asceticism are found side by side here as well, for the Marcionites also preached against marriage and abstained from animals.[114]

Whether Celsus had any experience of Montanists is debatable. His parodying description of the typical Near Eastern wandering prophet, however, does give one pause.

> As Celsus professes to describe the style of prophecy in Phoenicia and Palestine . . . There are many, he says, who are nameless, who prophesy at the slightest excuse for some trivial cause both inside and outside temples; and there are some who wander about begging and roaming around cities and military camps; and they pretend to be moved as if giving some oracular utterance. It is an ordinary and common custom for each one to say: "I am God (or a son of God, or a divine Spirit). And I have

111. See H. Chadwick, "The Domestication of Gnosis," in *The Rediscovery of Gnosticism*, vol. 1, *The School of Valentinus*, Studies in the History of Religions 41 (Leiden, 1980), 3–16, and R. McL. Wilson, "Alimentary and Sexual Encratism in the Nag Hammadi Texts," in *La tradizione dell'Enkrateia, motivazione ontologiche e protologiche: Atti del Colloquio internazionale, Milano 20–23 aprile 1982*, ed. U. Bianchi (Rome, 1985), 317–39. A. B. Kolenkow remarks on the Gnostic argument that the right following of Jesus lay in asceticism, not martyrdom, in "Relationship between Miracle and Prophecy in the Graeco-Roman World and Early Christianity," *ANRW* II.23.2 (1980): 1498.

112. H. Chadwick, *Early Christian Thought and the Classical Tradition* (Oxford, 1966), 26.

113. For sources on Marcion in this passage see Chadwick's notes on the passage, and, in general, A. von Harnack, *Marcion: Das Evangelium von fremden Gott*, 2d ed. (Leipzig, 1924).

114. Iren., *Adv. Haer.* I.28.1, cited also in Eus., *HE* IV.xxix.2.

come. Already the world is being destroyed. And you, O men, are to perish because of your iniquities. But I wish to save you. And you shall see me returning again with heavenly power. Blessed is he who has worshipped me now!". . . . Having brandished these threats they then go on to add incomprehensible, incoherent, and utterly obscure utterances, the meaning of which no intelligent person could discover; for they are meaningless and nonsensical, and give a chance for any fool or sorcerer to take the words in whatever sense he likes. (VII.9)[115]

R. Reitzenstein entertained the idea that this was a description of Montanist prophecy—specifically that of Maximilla in Eus., *HE* V.xvi–xvii—but concluded that the evidence was insufficient.[116] That this description can easily reflect enthusiastic Christian preaching generally is clear. A fundamental issue involved is the date at which Montanus's new prophecy arose.[117] That there are, at least, certain affinities between Celsus's description of the Christians and the Montanists is apparent.

The first, as Reitzenstein noted, is prophecy. Celsus's depiction of Christian missionary activity is that of wandering prophets, preaching on streetcorners and announcing a message of doom, underscoring their point with "possessed" behavior. So Montanus fell into frenzy and convulsions and spoke in strange language (*HE* V.xvi.7); his fellow prophetess Maximilla announced, "I am word and spirit and power" and prophesied great wars and revolutions (V.xvi.17f.). As in Celsus's description of Christian missionaries seducing women, claiming to teach them truth (*C. Cels.* III.44, 55), Eusebius reports that Montanus's prophetesses deserted their husbands the moment they themselves were filled with the spirit (*HE* V.xviii.3). For both Montanus and Marcion, who esteemed virginity and single marriage, women were allowed to

115. Cf. Lucian, *Lover of Lies* 16, for his description of a Syrian exorcist operating in Palestine.

116. R. Reitzenstein, *Hellenistische Mysterien-religionen nach ihren Grundgedanken und Wirkungen*, 3d ed. (Leipzig, 1927), 316; see also Chadwick, *Contra Celsum*, 402 n. 6, for further discussion.

117. An early date, based upon Epiphanius's *Panarion*, would place the rise of Montanism c. 157. A later date, based on Eusebius, places the event c. 182. Attempts to solve the difficulty have yielded further suggestions of c. 177 and c. 170. There is no consensus; discussion in T. D. Barnes, "The Chronology of Montanism," *JTS* 21 (1970): 403–8, and A. Birley, *Marcus Aurelius: A Biography*, 2d ed. (New Haven, 1987), 259f. M. Sordi, "Le polemiche intorno al cristianesimo nel II secolo e la loro influenza sugli sviluppi della politica imperiale verso la Chiesa," *Rivista di Storia della Chiesa in Italia* 16 (1962): 1–28, argues that Montanism was singularly influential in giving imperial authorities a negative impression of Christianity as a whole. Her arguments, however, require the early date for the rise of the prophecy.

teach, baptize, exorcise, and hold office. Contemporary deaconesses
among the conservatives were left with prayer, charity, and tending to
women's needs.[118]

The ascetical element is also present. Montanus taught the dissolution
of marriage (thus allowing the former partners to live in chastity) and
decreed the observance of fasts (*HE* V.xviii.2). Asceticism and prophecy
were accompanied by charismatic leadership on a grand scale. Very
much in the manner of Alexander at Abonuteichos, Montanus transformed his little Pepuza into a religious capital, holding assemblies, ap-
pointing officials to collect money and organize offerings, and salary-
ing preachers of his doctrine (V.xviii.2). Like Alexander's corporation,
Montanus's religious establishment must have appeared frightening to
those who did not share its doctrine. Elements of Celsus's description of
Christian missionaries are also reminiscent of Cynic street preachers
and of Peregrinus, especially in his farewell performance at Olympia,
while Aelius Aristides, another contemporary, compared the Cynics' behavior to that of the "impious in Palestine."[119]

In his masterly analysis of the social world of the Apocryphal Acts of
the Apostles, S. Davies describes a form of Christianity that brings all
the elements seen thus far into sharp focus. Fundamental to his argument is that the Apocryphal Acts are representative of a social reality,
of a religious community of charismatic leaders, celibate women, and
itinerant prophets, characterized by the flagrant abandonment of traditional social codes.[120] Written in the later second and early third centuries in Greece and Asia Minor, the Acts are an important witness to the
diversity of Christianity in the period.[121]

118. Lane Fox, 372, 407.

119. τοῖς ἐν τῇ Παλαιστίνῃ δυσσεβέσι (*Or.* 3.671 in Behr = *Or.* 46 in Dindorf,
2:402). Whether Aristides intended the Christians, Jews, or some particularly eccentric
group within either faith is still debated, though with Behr, *Aristides. Complete Works,*
1:477 n. 745, the Christians in general appear the most likely.

120. Davies's most controversial thesis, that these Acts were written by women in a
loose community of celibates, *Revolt,* 95–129, need not be accepted in recognizing that
the documents themselves refer to an actual social situation. Davies's arguments regarding
authorship are not entirely convincing, but those of Brown, *Body,* 153, that the Acts were
written by men is even less so and entirely too dogmatic. See also V. Burrus, *Chastity as
Autonomy: Women in the Stories of the Apocryphal Acts,* Studies in Women and Religion
23 (Lewiston, N.Y., 1987).

121. On the general consensus on date and place, Davies, *Revolt,* 3–10. Valuable discussions are found in the introductions to the texts in *New Testament Apocrypha,* vol. 2,
ed. E. Hennecke and W. Schneemelcher, Eng. trans. J. B. Higgins, et al. (Philadelphia,
1965). See also Y. Tissot, "Encratisme et Actes Apocryphes," in *Les Actes Apocryphes des
Apôtres: Christianisme et monde païen,* ed. F. Bovon et al., Publications de la Faculté de

Origen is himself familiar with the transient Christian missionary living in poverty (III.9). Earlier, the second-century *Didache* had given clear instructions as to how wandering prophets and apostles are to be tested and treated (*Did.* 11). In the Apocryphal Acts, Jesus' apostles are roaming preachers and miracle workers who condemn not only wealth, but even ownership (A.Jn. 16, ed. James), and urge the giving up of not only homes and possessions, but fathers, mothers, and children (A.Th. 6.61). They themselves renounce and preach the renunciation of the entire social order:

> The apostle's freedom to oppose the normal social order denies to the established authorities moral right to uphold that order. . . . The apostle is set up as a rival to proconsuls, high priests, and kings. Indeed, he represents opposition to any established authority, be it religious, imperial, or local. In his opposition to families the apostle represents opposition to the *sine qua non* of social life; in his opposition to figures of authority he represents opposition to social control.[122]

Had Celsus encountered just one such figure, it would have supplied him with all the ammunition he needed for his polemic. Such was certainly the case for Lucian with Peregrinus. In fact, Davies's description of the apostle's rejection of social life and authority applies equally to the Cynic preachers. The appeal of both apostle and Cynic was based on personal, charismatic authority manifested and confirmed by an ascetical manner of life.

The central focus of the ministry of the apostle in the Apocryphal Acts is the conversion of a woman or women to a life of chastity. The most famous of many such figures is Thecla, the disciple of Paul who, upon hearing the apostle preach, abandons her betrothed and gives up all to follow the apostle in virginity. All the forces of authority are brought against Paul and Thecla as her betrothed, one of the first men of the city, hauls the apostle before the proconsul. Thecla is summoned and, upon displaying her utter devotion to Paul, her own mother demands she be burned! (A.Pl. 2.7–21). Here and throughout the other Acts, the apostle is repeatedly accused of *goeteia*, particularly for en-

---

théologie de l'Université de Genève 4 (Geneva, 1981), 109–19; J. Perkins, "The Apocryphal Acts and the Early Christian Martyrdom," *Arethusa* 18 (1985): 211–30; and the limited bibliography in Davies, 131–34.

122. Davies, *Revolt*, 34.

couraging women to abandon their men and devote themselves to chastity (e.g., A.Th. 10.130, 11.134, passim). In this regard, the Apocryphal Acts reflect an accurate historical picture, as this same accusation was used regularly against pagan ascetics and social deviants. The theme of the seduction of women also recurs, as it had with the Montanist prophetesses, Celsus's stories of Christian missionaries, various pagan women involved in cults of *superstitio,* and in the Cynics of Lucian's *Fugitives* who "claim to turn women too into philosophers" (18f.).[123]

The Apocryphal Acts, perhaps more clearly than any other source, illustrate the paradox concerning women in antiquity. By renouncing marriage, women released themselves from a plethora of social bonds, roles, and expectations and opened for themselves new areas of independent achievement. Women in the Acts possess definite religious power: Drusiana raises Fortunatus from the dead (A.Jn. 81ff.), Thecla baptizes herself (A.Pl. 2.34) and her prayer translates the departed soul of a young girl to Paradise (A.Pl. 2.28). Both characters become confessors facing the threat of martyrdom for the sake of their chastity— Drusiana out of conscience (A.Jn. 64), Thecla out of refusal to play her expected social role (A.Pl. 3.26f.)—saving themselves from the desires of lustful men. Such "liberation," especially when coupled with devotion to a *superstitio prava et externa,* was greeted by the men of this society with horror.[124]

It is evident, therefore, that Celsus would have found sufficient grounds for his contention that Christians posed a threat to the social fabric of the empire among the radical, ascetical factions of the new religion. The groups Celsus specifically mentions and contemporary apocryphal literature manifest a form of Christianity that emphasized personal charismatic authority, enthusiastic prophecy and / or secret and arcane knowledge, sexual renunciation, and the promotion of women to positions of responsibility. All these phenomena lay outside the *nomos* of the received culture and, therefore outside the control of its social norms. As such, they constituted a threat, especially since they subverted society at its very foundations: overturning traditional sexual roles, rejecting commonly held values, and supplanting traditional wis-

---

123. Meeks, 23ff., offers a brief, insightful résumé of the issues involved in women and pagan religion during the period.

124. Brown, *Body,* 61, on chastity as conveying a status "open to talent." This paradox of feminine advancement as it evolved in the fourth and fifth centuries has received an outstanding treatment in E. A. Clark, "Ascetic Renunciation and Feminine Advancement: A Paradox of Late Antique Christianity," *Anglican Theological Review,* 9 (1981): 240– 257 = *Ascetic Piety and Women's Faith: Essays in Late Ancient Christianity,* Studies in Women and Religion 20 (New York, 1986), 175–208.

dom by new revelations. Given the varieties of second-century Christianity, there is no reason to assume that Celsus either misrepresented or exaggerated the threat he perceived.

Evidence from orthodox Christian sources further confirms this view and reveals similarities in attitude and argument between ecclesiastical conservatives and pagan intellectuals. Davies notes that the social situation within the Church represented by the Acts is triangular, composed of charismatic apostles, continent women, and men whose authority stemmed from holding ecclesiastical office.[125] As established authority figures whose power came not from charismatic inspiration but from hierarchical structure, ecclesiastical leaders are painted in the same negative light as traditional social and political authorities. This antithesis exists among the earliest surviving records of the Christian community. Ignatius of Antioch, en route to his martyrdom c. 100, wrote to a fellow bishop:

> Tell my sisters to love the Lord and to be altogether contented with their husbands. Similarly urge my brothers in the name of Jesus Christ "to love their wives as the Lord loves the Church." If anyone can live in chastity for the honor of the Lord's flesh, let him do so without ever boasting. If he boasts of it, he is lost; and if he is more highly honored than the bishop, his chastity is as good as forfeited. (*Poly.* 4.2)[126]

The passage clearly illustrates not only the tension between the charismatic authority of the celibate and the hierarchical authority of the bishop, but also how this issue relates to the preservation of accepted social norms and roles. Ignatius's first admonition is for women to be contented in their marriages. If marriage and traditional family life are stressed as positive Christian virtues, the challenge posed by the celibates to institutional ecclesiastical authority would be diminished.[127]

The ascetics and radicals clearly recognized this alternative source of authority. When their new prophecy had been questioned by the bishops, the Montanists appealed for support to the confessors of Lyon (Eus., *HE* V.iii.4). Confronted by hierarchical authority, the radicals

---

125. Davies, *Revolt,* 87.

126. Translation by C. C. Richardson in *Early Christian Fathers,* ed. C. C. Richardson (New York, 1970), 119.

127. On this issue, see E. H. Pagels, "Adam and Eve, Christ and the Church: A Survey of Second Century Controversies Concerning Marriage," in *The New Testament and Gnosis: Essays in Honor of Robert McL. Wilson,* ed. A. H. B. Logan and A. J. M. Wedderburn (Edinburgh, 1983), 146–75.

appealed to the higher charismatic authority of those who had proved steadfast in the face of martyrdom.[128]

Foremost among the conservative figures of the second-century Church is Clement of Alexandria (c. 150–c. 215), Origen's predecessor in the catechetical school of that city. Three of his works are of particular importance here. The first, *Stromateis*, Book III, contains a lengthy discussion defending marriage. Clearly the conservatives perceived themselves under attack on this point. That celibacy was *recommended* by the Scriptures could not be denied; the issue at stake was to argue that it was not *required* for salvation. Clement's ultimate answer lies in chaste marriage, which is described as freedom from passion—*apatheia* (*Strom.* III.7.58).[129] What Clement does, in effect, is allow virginity to remain an ethical ideal in a way that does not violate social norms. The appearance of marriage is maintained, as are the roles and expectations for women that are implied in marriage.[130]

Conformity to social norms is of great importance to Clement, as seen in his *Paedagogos*, Books II and III. Here Clement offers a vastly elaborated "household code," distinctly bourgeois in tone and clearly reflective of what Fiorenza terms the orthodox "patriarchal" tradition.

128. The most notable instance of the exercise of authority by the confessors is the *libelli* controversy with Cyprian, bishop of Carthage (Cyp., *Epp.* IX, X, XV–XVI, XIX, XXIX). Confessors of the Decian persecution (249 C.E.), on their own authority and by the merits of the martyrs, were reconciling Christians who had falsely obtained certificates of sacrifice to avoid persecution. Thus, even well into the third century Christians could still look to sources of religious authority alternative to that of the bishops. The same is true regarding prophecy; see Lane Fox, 410. The radical and ascetical character of Christianity was preserved in Syria even longer, see M. Vööbus, *A History of Asceticism in the Syrian Orient: A Contribution to the History of Culture in the Near East*, 3 vols., Corpus Scriptorum Christianorum Orientalium (CSCO) 184, 197, 500; Subsidia 14, 17, 81 (Louvain, 1958–88). Consequently, Lane Fox is incorrect when he describes the danger posed by the Apocryphal Acts as expressing "ideals that came near to *accepted* Christian perfectionism" (358). The entire issue is that the proper place and expression of asceticism within Christianity had not yet been established. The Apocryphal Acts reflect the fact that the debate was still open in the mid-second century. In general, Lane Fox places the establishment of "orthodoxy" too early (see 332) and thus fails to give full significance to the debates that continued well on through the third century over issues of asceticism and authority.

129. In response to Celsus's argument that Christians should not marry or bear children since they do not honor the *daimones* (VIII.55), Origen states that marriage is *allowed* only for those who are not capable of the superior life of celibacy. It is, of course, this solution to the problem—the creation of two "classes" of believers, of which the superior follows the radical counsels of perfection—that ultimately triumphs. This solution, too, preserves the social norm of marriage and offspring, but only as an inferior status.

130. A convenient summary of Clement's views on women and sexuality is offered by Brown, *Body*, 122–39.

Pagan literature, especially the comic poets, and Christian Scripture are quoted side by side. The aim is clearly to show the commonality of values between pagan culture and Christian doctrine, but the level is hardly exalted. One example may suffice. *Paed.* II.2.4–14 is a long discourse against vanity, aimed at women. Though an opportunity for lofty moralizing presents itself, Clement prefers to argue in mundane, practical terms: vain women have little care for managing the household expenses for their husbands (II.2.5).

Clement's acceptance of the prevailing social order is most evident in a treatise aimed against the advocates of evangelical poverty: *Who Is The Rich Man Who Shall Be Saved?* The question of property and wealth is approached with the same method of internalization seen earlier in the Stoics,[131] and with the same care to preserve both the spiritual virtue and societal norm seen in his teaching on marriage. Jesus' command to the rich young man (Matt. 19:16–26; Mark 10:17–26; Luke 18:18–27) is not to become destitute, but to be *spiritually detached* from wealth (*Rich Man* 11). That is why the disciples, who were themselves poor, were troubled by this saying (20). Wealth is indifferent in itself (14); the real issue lies with the inner disposition of the individual and with passion (12, 15). Wealth can even be a blessing when used for almsgiving (13f., 22, 24).[132] In his defense of the prevailing social order and his emphasis on the internal aspects of virtue, Clement can rightly be termed the last of the Christian Stoics.[133]

Christian ascetics, and the radical social agenda that grew out of their beliefs, were perceived as a threat by educated conservatives both within and without the Church. It is certainly not surprising that acceptance of the new faith would actually do little to change the pride in the accomplishments of *paideia* and of the empire that was the hallmark of the cultured. The opponents of the radical separatists in the Church were the conservative integrationists, those with a vested interest, by virtue of education or class, in the preservation of the social structure.[134]

131. See Chapter 2, page 36 and note 41.

132. On the trajectory of this line of thinking among the Church Fathers, see G. E. M. de Ste. Croix, *The Class Struggle in the Ancient Greek World*, corrected ed. (Ithaca, N.Y. 1989), 433–48. On this subject in general, see the excellent treatment by L. W. Countryman, *The Rich Christian in the Church of the Early Empire: Contradictions and Accommodations* (Lewiston, N.Y., 1980).

133. J. M. Rist, *Stoic Philosophy* (Cambridge, 1969), 289.

134. Fiorenza, *In Memory*, identifies these as "middle class males," 90–92, or "the propertied class," 253. Lane Fox, 509f., speaks of the laity's preference for men of social position and property as candidates for the episcopate, men who were brought up in an atmosphere of responsibility and leadership. Cyprian himself is a prime example of this phenomenon. Origen has harsh words for haughty bishops and for the snobbishness of

Despite their profession of Christianity, figures such as Clement of Alexandria must be counted among Aurelius, Lucian, Dio Chrysostom, and—paradoxically—even Celsus in their opposition to radical asceticism and its concomitant social values and behaviors.

Toward a United Front

In his attack upon Christianity, Celsus gives further articulation to the social and cultural assumptions and values of men like Aurelius, Lucian, and Philostratus. His defense of his civilization is not only an apology for its religion, society, politics, and culture. It is above all an exposition of the very concept of classical civilization—the unbreakable and inviolable unity of all its component parts. This is the *alethes logos*: the unity that both expresses and transcends religion, society, politics, and culture, and that *paideia* which, being far more than simply "education," was the means of initiation into the attitudes, values, and life of classical civilization at its fullest. If Celsus is an intellectual aristocrat, it is because only such an aristocrat could have a full appreciation for the complex values and accomplishments of his culture and society.

But the *alethes logos* should not be confined to so few. Celsus realized this, though scholars have failed to see the point. By his use of allegory and his defense of oracles, popular cults, and prodigies such as the healings of Asclepius, Celsus brings common pagan belief into the philosophically refined true doctrine. The unity of Celsus's system applies not only to the various aspects of his civilization, but to the various levels of his society. *True Doctrine* is an expression of the attempt to reunify higher and lower religion and culture, philosophical and popular belief, into one embracing system. Divided since the days of the birth of Ionian science and Attic philosophy, intellectual culture and popular practice existed side by side in an often uneasy mixture, of which Cicero's *de Natura Deorum* is a prime example.

Beginning in the second century, an attempt was made to resolve this dichotomy. It is not a sign of the decadence of intellectual life, but of its very vigor, that the educated sought to reincorporate what post-Enlightenment scholars have disdainfully termed "magic and superstition," and

families with a long history in the faith, especially if there had been a bishop in their lineage (*Comm. in Matt.* 15.26, 16.6). Within a decade of Origen's death, Paul of Samosata was parading through the agora of his episcopal city surrounded by a choir of virgins and styling himself as a Roman governor; see Eus., *HE* VI.xliii.11–12, VII.xxx.8–9.

what are in fact traditional pagan religious expressions, into a single comprehensive and comprehensible belief system. Philostratus's *Life of Apollonius,* in uniting the popular and philosophical images of his hero, is another step in this process. Not all attempts were successful, as Iamblichus's combination of philosophy and theurgy and Julian's attempted revival of pagan cult demonstrate. In the opinion of one scholar, the task was finally consummated (but only after the triumph of Christianity) in a little pamphlet from the middle of the fourth century—Sallustius's *de Deis et Mundo.*

> It is more or less an intelligible whole, and succeeds better than most religions in combining the two great appeals. It appeals to the philosopher and the thoughtful man as a fairly complete and rational system of thought, which speculative and enlightened minds of any age might believe without disgrace. . . . At the same time this religion appeals to the ignorant and humble-minded. It takes from the pious villager no single object of worship that has turned his thoughts heavenwards. It may explain and purge; it never condemns or ridicules. In its own eyes that was its greatest glory, in the eyes of history perhaps its most fatal weakness. Christianity, apart from its positive doctrines, had inherited from Judaism the noble courage of its disbeliefs.[135]

The Christians threatened to destroy this supreme accomplishment on the very verge of its consummation. In its endeavor to replace the unity of religion, society, and culture with supreme allegiance to a god who transcended civilization, radical Christian ascetics served as shock-troops. Their practice, even more than their beliefs, imperiled the survival of Celsus's society. One may wonder whether Celsus could have "negotiated" with someone like Clement, but the very existence of the radicals who also bore the "name" eliminated the hope of any compromise with Christians. Experience with pagan ascetics, deviants, radicals, and holy men proved this. The radical Christians bore all the worst characteristics of a Peregrinus or Alexander, but were even more dangerous since they were an organized group—a corporate *goes* or mass movement of *goeteia.* In the long term, it would be up to the bishops and theologians, leaders and intellectuals with an interest in established society and the empire, to do something themselves about the Christian radicals if their own hopes of a Christian Empire were to be fulfilled.

135. G. Murray, 184. The author appends a translation of Sallustius to his work, 191–212.

C h a p t e r   S i x

ॐ

ASCETICS AND HOLY MEN:

Conflict, Change, and Continuity

THE SECOND CENTURY WAS, in many ways, a watershed in the history of asceticism in antiquity. It began with the physical moderation and cerebral moral rigor of Epictetus and ended with Philostratus's exaltation of a miracle-working, physically rigorous Pythagorean in Apollonius of Tyana. Between these two poles lies a conflict in social and cultural norms and values between the practitioners of self-conscious physical asceticism and the upholders of traditional authority.

Inheriting and amplifying the Roman Stoicism that was his intellectual patrimony, the emperor Marcus Aurelius simultaneously manifests respect for ascetical ideals and dogmatic adherence to the political and social status quo. The latter takes clear precedence over the former, and any sympathy for ascetic ideals ends when it verges on deviance or dissent. The great paradox is that both these attitudes derive from the same Stoic doctrines of adherence to reason and nature, the practice of *apatheia* and *ataraxia,* and submission to fate. Deviants or dissenters show, by their very actions, their rejection of these precepts common to all humanity. Spurning the common law of humanity, they bring upon themselves the most severe punishments as rebels from the cosmos itself. Aurelius's relentless pursuit of the logic of these principles in his own mind resulted in a new degree of severity and a new emphasis on the force of law. The final paradox is that this conscientious and altruistic ruler thus left to posterity, in his *Meditations,* a philosophical justification for totalitarianism. Aurelius may well be seen as the intellectual forerunner of the systematic persecutions of Christians in the third century and of the rigidity and domination that was to characterize the new empire of Diocletian and Constantine. The voice of authority could find no more eloquent spokesman.

The distinction, then, between acceptable and unacceptable asceticism hinged upon adherence to traditional norms and values. The sort of asceticism advocated by the Stoics and practiced by Aurelius, with its emphasis on ethics and the internal dynamics of the individual psyche, was constituted precisely to allow individuals to better perform their traditional social roles and functions. Indeed, it elevated these conventions to the level of moral obligations. Physical asceticism, however, tended to do just the opposite. In manifestly rejecting such institutions as property and marriage, radical ascetics placed themselves in opposition to accepted values and thereby posed a threat to the social order.

These ascetics are found in a variety of forms in the second century. Foremost among them were the Cynics who, from the days of Diogenes, used the practice of rigorous physical asceticism as a witness to their anarchic doctrines, which rejected political authority, private property, marriage, and social decorum. In publishing these beliefs, their street-corner demagoguery posed a repeated threat to civic order. In the person of Peregrinus, however, traditional Cynicism took on a new coloring. To the rejection of constituted authority, Peregrinus adds his own claim to personal, charismatic leadership—culminating in and sealed for posterity by his suicide at Olympia and the miraculous stories told after his death. In the person of Peregrinus, enmity to social norms and demagoguery assumes the characteristics of personality cultism and religious superstition, validated and expressed as a whole by ostentatious ascetical accomplishments. In this way, Lucian was able to connect Peregrinus's asceticism with *goeteia* and to portray the ascetic as but another species of that throng of charlatans, wonderworkers, and prophets that traveled the empire of the second century. As Lucian's flattering portrait of Demonax makes clear, it is not so much Cynic doctrine that irked Lucian, but the degree to which Peregrinus practiced it and the use to which he put the credentials gained from it. Peregrinus's combination of Cynic social nihilism with the methods and appeal of the *goes* constituted an attack upon the very ideals and idea of classical culture. A world left to the likes of ascetics such as Peregrinus would have no room for the vanities of art, literature, reason, or education, or for those living embodiments of classical *paideia* such as Antoninus Pius and Herodes Atticus, men whom Peregrinus publicly ridiculed.

This connection of asceticism and *goeteia* is further elaborated by the figure of Apollonius of Tyana. In the negative traditions concerning him prior to Philostratus, it is clear that Apollonius's practice of Pythagorean asceticism laid him open to charges of atheism, sinister magic, and pretensions to divinity. His distinctive manner of life, embracing poverty, vegetarianism, chastity, and idiosyncratic religious practice, brought him under suspicion as displaying the sort of extreme behavior the Stoics considered both irrational and antisocial. It is no accident that in Philostratus, Apollonius's nemesis is the foremost Stoic of his time: Euphrates. Intimately connected with Apollonius's asceticism were his *thaumata:* prophecy, healing, and miracle working, which only served to increase suspicion and confirm the verdict that he was nothing more than a *magos* and "false philosopher." Thus Philostratus, in writing his biography, had first to face the task of exonerating his hero of these suspicions and accusations.

The pagan society of the second-century empire had ample experience of the danger ascetics could pose, and a clear criterion for determining acceptable ascetical practice. So it was that the historical Jesus and his contemporary followers presented themselves to the eyes of Celsus as known quantities.[1] The Nazarene is simply a *goes* in the manner of a Peregrinus, Alexander, or Apollonius. The Christians are a dangerous rabble, seduced and suborned by their preachers in the manner of Cynic demagogues or by the mumbo-jumbo characteristic of the *goetes*. They reject reason and the classical tradition, making themselves enemies of culture. They are disloyal to the emperor, making themselves rebels. Most important, they attack the very foundations of society, seducing women and children, turning them from the authority of fathers, husbands, and teachers. They abstain from normal social intercourse, believing themselves an elect and separate society. Celsus's descriptions and condemnations echo the social thought of Aurelius, so much so that it has been suggested that the former was actually a mouthpiece for the emperor, delineating his reasons for a harsh policy against the adherents

---

1. Thus the characterization of Christian asceticism as a "flagrant antithesis to the norms of civilized life in the Mediterranean," P. R. L. Brown, *The World of Late Antiquity* (London, 1971), 98f., and P. Cox, *Biography in Late Antiquity: A Quest for the Holy Man* (Berkeley and Los Angeles, 1983), 28 n. 53, applies equally as well to numerous forms of pagan asceticism. It is vital to keep this in mind lest Christian asceticism be portrayed as an utterly new phenomenon to the Roman world, and the important point of its familiarity to pagan observers—and thus the prejudice of suspicion against it—be overlooked.

of the new religion.[2] Experience with their own ascetics confirmed the
reality of this threat to pagan observers, and the behavior of radical
ascetical groups among the Christians made the danger all the more
alarming.

Marcus Aurelius, Lucian, and Celsus present an attitude toward ascetics that can be taken as characteristic of the educated and ruling
classes of the period. It is one of suspicion of deviants who, by their
statements and personal example, express discontent with the status
quo, advocate alternative norms and values to those of the prevailing
culture, and arrogate to themselves a personal authority superior to that
of the structures and institutions of their society. Whether springing
from Aurelius's Stoic philosophy, Lucian's veneration of the culture of
paideia, or Celsus's insistence on the demands of historical tradition,
this attitude has as its hallmark an aggressive social conservatism that,
in all cases, entailed severe repercussions for those who would not conform.

The dominance of social and cultural issues in this conflict is further
demonstrated by Philostratus's rehabilitation of Apollonius. Throughout the *VA*, Philostratus seeks to prove that the very behaviors that
bring Apollonius under suspicion are, to the contrary, rooted in classical tradition and serve to promote prevailing norms and values. Apollonius's doctrine and practice are that of Pythagoras, and no stranger
than that of the hallowed figures of Empedocles, Democritus, and Plato.
His *thaumata* stem not from magic but from his philosophical life and
particularly from his ascetical practice. His life, in Philostratus's depiction, is characterized by the ardent promotion of civic harmony, ancestral religion, and the old-time virtues. Thus Philostratus defenced his
hero against the slanders and accusations that clustered around his ascetic manner of life precisely by portraying him as a veritable evangelist
of social conservatism. Apollonius is made not only to conform to, but
to champion, the attitudes and values of Aurelius, Lucian, and Celsus.

Apollonius's relations with emperors are particularly illustrative. In
the face of Nero, he is the heroic martyr, ready to face the enemy in his
stronghold. He is a figure of opposition, but in the consecrated tradition
of the Stoic "martyrs" of the first century. In associating Apollonius in
this way with these Stoics, he is shown to be not a revolutionary but, to
the contrary, a defender of political tradition. Apollonius was an active
participant in the intrigues against Domitian that eventually brought

2. See M. Sordi, "Le polemiche intorno al cristianesimo nel II secolo e la loro influenza
sugli sviluppi della politica imperiale verso la Chiesa," *Rivista di Storia della Chiesa in
Italia* 16 (1962): 17ff.

Nerva to the throne, a case that again allied him with the senatorial aristocracy. Yet, Philostratus is careful to portray his hero as no archaizing republican. When not dealing with a tyrant, Apollonius is a hearty advocate of monarchy. Dismissing the arguments advanced, significantly, by the Stoic Euphrates, it is he who presents the clinching argument in favor of Vespasian's taking the throne. In arguing that the rule of the best man is the equivalent of democracy, Apollonius offers a philosophical justification for the Roman political ideology that would have made even Panaetius envious.

In focusing on the conflict and polemic between asceticism and authority, this study may have insufficiently emphasized one important fact. The very existence of conflict and polemic means that the deviant ascetics were, to a large measure, successful. Cynic preachers did attract the popular following they sought in the cities. Lucian's diatribe against the deceased Peregrinus was obviously aimed at his living devotees. Apollonius possessed a notoriety that allowed him to be resurrected in literature a century after his death. The followers of Jesus eventually took over the empire itself. The prominence of this conflict in the second century is not simply apparent, produced by the chance survival of evidence or mere cultural trends and literary tastes. The ascetical conflict of the second century was a social reality and an urgent matter for the defenders of the status quo. Asceticism had held a constant appeal to those who were in some way disenchanted with the prevailing mores and structures of their societies. The forces and issues that clustered about asceticism in antiquity—ever since Diogenes moved into his clay tub and snubbed Alexander the Great—came to a head at this time.

The conflict over, and eventual triumph of, asceticism should not be cast in terms of a debate on the holy, or of a reaction against rationalism and a rise in superstition and credulity, but in terms of the nature of power in society. On the one side is structure, institution, authority, and accepted norms, on the other is inspiration, individualism, charismatic leadership, and alternative values. So long as the latter nexus was perceived as antithetical to and destructive of the former, the radical ascetic, who was the locus of these phenomena, would remain suspect and an enemy to the prevailing social order.

Herein lies the importance of Philostratus's work. By depicting Apollonius as the defender of traditional norms and values, a model was created whereby the appeal of the ascetic and the power of his charismatic authority could be allied to the status quo. Apollonius is, in his private life, deviant, but he is no apostle of Pythagoreanism. His manner of life is a personal choice, suitable only for him. Indeed, his life is portrayed as heroic, extraordinary, beyond the capabilities of the average person. Superiority is accompanied by separatism. Deviance is thus safely locked away as the prerogative earned by the accomplishments of the ascetic few, and emphatically not a prescription for the many.[3] The power that accrues to Apollonius from his manner of life is explicitly not used for self-glorification or to seize leadership of a group. Instead it is wielded to urge others to conform to the established dictates of social, religious, and political conduct. Philostratus does not depict a philosopher as a charismatic holy man. Rather, he portrays a figure already invested with many of the characteristics of the charismatic holy man found throughout antiquity as a "philosopher," which, in this case, specifically means a traditional figure subscribing to traditional ideals. What then constitutes the novelty of the "Late Antique Holy Man," about which so much has been written, is not his charismatic authority or his *thaumata*, but his society's perception and judgment of him. It is this change in perception and judgment that allowed him to be transformed from a suspicious, liminal figure into a bulwark of the established order.[4]

This transformation of the ascetic corresponds to other developments in the second century. As seen in Celsus, a process was under way to reconcile the dichotomy that had existed in pagan religion from the fifth century B.C.E. onward of "rationalism for the few, magic for the many."[5] Celsus posits a religious system that, through the use of alle-

3. G. Fowden, "The Pagan Holy Man in Late Antique Society," *JHS* 102 (1982): 33–59, notes the progressive marginalization of pagan holy men, especially Neoplatonic philosophers, in the third century and beyond. This would appear to be a development from the initial separatism discussed here. Yet it is important to realize, as Fowden, 56–59, admits, that these figures still possessed recognized position in, and performed important services for, their society. These holy men remained "connected" to the social order; marginalization does not necessarily mean withdrawal. Furthermore, in those cases Fowden adduces of genuine flight from the world among pagans, it is possible to see some form of influence from the Christian monastic ideal of *anachoresis*. His broader argument, however, that this marginalization of its leadership hamstrung any attempt at pagan revival in relation to Christianity, is acute and accurate. Perhaps it can be said that Athanasius was more clever and successful than Philostratus and his pagan successors in exploiting marginal ascetic figures for their leadership potential; see the end of this chapter.

4. If, as stated by P. R. L. Brown, *The Making of Late Antiquity* (Cambridge, Mass., 1978), 8, "the changes that came about in Late Antiquity can best be seen as a redistribution and a reorchestration of components that had already existed in the Mediterranean world," the so-called rise of the holy man offers a prime example of this. The holy man had existed for centuries with essentially the same set of characteristics and behaviors. What changed was his society's view of him. He did not so much rise of his own accord as he was elevated, once the threatening aspects of his power and behavior were safely defused.

5. E. R. Dodds, *The Greeks and the Irrational*, Sather Classical Lectures, 25 (Berkeley and Los Angeles, 1951), 192, borrowing an elegant phrase from Jacob Burckhardt.

gory and historical argument, unites philosophical doctrine and popular belief as merely different expressions of the one ancient and established doctrine (*alethes logos*) regarding the nature of the gods and their relation to humanity. The process was one of fusion, in which modern labels and prejudices regarding reason and superstition cease to apply.[6] Likewise, the figure castigated as a *goes* by skeptics and revered as a holy man by believers was essentially a product of popular, "irrational" belief. Thus his followers were disdained as yokels, rabble, or slaves. By rehabilitating this figure as a philosopher, Philostratus's *Life* parallels developments in philosophy and religion by uniting in one person the religious "hero" of the upper and lower classes. Again, the work is one of fusion—a work that, as stated earlier, is correctly characterized as one of intellectual vigor rather than degeneration. These developments are not only parallel, but connected. As the difference between upper- and lower-class religion narrowed, and their division became more a matter of complexity or depth of explanation, intercessors for divine favor became more widespread in persons who were, at once, both holy men and philosophers. The difference is one of emphasis rather than innovation.[7]

Shorn of his social threat and exalted into a hero beyond the reach of ordinary mortals, the ascetic philosopher *cum* holy man became central to Neoplatonism in the persons of Plotinus, Porphyry, and Iamblichus. The defense of the status quo thus continued in the same way it had been conducted in the second century, but with a new source of authority to bolster traditional values in model, heroic ascetics. Such is the case in Hierocles' biography of Apollonius, *Philalethes,* the work that so enraged Eusebius, written by one of the leading forces behind Diocletian's persecution. In a final process of fusion, the forces of political authority, traditional religion, cutting-edge philosophy, and asceticism all unite in defense of the pagan Roman social order against its ultimate enemy: Christianity.

6. The same process may be seen in second-century medicine, where both scientific and spiritual healing made advances, existing side by side with no perceived contradiction or competition; see G. W. Bowersock, *Greek Sophists in the Roman Empire* (Oxford, 1969), 70.

7. R. MacMullen, *Paganism in the Roman Empire* (New Haven, 1981), 72f. MacMullen, however, sees this development as evidence for the "decline in rationalism," a position that, I hope, has been sufficiently discredited. See, for example, the view of C. Robinson, *Lucian and His Influence in Europe* (Chapel Hill, N.C., 1979), 46, that reaction against rationalism as an explanation for the second century's interest in the metaphysical would, at most, only hold true for the intelligentsia, and that the broader influences on this development were social in nature.

These issues regarding pagan asceticism have important ramifications
for the understanding of the growth and development of Christian asceticism as well. Conservative men of culture within the Church found
radical Christian ascetics objectionable in the same way as their counterparts outside the Church. Within Christianity, the ascetics, with their
claims to charismatic authority, posed the same sort of threat to hierarchical authority as they did to the institutional authority of the state.
Faced with a similar conflict, Christianity effected a similar resolution.
Conservative Christian missionaries developed a way of sidestepping
the "hard sayings" of the Gospels—the proof texts of the radical ascetics—by spiritualizing the ideals of poverty, chastity, and equality. In
this they borrowed the concepts of *apatheia* and *ataraxia* from the
Stoics, making virtue more an internal question of attitude than an external matter of physical practice. These ideals were thus stripped of
their radical social character and their threat to the social order. This
also allowed Christianity to appeal to many more people of higher rank
and property than if it had attacked their riches and status in plain
material terms. It showed that the "rich man" could, indeed, be saved.[8]

If a Christian equivalent to the *Life of Apollonius* is to be found, it is
the *Life of Antony* written by Athanasius, patriarch of Alexandria (c.
296–373). Athanasius's work clearly parallels Philostratus in literary
form and in the characterization of Antony as ascetic, wonderworker,
and philosopher.[9] The most important parallel between the two lives
runs even deeper. The *Life of Antony* performed the same *function* for
the society of the Church as the *Life of Apollonius* did for the society
and culture of the empire. The same sort of controversy that took place
in broader imperial society between ascetic radicals and authoritarian
conservatives occurred within the Church itself, and just as pagan society ultimately found a way to incorporate the radicals into its ranks, so
did the Church. In both, radical ascetics were shorn of their threat,
liminized, heroized, and transformed from rivals to authority (whether
of emperor or bishop) into allies of that authority and paragons of its
values. Seen in this perspective, Christian monasticism amounts to an
institutional domestication and incorporation of radicalism—a theory
that would profoundly affect the study of Church history.

8. R. Lane Fox, *Pagans and Christians* (New York, 1987), 325.
9. These parallels were first discussed by R. Reitzenstein, *Hellenistische Wundererzählungen,* 2d ed. (Leipzig, 1906), and have been the subject of voluminous work
ever since. A convenient bibliography may be found in Cox, *Biography.*

"Antony and the monks of the fourth century inherited a revolution; they did not initiate one."[10] This much is true. Yet, the true nature and source of this revolution has not been recognized. It is less intellectual, and even religious, in nature than it is social, and its source lies less in the philosophical developments of the third century than in the ascetical controversy of the second. As with most revolutions, the issues at stake concerned social norms and authority. These issues were defined in the course of the second century by the process described in this study, and their first resolution was offered by Philostratus at the close of the period. As such, the ideals, attitudes, and tolerance of these second-century pagans not only mark a watershed in the history of asceticism in pagan antiquity, but also set the tone Western Civilization would inherit in the succeeding Christian ages.

10. Brown, *Body*, 208. For the further development of the issues of asceticism and authority within the Church during the fourth century and beyond, see Rousseau, *Ascetics*. I would, however, note that his view of ascetics as possessing a *new* form of social and religious power (9–11) is incorrect in view of the analysis presented here.

Select Bibliography

Primary Sources

The following lists ancient authors and texts that figure prominently in this work. The edition or translation is cited only when it does not occur in standard series of classical or patristic texts, or might otherwise be difficult to identify or locate.

Acts of the Christian Martyrs.
H. A. Musurillo, ed. *The Acts of the Christian Martyrs*. Oxford: Clarendon Press, 1972.
Acts of the Pagan Martyrs.
H. A. Musurillo, ed. *The Acts of the Pagan Martyrs: Acta Alexandrianorum*. Oxford: Clarendon Press, 1954.
Apocryphal Acts of the Apostles.
R. A. Lipsius and M. Bonnet, eds. *Acta Apostolorum Apocrypha*. 3 vols. Leipzig: H. Mendelssohn, 1891–1903. Reprint. Hildesheim: G. Olms, 1959 and 1990.
M. R. James, ed. *The Apocryphal New Testament: Being the Apocryphal Gospels, Acts, Epistles and Apocalypses, with other Narratives and Fragments*. Revised ed. Oxford: Clarendon Press, 1953.
E. Hennecke and W. Schneemelcher, eds. *New Testament Apocrypha*. Vol. 2. Translated by J. B. Higgins et al. Philadelphia: Westminster, 1963–65.
Apollonius of Tyana.
R. J. Panella. *The Letters of Apollonius of Tyana: A Critical Text with Prolegomena, Translation and Commentary*. Mnemosyne suppl. 56. Leiden: E. J. Brill, 1979.
Appian. *Civil Wars (Bella Civilia)*.
Apuleius. *Apology*.
Aristides, Aelius.
W. Dindorf, ed. *Aristides*. 3 vols. Leipzig: G. Reimer, 1829. Reprint. Hildesheim: G. Olms, 1964.
C. A. Behr and F. W. Lenz, eds. *P. Aelii Aristides: Opera Quae Extant Omnia*. 2 vols. Leiden: E. J. Brill, 1976–81.
C. A. Behr, trans. *P. Aelius Aristides: The Complete Works*. 2 vols. Leiden: E. J. Brill, 1981–86.
Aurelius, Marcus. *Meditations*.
Cassius Dio. *Roman History*.
Cicero, Marcus Tullius. *Laws (de Legibus); On Duties (de Officiis); On the Nature of the Gods (de Natura Deorum)*.
Clement of Alexandria. *Stromateis; Paedagogos; Who Is The Rich Man Who Shall Be Saved? (Quis Divis Salvetur?)*
Dio Chrysostom (Dio of Prusa). *Oration 32 (Alexandrian)*.

Epictetus. *Enchiridion; Discourses* (Arrian, *Epicteti Dissertationes*).
Eusebius. *Against Hierocles (Contra Hieroclem)*.
     M. Forrat. *Contre Hiéroclès*. Greek text edited by E. des Places. *Scurces chrétiennes* 333. Paris: Editions du Cerf, 1986.
     F. C. Conybeare, trans. *The Life of Apollonius of Tyana, the Episiles of Apollonius, and the Treatise of Eusebius*. Vol. 2. Revised ed. Loeb Classical Library 17. Cambridge: Harvard University Press, 1950.
————. *Ecclesiastical History*.
Fronto, Marcus Cornelius. *Letters*.
Galen.
     P. Kraus and R. Walzer. *Plato Arabus*. Vol. 1, *Galeni compendium Timaei Platonis aliorum dialogorum synopsis quae extant fragmenta.* ed. P. Kraus and F. Rosenthal. London: Warburg Institute, 1943.
     R. Walzer. *Galen on Jews and Christians*. Oxford: Oxford University Press, 1949.
————. *On Prognosis (de Praecognitione)*.
     V. Nutton, ed. and trans. *On Prognosis*. Corpus medicorum Graecorum. Vol. 5, part. 8, fasc. 1. Berlin: Akademie-Verlag, 1979.
Gellius, Aulus. *Attic Nights (Noctes Atticae)*.
Historia Augusta.
Ignatius of Antioch. *Letter to Polycarp*.
Josephus, Flavius. *Antiquities of the Jews (Antiquitates Judaicae)*.
Justin Martyr. *Apologies*.
Lucian. *Alexander* or *The False Prophet; Apology; Demonax; The Dream* or *Lucian's Career; Double Indictment; The Fugitives; Lover of Lies; Menippus; Nigrinus; On Salaried Posts; The Death of Peregrinus (Proteus); Philosophies for Sale*.
Pseudo-Lucian. *Cynic*.
Musonius Rufus.
     C. E. Lutz. "Musonius Rufus: 'The Roman Socrates.'" In *Yale Classical Studies* 10, ed. A. R. Bellinger, 3–150. New Haven: Yale University Press, 1947.
Origen. *Against Celsus (Contra Celsum)*.
Philostratus. *Life of Apollonius of Tyana (Vita Apollonii); Lives of the Sophists (Vitae Sophistarum)*.
Pliny the Younger. *Letters*.
Porphyry. *Against the Christians*.
     A. von Harnack. *Porphyrius, "Gegen die Christen," 15 Bücher: Zeugnisse, Fragmente und Referate*. Abhandlungen der königlichen preussischen Akademie der Wissenschaften 1916. No. 1. Berlin: Verlag der köngl. Akad. in Kommission bei G. Reimer, 1916.
————. *Life of Plotinus (Vita Plotini); On Abstinence (de Abstinentia)*.
Sallustius. *de Deis et Mundo*.
     G. Murray. *Five Stages of Greek Religion*. 3d ed. Garden City, N.Y.: Doubleday, 1951.
Seneca, Lucius Annaeus. *Letters*.
Suetonius. *Caesars (de Vita Caesarum)*.
Tacitus. *Agricola; Annals; Histories*.
Tatian. *Oration to the Greeks (Oratio ad Graecos)*.
     M. Whittaker, ed. and trans. *Oratio ad Graecos and Fragments*. Oxford: Clarendon Press, 1982.

Secondary Sources

English translations of works in other languages are cited in the entry under the original title. Infrequently printed older works are listed along with their most recent reprints.

Alföldy, G. "The Crisis of the Third Century as Seen by Contemporaries." *GRBS* 15 (1974): 89–111.

Allinson, F. G. *Lucian Satirist and Artist*. Boston: Marshall Jones, 1926.

Ameling, W. *Herodes Atticus*. 2 vols. Subsidia epigraphica 11. Hildesheim: G. Olms, 1983.

Anderson, G. *Lucian, Theme and Variation in the Second Sophistic*. Mnemosyne suppl. 41. Leiden: E. J. Brill, 1976.

———. *Philostratus: Biography and Belles Lettres in the Third Century A.D.* London: Croom Helm, 1986.

———. *Studies in Lucian's Comic Fiction*. Mnemosyne suppl. 43. Leiden: E. J. Brill, 1976.

André, J. M. "Les Ecoles philosophiques aux deux premiers siècles de l'Empire." *ANRW* II.36.1 (1987): 5–77.

Andresen, C. *Logos und Nomos: Die Polemik des Kelsos wider das Christentum*. Arbeiten zur Kirchengeschichte 30. Berlin: W. de Gruyter, 1955.

Arbesmann, R. "Fasting and Prophecy in Pagan and Christian Antiquity." *Traditio* 7 (1949–51): 1–71.

Armstrong, A. H. "The Self-Definition of Christianity in Relation to Later Platonism." In *Jewish and Christian Self-Definition*, ed. B. F. Meyer and E. P. Sanders, 1:74–99. Philadelphia: Fortress, 1980.

Arnim, H. von. *Leben und Werke des Dio von Prusa*. Berlin: Weidmann, 1898.

Arnold, E. V. *Roman Stoicism*. Cambridge: Cambridge University Press, 1911.

Asmis, E. "The Stoicism of Marcus Aurelius." *ANRW* II.36.3 (1988): 2228–52.

Attridge, H. W. "The Philosophical Critique of Religion under the Early Empire." *ANRW* II.16.1 (1978): 45–78.

Aune, D. E. "Magic in Early Christianity." *ANRW* II.23.2 (1980): 1507–57.

Bader, R. *Der Ἀληθὴς Λόγος des Kelsos*. Tübinger Beiträge zur Altertumswissenschaft. Heft 33. Stuttgart: W. Kohlhammer, 1940.

Bagnani, G. "Peregrinus Proteus and the Christians." *Historia* 4 (1955): 107–12.

Baldwin, B. "Lucian as Social Satirist." *CQ*, n.s. 11 (1961): 199–208.

———. *Studies in Lucian*. Toronto: Hakkert, 1973.

Ballanti, A. "Documenti sull'opposizione degli intellettuali a Domiziano." *Phoenix* 18 (1964): 39–48.

Bardy, G. "Origène et la magie." *Recherches de science religieuse* 18 (1928): 126–42.

———. " 'Philosophie' et 'philosophe' dans le vocabulaire chrétien des premiers siècles." *Revue d'ascétique et de mystique* 25 (1949): 97–108.

Barnes, T. D. "The Chronology of Montanism." *JTS* 21 (1970): 403–8.

———. *Constantine and Eusebius*. Cambridge: Harvard University Press, 1981.

———. "Legislation Against the Christians." *JRS* 58 (1968): 32–50.

———. "Pagan Perceptions of Christianity." In *Early Christianity: Origins and Evolution to A.D. 600, In Honor of W. H. C. Frend*, ed. Ian Hazlett, 231–43. Nashville, Tenn.: Abingdon, 1991.

————. "Sossianus Hierocles and the Antecedents of the Great Persecution." *Harvard Studies in Classical Philology* 80 (1976): 239–52.

————. *The Sources of the Historia Augusta.* Collection Latomus 155. Brussels: Latomus, 1978.

————. *Tertullian: A Historical and Literary Study.* 2d ed. Oxford: Clarendon Press, 1985.

Bauer, W. *Rechtgläubigkeit und Ketzerei im ältesten Christentum.* Beiträge zur historischen Theologie 10. Tübingen: Mohr, 1934. Translated by a team from the Philadelphia Seminar on Christian Origins, as *Orthodoxy and Heresy in Earliest Christianity,* ed. R. A. Kraft and G. Krodel. Philadelphia: Fortress, 1971.

Bauman, R. A. "The Suppression of the Bacchanals: Five Questions." *Historia* 39 (1990): 334–48.

Baumeister, T. "Gotteslaube und Staatsauffassung—ihre Interdependenz bei Celsus und Origenes." *Theologie und Philosophie* 53 (1978): 161–78.

Baur, F. C. *Apollonius von Tyana und Christus, oder das Verhältniss des Pythagoreismus zum Christentum.* Tübingen: L. F. Fues, 1832. Reprint. *Apollonius und Christus: ein Beitrag zur Religionsgeschichte der ersten Jahrhunderte nach Christus.* Hildesheim: G. Olms, 1966 = *Drei Abhandlungen zur Geschichte der alten Philosophie und ihres Verhältnisses zum Christentum,* ed. E. Zeller, 1–227. Leipzig: L. F. Fues, 1876. Reprint. Aalen: Scientia-Verlag, 1978.

Beaujeu, J. "Le Paganisme romain sous le Haut Empire." *ANRW* II.16.1 (1978): 3–26.

————. "La Religion de la classe sénatoriale à l'époque des Antonins." In *Hommages à Jean Bayet,* ed. M. Renard and R. Schilling, 54–75. Collection Latomus 70. Brussels: Latomus, 1964.

————. *La Religion romaine à l'apogée de l'empire.* Vol. 1, *La politique religieuse des Antonins (96–192).* Paris: Belles Lettres, 1955.

Behr, C. A. *Aelius Aristides and the Sacred Tales.* Amsterdam: Hakkert, 1968.

Béliard, O. "Un Saint païen. Apollonius de Tyane." *Annales* 53 (1936): 584–86.

Belloni, L. "Aspetti dell'antica σοφία in Apollonio di Tiana." *Aevum* 54 (1980): 140–49.

Benko, S. "Pagan Criticisms of Christianity During the First Two Centuries A.D." *ANRW* II.23.2 (1980): 1054–1118.

————. *Pagan Rome and the Early Christians.* Bloomington: Indiana University Press, 1984.

Benoît, A. "Le 'Contra Christianos' de Porphyre: Où en est la collecte des fragments." In *Paganisme, Judaïsme, Christianisme: Influences et affrontements dans le monde antique. Mélanges offerts à Marcel Simon,* 261–75. Paris: de Boccard, 1978.

Bernays, J. *Lucian und die Kyniker.* Berlin: W. Hertz, 1879.

Betz, H. D. "Lukian von Samosata und das Christentum." *Novum Testamentum* 3 (1959): 226–37.

————. *Lukian von Samosata und das Neue Testament: Religionsgeschichte und paränetische Parallelen. Ein Beitrag zum Corpus Hellenisticum Novi Testamenti.* Texte und Untersuchungen zur Geschichte der altchristlichen Literatur 76 (Reihe 5, Band 21). Berlin: Akademie-Verlag, 1961.

Bieler, L. ΘΕΙΟΣ ΑΝΗΡ: *Das Bild des "Göttlichen Menschen" in Spätantike und Frühchristentum.* 2 vols. Vienna: O. Höffels, 1935–36. Reprinted as two volumes in one, Darmstadt: Wissenschaftliche Buchgesellschaft, 1976.

Billerbeck, M. *Vom Kynismus / Epiktet.* Philosophie Antiqua 34. Leiden: E. J. Brill, 1978.

Birley, A. *The African Emperor: Septimius Severus.* 2d ed. London: B. T. Batsford, 1988.

———. *Marcus Aurelius: A Biography.* 2d ed. New Haven: Yale University Press, 1987.

———. "Some Teachers of Marcus Aurelius." *Bonner Historia–Augusta Colloquium 1966/67,* ed. J Straub, 39–42. Antiquitas Reihe 4: Beiträge zur Historia-Augusta Forschung, Band 4. Bonn: R. Habelt, 1968.

Blanchetière, F. *Le Christianisme Asiate aux IIème et IIIème siècles.* Lille: Service de reproduction des thèses, 1981. (Originally presented as the author's doctoral dissertation at the University of Lille, 1977)

Boer, W. den. "Gynaeconitis: A Center of Christian Propaganda." *Vig. Chr.* 4 (1950): 61–64.

———. "La Polémique anti-chrétienne du IIe siècle. La Doctrine de vérité de Celse." *Athenaeum* 54 (1976): 300–318.

Bompaire, J. *Lucien écrivain: imitation et création.* Bibliothèque des Ecoles Françaises d'Athènes et de Rome 190. Paris: de Boccard, 1958.

———. "Travaux récents sur Lucien." *Revue des études grecques* 88 (1975): 224–29.

Borret, M. *Contre Celse.* 5 vols. Sources chrétiennes 132, 136, 147, 150, and 227. Paris: Editions du Cerf, 1967–76.

———. "L'Ecriture d'après le païen Celse." In *Le Monde grec ancien et la Bible,* ed. C. Mondésert, 171–93. Bible de tous les temps 1. Paris: Beauchesne, 1984.

Bowersock, G. W. *Greek Sophists in the Roman Empire.* Oxford: Clarendon Press, 1969.

———. Introduction to *Life of Apollonius,* by Philostratus. Translated by C. P. Jones. Harmondsworth, Middlesex: Penguin, 1970.

———, ed. *Approaches to the Second Sophistic: Papers Presented at the 105th Annual Meeting of the American Philological Association.* University Park, Pa.: A.P.A., 1974.

Bowie, E. L. "Apollonius of Tyana: Tradition and Reality." *ANRW* II.16.2 (1978): 1652–99.

———. "The Greeks and Their Past in the Second Sophistic." *Past and Present* 46 (1970): 3–41.

Bradley, K. R. *Discovering the Roman Family: Studies in Roman Social History.* New York: Oxford University Press, 1991.

Branham, R. B. "The Comic as Critic: Revenging Epicurus—a Study of Lucian's Art of Comic Narrative." *Classical Antiquity* 3 (1984): 143–63.

———. *Unruly Eloquence: Lucian and the Comedy of Traditions.* Cambridge: Harvard University Press, 1989.

Bremmer, J. N. "Symbols of Marginality from Early Pythagoreans to Late Antique Monks." *Greece and Rome,* n.s. 39 (1992): 205–14.

Brown, P. R. L. "Approaches to the Religious Crisis of the Third Century A.D." *English Historical Review* 83 (1968): 542–58 = *Religion and Society in the Age of St. Augustine,* 74–93. New York: Harper and Row, 1972.

————. *The Body and Society: Men, Women, and Sexual Renunciation in Early Christianity.* New York: Columbia University Press, 1988.

————. *The Making of Late Antiquity.* Cambridge: Harvard University Press, 1978.

————. "The Rise and Function of the Holy Man in Late Antiquity." *JRS* 61 (1971): 80–101 = *Society and the Holy in Late Antiquity,* 103–52. Berkeley and Los Angeles: University of California Press, 1982.

————. "The Saint as Exemplar in Late Antiquity." *Representations* 1, no. 2 (Spring 1983): 1–26.

————. *A Social Context for the Religious Crisis of the 3rd Century A.D.* Protocol Series of the Colloquies of the Center for Hermeneutical Studies in Hellenistic and Modern Culture 14. Berkeley, 1975.

————. "Sorcery, Demons and the Rise of Christianity: From Late Antiquity into the Middle Ages." In *Witchcraft: Confessions and Accusations,* ed. M. Douglas, 17–45. Association of Social Anthropologists Monographs 9. London: Tavistock, 1970. = *Religion and Society in the Age of St. Augustine,* 119–46. New York: Harper and Row, 1972.

————. *The World of Late Antiquity,* A.D. *150–750.* New York: Harcourt, Brace, Jovanovich, 1971. Reprint. New York: Norton, 1989.

Brox, N. "Der einfache Glaube und die Theologie: zur altkirchlichen Geschichte eines Dauerproblems." *Kairos* 14 (1972): 161–87.

Brunt, P. A. "Aspects of the Social Thought of Dio Chrysostom and of the Stoics." *Proceedings of the Cambridge Philosophical Society,* n.s. 19 (1973): 9–34.

————. "Marcus Aurelius and the Christians." In *Studies in Latin Literature and Roman History,* ed. C. Deroux, 1:484–98. Collection Latomus 164. Brussels: Latomus, 1979.

————. "Marcus Aurelius in his Meditations." *JRS* 64 (1974): 1–20.

————. Review of *The Meditations of Marcus Aurelius: A Study,* by R. B. Rutherford. In *JRS* 80 (1990): 218–19.

————. "Stoicism and the Principate." *PBSR* 43, n.s. 30 (1975): 7–35.

Burke, G. T. "Celsus and Late Second-Century Christianity." Ph.D. dissertation, University of Iowa, 1981.

————. "Walter Bauer and Celsus: The Shape of Late Second-Century Christianity." *Second Century* 4 (1984): 1–7.

Burkert, W. "Craft Versus Sect: The Problem of Orphics and Pythagoreans." In *Jewish and Christian Self-Definition,* ed. B. F. Meyer and E. P. Sanders, 3:1–22. Philadelphia: Fortress, 1982.

————. "Γόης. Zum Griechischen 'Schamanismus.'" *Rheinisches Museum* 150 (1962): 36–55.

————. "Hellenistische Pseudopythagorica." *Philologus* 105 (1961): 16–43.

————. *Weisheit und Wissenschaft: Studien zu Pythagoras, Philolaus, und Platon.* Nuremberg: H. Carl, 1962. Translated by E. L. Minar, Jr., as *Lore and Science in Ancient Pythagoreanism.* Cambridge: Harvard University Press, 1972.

Burrus, V. *Chastity as Autonomy: Women in the Stories of the Apocryphal Acts.* Studies in Women and Religion 23. Lewiston, N.Y.: E. Mellen, 1987.

Butler, H. E., and A. S. Owen. *Apulei Apologia, Sive pro se de magia liber.* Oxford: Clarendon Press, 1914.

Calderini, A. "Teoria e pratica politica nella 'Vita di Apollonio di Tiana.'" *Rendiconti dell'Istituto Lombardo* 74 (1940–41): 213–41.

Cangh, J. M. van. "Santé et salut dans les miracles d'Epidaure, d'Apollonius de Tyane et du Nouveau Testament." In *Gnosticisme et monde hellénistique: Actes du Colloque de Louvain-la-Neuve, 11–14 mars 1980*, ed. J. Reis et al., 263–77. Publications de l'Institut Oriental de Louvain 27. Louvain: Institut Oriental, 1982.

Caster, M. *Etudes sur Alexandre ou Le Faux Prophète de Lucien*. Paris: Belles Lettres, 1938. Reprint; see below.

———. *Lucien et la pensée religieuse de son temps*. Paris: Belles Lettres, 1937. Reprinted with *Etudes sur Alexandre* in one volume in the Ancient Greek Literature Series. New York: Garland, 1987.

Chadwick, H. "The Domestication of Gnosis." In *The Rediscovery of Gnosticism*. Vol. 1, *The School of Valentinus*, ed. B. Layton, 3–16. Leiden: E. J. Brill, 1980.

———. *Early Christian Thought and the Classical Tradition: Studies in Justin, Clement, and Origen*. New York: Oxford University Press, 1966.

———. "Origen, Celsus, and the Resurrection of the Body." *Harvard Theological Review* 41 (1948): 83–102.

———. "Origen, Celsus, and the Stoa." *JTS* 48 (1947): 34–49.

———, ed. *Contra Celsum*. Revised ed. Cambridge: Cambridge University Press, 1980.

Champlin, E. "The Chronology of Fronto." *JRS* 64 (1974): 136–59.

———. *Fronto and Antonine Rome*. Cambridge: Harvard University Press, 1980.

Clark, E. A. "Ascetic Renunciation and Feminine Advancement: A Paradox of Late Antique Christianity." *Anglican Theological Review* 6 (1981): 240–57 = *Ascetic Piety and Women's Faith: Essays on Late Ancient Christianity*, 175–208. Studies in Women and Religion 20. Lewiston, N.Y.: E. Mellen, 1986.

Clarke, G. W. *The Octavius of Marcus Minucius Felix*. Ancient Christian Writers 39. New York: Newman, 1974.

Clay, D. "Lucian of Samosata: Four Philosophical Lives (Nigrinus, Demonax, Peregrinus, Alexander Pseudomantis)." *ANRW* II.36.5 (1992): 3406–50.

———. "The Philosophical Inscription of Diogenes of Oenoanda: New Discoveries 1969–1983." *ANRW* II.36.4 (1990): 2446–559.

Cochrane, C. N. *Christianity and Classical Culture: A Study of Thought and Action from Augustus to Augustine*. Revised and corrected ed. Oxford: Oxford University Press, 1944.

Corno, D. del. "Lo scritto di Filostrato su Apollonio Tianeo e la tradizione della narrativa." In *La struttura della fabulazione antica*, 65–87. Università di Genova Pubblicazioni dell'Istituto di filologia classica e medioevale 54. Genoa: Università di Genova, 1979.

Countryman, L. W. *The Rich Christian in the Church of the Early Empire: Contradictions and Accommodations*. Lewiston, N.Y.: E. Mellen, 1980.

Courcelle, P. "La figure du philosophe d'après les écrivains latins de l'Antiquité." *Journal des Savantes* (1980): 85–101.

Cox, P. *Biography in Late Antiquity: A Quest for the Holy Man*. Berkeley and Los Angeles: University of California Press, 1983.

———. "The Ideal of the Holy Philosopher in Pagan and Christian Biographies (2nd–4th Centuries)." Forthcoming in *ANRW*.

Cramer, F. H. *Astrology in Roman Law and Politics.* Memoirs of the American Philosophical Society 37. Philadelphia, 1954.

Croiset, M. *Essai sur la vie et les oeuvres de Lucien.* Paris: Hachette, 1882.

Crouzel, H. *Bibliographie critique d'Origène.* Instrumenta Patristica 8. The Hague: Nijhoff, 1971. Continued in *Bibliographie critique d'Origène: Supplément I.* Instrumenta Patristica 8A. The Hague: Nijhoff, 1982.

———. "Conviction intérieure et aspects extérieures de la religion chez Celse et Origène." *Bulletin de littérature ecclésiastique* 77 (1976): 83–98.

———. *Origène.* Paris: Lethielleux, 1985. Translated by A. S. Worrall, as *Origen.* San Francisco: Harper and Row, 1989.

———. *Origène et la "connaissance mystique."* Toulouse: Desclée de Brouwer, 1961.

———. *Origène et la philosophie.* Paris: Aubier, 1962.

Crouzel, H., and A. Quacquarelli, eds. *Origeniana secunda: Second colloque internationale des études origéniennes, Bari, 20–23 Sept. 1977.* Quaderni di "Vetera Christianorum" 15. Rome: Edizioni dell'Ateneo, 1980.

Cumont, F. "Alexandre d'Abonoteichos et le Néo-Pythagorisme." *Revue de l'histoire des religions* 86 (1922): 202–10.

———. *Alexandre d'Abonoteichos: Un Episode de l'histoire de paganisme au IIe siècle de notre ère.* Mémoires couronés et autres mémoires publiés par l'Académie Royale des sciences, des lettres et des beaux-arts de Belgique 40. Brussels, 1887.

Davies, E. L. "Ascetic Madness." In *Pagan and Christian Anxiety: A Response to E. R. Dodds,* ed. R. C. Smith and J. Lounibos, 13–26. Lanham, Md.: University Press of America, 1984.

———. *The Revolt of the Widows: The Social World of the Apocryphal Acts.* Carbondale: Southern Illinois University Press, 1980.

Delatte, A. *Etudes sur la littérature pythagoricienne.* Bibliothèque de l'Ecole des hautes études—Sciences historiques et philologiques 217. Paris: E. Champion, 1915. Reprint. Geneva: Slatkine, 1974.

Detienne, M. "Les Chemins de la déviance: Orphisme, Dionysisme, et Pythagorisme." In *Orfismo in Magna Grecia: Atti del Quattrodicesimo Convegno di Studi sulla Magna Grecia, Taranto, 6–10 Ottobre 1974,* 49–78. Naples: Arte tipog., 1975.

———. *Dionysos mis à mort.* Paris: Gallimard, 1977. Translated by M. and L. Muellner, as *Dionysus Slain.* Baltimore: Johns Hopkins University Press, 1979.

Dill, S. *Roman Society from Nero to Marcus Aurelius.* 2d ed. London: Macmillan, 1905.

Dodds, E. R. *The Ancient Concept of Progress and Other Essays in Greek Literature and Belief.* Oxford: Clarendon Press, 1973.

———. *The Greeks and the Irrational.* Sather Classical Lectures 25. Berkeley and Los Angeles: University of California Press, 1951.

———. *Pagan and Christian in an Age of Anxiety: Some Aspects of Religious Experience from Marcus Aurelius to Constantine.* Cambridge: Cambridge University Press, 1965.

Dörrie, H. "Die platonische Theologie des Kelsos in ihrer Auseinandersetzung mit der christliche Theologie: auf Grund von Origenes c. Celsum 7.42ff." *Nachrichten der Akademie der Wissenschaffen in Göttingen,* Philologische-historische Klasse 1 (1967): 23–55.

Douglas, M. *Natural Symbols: Explorations in Cosmology.* 2d ed. London: Barrie and Jenkins, 1973.

Downing, F. G. *Christ and the Cynics: Jesus and other Radical Preachers in the First Century Tradition.* JSOT Manuals 4. Sheffield: JSOT Press (Sheffield Academic Press), 1988.

Dressler, H. *The Usage of Ἀσκέω and its Cognates in Greek Documents to 100 A.D.* Catholic University of America Patristic Series 78. Washington, D.C.: Catholic University of America Press, 1947.

Dubuisson, M. "Lucien et Rome." *Ancient Society* 15–17 (1984–86): 185–207.

Dudley, D. R. *A History of Cynicism from Diogenes to the 6th Century.* London: Methuen, 1937.

Dulière, W. L. "Protection permanente contre des animaux nuisibles assurée par Apollonius de Tyane dans Byzance et Antioche. Evolution de son mythe." *Byzantinische Zeitschrift* 63 (1970): 247–77.

Dzielska, M. *Appoloniusz z Tiany: legenda i rzeczywistość.* Rozprawy habilitacyjne Uniwersytet Jagielloński 78. Cracow: Nak. Uniwersytetu Jagiellońskiego, 1983. Translated by P. Pieńkowski, as *Apollonius of Tyana in Legend and History.* Problemi e Ricerche di Storia Antica 10. Rome: "L'Erma" di Bretschneider, 1986.

———. "Les Idées politiques dans la morale stoïcienne de Marc Aurèle." *Eos* 59 (1971): 241–54.

———. "La Participation du milieu d'Alexandrie à la discussion sur l'idéal du souverain dans les deux premiers siècles de l'Empire Romaine." *Eos* 59 (1971): 241–54.

Easterling, P. E., and B. M. W. Knox, eds. *The Cambridge History of Classical Literature.* Vol. 1, *Greek Literature.* Cambridge: Cambridge University Press, 1985.

Edwards, M. J. "Satire and Verisimilitude: Christianity in Lucian's *Peregrinus.*" *Historia* 38 (1989): 89–98.

Erskine, A. *The Hellenistic Stoa: Political Thought and Action.* Ithaca: Cornell University Press, 1990.

Farquharson, A. S. L. *Marcus Aurelius: His Life and His World.* Edited by D. A. Rees. New York: William Galloch, 1951.

———. *The Meditations of the Emperor Marcus Aurelius.* 2 vols. Oxford: Clarendon Press, 1944. Reprint. 1968.

Festugière, A. J. *Personal Religion Among the Greeks.* Sather Classical Lectures 26. Berkeley and Los Angeles: University of California Press, 1954.

———. Review of *Etudes sur Alexandre ou Le Faux Prophète de Lucien,* by M. Caster. In *Revue des études grecques* 52 (1939): 230–33.

———. "Trois rencontres entre la Grèce et l'Inde." *Revue de l'histoire des religions* 125 (1943): 32–47.

Fiorenza, E. S. *In Memory of Her: A Feminist Theological Reconstruction of Christian Origins.* New York: Crossroad, 1984.

———. "Miracles, Mission, and Apologetics: An Introduction." In *Aspects of Religious Propaganda in Judaism and Early Christianity,* ed. E. S. Fiorenza, 1–25. Notre Dame: University of Notre Dame Press, 1976.

Forrat, M. *Contre Hiéroclès.* Greek text edited by E. des Places. Sources chrétiennes 333. Paris: Editions du Cerf, 1986.

Foucault, M. *Histoire de la sexualité.* Vol. 3, *Le Souci de soi.* Paris: Gallimard,

1984. Translated by R. Hurley, as *The History of Sexuality*. Vol. 3, *The Care of the Self*. New York: Pantheon Books, 1986.

Fowden, G. "The Pagan Holy Man in Late Antique Society." *JHS* 102 (1982): 33–59.

Fraade, S. D. "Ascetical Aspects of Ancient Judaism." In *World Spirituality*. Vol. 13, *Jewish Spirituality: From the Bible to the Middle Ages* ed. A. Green, 253–88. New York: Crossroad, 1986.

Francis, J. A. "Pagan and Christian Philosophy in Athanasius' *Vita Antonii*." *American Benedictine Review* 32 (1981): 100–113.

Frank, K. S. *Askese und Mönchtum in der alten Kirche*. Darmstadt: Wissenschaftliche Buchgesellschaft, 1975.

Frend, W. H. C. "Athanasius as an Egyptian Christian Leader in the Fourth Century." *New College Bulletin* (University of Edinburgh) 8, no. 1 (1974): 20–37.

———. "The Gnostic Sects and the Roman Empire." *Journal of Ecclesiastical History* 5 (1954): 25–37. Reprinted with original page numbers in *Religion Popular and Unpopular in the Early Christian Centuries*. Collected Studies 45. London: Variorum Reprints, 1976.

———. *Martyrdom and Persecution in the Early Church: A Study of a Conflict from the Maccabees to Donatus*. Oxford: Blackwell, 1965.

———. "Prelude to the Great Persecution: The Propaganda War." *Journal of Ecclesiastical History* 38 (1987): 1–18.

———. "Religion and Social Change in the Late Roman Empire." *Cambridge Journal* 2 (1949): 487–97.

Fridrichsen, A. *Le problème du miracle dans le Christianisme primitif*. Etudes d'histoire et de philosophie religieuses 12. Strasbourg: Librarie Istra, 1925. Translated by R. Harrisville and J. Hanson, as *The Problem of Miracle in Early Christianity*. Minneapolis, Minn.: Augsburg, 1972.

Fritz, K. von. "Peregrinus (Proteus) (16)." *RE* 19.1 (1937): 656–63.

Gager, J. C. "The Dodds Hypothesis." In *Pagan and Christian Anxiety: A Response to E. R. Dodds,* ed. R. C. Smith and J. Lounibos, 1–11. Lanham, Md.: University Press of America, 1984.

Gallagher, E. V. *Divine Man or Magician? Celsus and Origen on Jesus*. SBL Dissertation Series 64. Chico, Calif.: Scholars, 1982.

Geffcken, J. *Der Ausgang des griechisch-römischen Heidentums*. Revised ed. Heidelberg: C. Winter, 1929. Translated by S. MacCormack with updated references and index, as *The Last Days of Greco-Roman Paganism*. New York: North Holland, 1978.

Georgi, D. "Socioeconomic Reasons for the 'Divine Man' as a Propagandistic Pattern." In *Aspects of Religious Propaganda in Judaism and Early Christianity,* ed. E. S. Fiorenza, 27–42. Notre Dame: University of Notre Dame Press, 1976.

Geytenbeek, A. C. van. *Musonius Rufus en de griekse diatribe*. Revised ed. Amsterdam: H. J. Paris, 1948. Translated by B. L. Hijmans, as *Musonius Rufus and Greek Diatribe*. Assen: Van Gorcum, 1963.

Gibbon, E. *The Decline and Fall of the Roman Empire*. Modern Library. New York: Random House, 1932.

Glöckner, O. *Celsi ΑΛΗΘΗΣ ΛΟΓΟΣ*. Kleine Texte für Vorlesungen und Übungen 151. Bonn: A. Marcus and B. Weber, 1924.

————. "Die Gottes- und Weltanschauung des Kelsos." *Philologus* 82 (1926–27): 329–52.

Gordon, R. L. "Mithraism and Roman Society: Social Factors in the Explanation of Religious Change in the Roman Empire." *Religion* 2 (1971): 92–121.

Göttsching, J. *Apollonius von Tyana.* Leipzig: Druck von M. Hoffman, 1889.

Goulet-Cazé, M.-O. *L'Ascèse Cynique: Un Commentaire de Diogène Laërce VI.70–71.* Histoire des doctrines de l'antiquité classique 10. Paris: J. Vrin, 1986.

————. "Le Cynisme à l'époque impériale." *ANRW* II.36.4 (1990): 2720–2833.

————. "Le Livre VI de Diogène Laërce: Analyze de sa structure et réflexions méthodologiques." Forthcoming in *ANRW*.

Grant, R. M. "Charges of 'Immorality' against Various Religious Groups in Antiquity." In *Studies in Gnosticism and Hellenistic Religions: Presented to Gilles Quispel on the Occasion of His 65th Birthday,* ed. R. van Den Broek and M. J. Vermaseren, 161–70. Leiden: E. J. Brill, 1981.

————. "Five Apologists and Marcus Aurelius." *Vig. Chr.* 42 (1988): 1–17.

————. "Paul, Galen, and Origen." *JTS* 34 (1983): 533–36.

————. "The Social Setting of Second-century Christianity." In *Jewish and Christian Self-Definition,* ed. B. F. Meyer and E. P. Sanders, 1:16–29. Philadelphia: Fortress, 1980.

Green, H. A. "Ritual in Valentinian Gnosticism: A Sociological Interpretation." *Journal of Religious History* 12 (1982): 109–24.

Greenslade, S. L. "Heresy and Schism in the Later Roman Empire." In *Studies in Church History.* Vol. 19: *Schism, Heresy, and Religious Protest: Papers Read at the 10th Summer Meeting and the 11th Winter Meeting of the Ecclesiastical History Society,* ed. D. Baker, 1–20. Cambridge: Cambridge University Press, 1972.

Griffin, M. T. *Nero: The End of a Dynasty.* New Haven: Yale University Press, 1985.

————. Review of *The Meditations of Marcus Aurelius: A Study,* by R. B. Rutherford. In *CR,* n.s. 41 (1991): 42–44.

————. *Seneca: A Philosopher in Politics.* 2d ed. Oxford: Oxford University Press, 1992.

Groningen, B. A. van. "Apollonius de Tyane." *Bulletin de la Faculté des Lettres de Strasbourg* 30 (1951–52): 107–16.

Grosso, F. "La 'Vita di Apollonio di Tiana' come fonte storica." *Acme* 7, fasc. 3 (1954): 333–52.

Hadot, P. *Exercices spirituels et philosophie antique.* 2d ed. Paris: Etudes Augustiniennes, 1987.

————. "Les Pensées de Marc Aurèle." *Bulletin de l'Association Guillaume Budé* 1 (1981): 183–91.

————. "La Physique comme exercice spirituel ou pessimisme et optimisme chez Marc Aurèle." *Revue de théologie et de philosophie* 22 (1972): 225–39 = *Exercices spirituels et philosophie antique*[2], 119–33.

Hägg, T. "Hierocles the Lover of Truth and Eusebius the Sophist." *Symbolae Osloenses* 67 (1992): 138–50.

Hall, J. A. *Lucian's Satire.* New York: Arno, 1981.

Hammond, M. *The Antonine Monarchy.* Papers and Monographs of the American Academy in Rome 19. Rome, 1959.

Harnack, A. von. *Marcion, das Evangelium vom fremden Gott.* 2d ed. Leipzig: J. C. Henrichs, 1924.

———. *Die Mission und Ausbreitung des Christentums in den ersten drei Jahrhunderten.* 2 vols. 4th ed. Texte und Untersuchungen zur Geschichte der altchristlichen Literatur 45. Leipzig: J. C. Hinrich, 1924. Reprint. Darmstadt: Wissenschaftliche Buchgesellschaft, 1985. Translation of the 2d ed. (1908) by J. Moffat, as *The Mission and Expansion of Christianity in the First Three Centuries.* 2 vols. Theological Translation Library 19–20. New York: Putnam, 1908.

———. *Der Vorwurf des Atheismus in den drei ersten Jahrhunderten.* Texte und Untersuchungen zur Geschichte der altchristlichen Literatur 28, no. 4 (n.s. 13). Leipzig: J. C. Henrichs, 1905.

Harris, B. F. "Apollonius of Tyana. Fact and Fiction." *Journal of Religious History* 5 (1969): 189–99.

Hauck, R. J. *The More Divine Proof: Prophecy and Inspiration in Celsus and Origen.* AAR Academy Series 69. Atlanta, Ga.: Scholars, 1989.

Helm, R. *Lucian und Menipp.* Leipzig: B. G. Teubner, 1906. Reprint. Hildesheim: G. Olms, 1967.

Hershbell, J. "The Stoicism of Epictetus: Twentieth Century Perspectives." *ANRW* II.36.3 (1989): 2148–63.

Hijmans, B. L. *ΑΣΚΗΣΙΣ: Notes on Epictetus' Educational System.* Wejsgerige teksten en studies 2. Assen: Van Gorcum, 1959.

Hinrichs, A. "Pagan Ritual and the Alleged Crimes of the Early Christians. A Reconsideration." In *Kyriakon, Festschrift Johannes Quasten,* ed. P. Granfield and J. A. Jungmann, 18–35. Münster: Aschendorff, 1970.

Hoïstad, R. *Cynic Hero and Cynic King: Studies in the Cynic Conception of Man.* Uppsala: C. Bloms, 1948.

Hoffman, R. J. *On the True Doctrine: A Discourse against the Christians.* New York: Oxford University Press, 1987.

Hopfner, T. "Apollonius von Tyana und Philostratos." In *Seminarium Kondakovianum (Seminar Kondakov).* Vol. 4, *Recueil d'études: Archéologie, histoire de l'art, études byzantines,* 135–64. Prague: Seminarium Kondakovianum, 1931.

Hornsby, H. M. "The Cynicism of Peregrinus Proteus." *Hermathena* 48 (1933): 65–84.

Hovland, C. W. "The Dialogue between Origen and Celsus." In *Pagan and Christian Anxiety: A Response to E. R. Dodds,* ed. R. C. Smith and J. Lounibos, 191–219. Lanham, Md.: University Press of America, 1984.

Hull, J. *Hellenistic Magic and the Synoptic Tradition.* Studies in Biblical Theology, 2d ser. 28. Naperville: A. R. Allenson, 1974.

Inge, W. R. "Origen." *Proceedings of the British Academy* 32 (1946): 123–45.

Jackson, H. M. "The Setting and Sectarian Provenance of the Fragment of the 'Celestial Dialogue' Preserved by Origen from Celsus' Αληθὴς Λόγος." *Harvard Theological Review* 85 (1992): 273–305.

Jackson, S. "Apollonius and the Emperors." *Hermathena* 137 (Winter 1984): 25–32.

Jaeger, W. *Paideia: Die Formung des griechischen Menschen.* 2d ed. 3 vols. Berlin: de Gruyter, 1936. Translated by G. Highet, as *Paideia: The Ideals of Greek Culture*. 2d ed. 3 vols. New York: Oxford University Press, 1945.

Janssen, L. F. "'Superstitio' and the Persecution of the Christians." *Vig. Chr.* 33 (1979): 131–59.

Jones, A. H. M. "The Social Background of the Struggle between Pagans and Christians." In *The Conflict between Paganism and Christianity in the Fourth Century A.D.*, ed. A. Momigliano, 17–37. Oxford: Clarendon Press, 1963.

———. "Were Ancient Christian Heresies Disguised Social Movements?" *JTS* 10 (1959): 280–98 = *The Roman Economy: Studies in Ancient Economic and Administrative History*, ed. P. A. Brunt, 308–29. Oxford: Blackwell, 1974. Reprinted as separate pamphlet. Philadelphia: Fortress, 1966.

Jones, C. P. *Culture and Society in Lucian*. Cambridge: Harvard University Press, 1986.

———. "The Date of Dio of Prusa's Alexandrian Oration." *Historia* 22 (1973): 302–9.

———. "An Epigram on Apollonius of Tyana." *JHS* 100 (1980): 190–94.

———. "A Martyria for Apollonius of Tyana." *Chiron* 12 (1982): 137–44.

———. *The Roman World of Dio Chrysostom*. Cambridge: Harvard University Press, 1978.

———. "Two Enemies of Lucian." *GRBS* 13 (1972): 475–87.

Jordan, H. "Celsus, die älteste umfassende Kritik des Christentums." In *Moderne Irrtümer im Spiegel der Geschichte: Bilder aus der Geschichte des Kampfes der religiösen Richtungen*, ed. W. Laible, 1–31. Leipzig: Dörffling und Franke, 1912.

Józefowicz, M. *See* Dzielska, M.

Józefowicz-Dzielska, M. *See* Dzielska, M.

Judge, E. A. "'Antike und Christentum': Towards a Definition of the Field. A Bibliographical Survey." *ANRW* II.23.1 (1979): 3–58.

———. "Christian Innovation and Its Contemporary Observers." In *History and Historians in Late Antiquity*, ed. B. Croke and A. Emmett, 13–29. Sydney: Pergamon, 1983.

———. "The Social Identity of the First Christians: A Question of Method in Religious History." *Journal of Religious History* 11 (1980): 201–17.

———. *The Social Pattern of Christian Groups in the First Century*. London: Tyndale, 1960.

Junod, E. "Etude critique. A propos de cinq traductions récents d'oeuvres d'Origène." *Revue de théologie et de philosophie* 21 (1971): 30–43.

———. "Polémique chrétienne contre Apollonius de Tyane." *Revue de théologie et de philosophie* 120 (1988): 475–82.

Junod, E., and J.-D. Kaestli. *L'Histoire des Actes Apocryphes du IIIème au IXème siècle: Le cas des Actes de Jean*. Cahiers de la revue de théologie et de philosophie 7. Lausanne: La Concorde, 1982.

Kahn, C. H. "Religion and Natural Philosophy in Empedocles' Doctrine of the Soul." *Archiv für Geschichte der Philosophie* 42 (1960): 3–35 = *Essays in Ancient Greek Philosophy*, ed. J. Anton and G. Kustas, 1:3–38. Albany: State University of New York Press, 1971.

Kee, H. C. "Aretalogy and Gospel." *JBL* 92 (1973): 402–22.

Keim, T. *Celsus' Wahres Wort: Älteste Streitschrift antiker Weltanschauung gegen das Christentum vom Jahr 178 n. Chr.* Zürich: Orell Füssli, 1873.

Keresztes, P. "The Imperial Roman Government and the Christian Church I. From Nero to the Severi." *ANRW* II.23.1 (1979): 247–315.

———. "Marcus Aurelius a Persecutor?" *Harvard Theological Review* 61 (1968): 321–41.

Kertsch, M. "Traditionelle Rhetorik und Philosophie in Eusebius' Antirrhetikos gegen Hierokles." *Vig. Chr.* 34 (1980): 145–71.

Kidd, I. G. "Moral Actions and Rules in Stoic Ethics." In *The Stoics*, ed. J. M. Rist, 247–58. Berkeley and Los Angeles: University of California Press, 1978.

———. "Stoic Intermediates as the End for Man." *CQ*, n.s. 5 (1955): 181–94 = *Problems in Stoicism*, ed. A. A. Long, 150–72. London: Athlone, 1971.

Kindstrand, J. F. "The Date of Dio of Prusa's Alexandrian Oration—A Reply." *Historia* 27 (1978): 378–83.

Klein, R., ed. *Marc Aurel*. Wege der Forschung 50. Darmstadt: Wissenschaftliche Buchgesellschaft, 1979.

Knoles, T. G. "Literary Techniques and Theme in Philostratus' *Life of Apollonius of Tyana*." Ph.D. dissertation, Rutgers University, 1981.

Koetschau, P. "Die Gliederung des Alethes Logos des Celsus." *Jahrbücher für protestantische Theologie* 18 (1892): 604–32.

Kolenkow, A. B. "A Problem of Power: How Miracle Workers Counter Charges of Magic in the Hellenistic World." *Society of Biblical Literature Seminar Papers* 1 (1976): 105–10.

———. "Relationship Between Miracle and Prophecy in the Graeco-Roman World and Early Christianity." *ANRW* II.23.2 (1980): 1470–1506.

Krill, R. M. "Roman Paganism under the Antonines and the Severans." *ANRW* II.16.1 (1978): 27–44.

Labriolle, P. de. *La Réaction païenne: Etude sur la polémique antichrétienne du Ier au IVe siècle*. Paris: Artisan du Livre, 1934.

Laffranque, M. *Poseidonios d'Apamée: Essai de mise au point*. Publ. de la Faculté des lettres et sciences humaines de Paris, serie "Recherches" 13. Paris: Presses Universitaires de France, 1964.

Lameere, W. "L'Empereur Marc Aurèle." *Problèmes d'histoire du Christianisme* 5 (1974–75): 5–54.

Lane Fox, R. *Pagans and Christians*. New York: Knopf, 1987.

Laurenti, R. "Musonio, maestro di Epitteto." *ANRW* II.36.3 (1989): 2105–46.

Lebreton, J. "Le Désaccord de la théologie savante et de la foi populaire dans l'Eglise chrétienne du IIIe siècle." *Revue d'histoire ecclésiastique* 19 (1923): 481–506; continued in 20 (1924): 5–37.

Leest, J. vander. "Lucian in Egypt." *GRBS* 26 (1985): 75–82.

Leipoldt, J. *Griechische Philosophie und frühchristlichen Askese*. Berlin: Akademie-Verlag, 1961.

Letocha, D. "L'Affrontement entre le christianisme et le paganisme dans le Contre Celse d'Origène." *Dialogue* 19 (1980), 373–95.

Lévy, I. *La Légend de Pythagore de Grèce en Palestine*. Paris: E. Champion, 1927.

———. *Recherches sur les sources de la légend de Pythagore*. Bibliothèque de l'Ecole des hautes études, sciences religieuses 42. Paris: E. Leroux, 1926. Reprint. New York: Garland, 1987.

Liebeschuetz, J. H. W. G. *Continuity and Change in Roman Religion*. Oxford: Clarendon Press, 1979.

Lo Cascio, F. *La forma letteraria della Vita di Apollonio Tianeo.* Quaderni dell'Istituto di filologia greca della Università di Palermo 6. Palermo: Università di Palermo, 1974.

Lohse, B. *Askese und Mönchtum in der Antike und in der alten Kirche.* Religion und Kultur der alten Mittelmeerwelt in Parallelforschungen 1. Munich: Oldenbourg, 1969.

Long, A. A. "Epictetus and Marcus Aurelius." In *Ancient Writers: Greece and Rome,* ed. T. J. Luce, 2:985–1002. New York: Scribner, 1982.

———. *Hellenistic Philosophy: Stoics, Epicureans, Sceptics.* 2d ed. Berkeley and Los Angeles: University of California Press, 1986.

———. "Heraclitus and Stoicism." *Philosophia* 5–6 (1975–76): 133–56.

Lowe, J. E. *Magic in Greek and Latin Literature.* Oxford: Blackwell, 1929.

Lutz, C. E. "Musonius Rufus: 'The Roman Socrates.'" In *Yale Classical Studies* 10, ed. A. R. Bellinger, 3–150. New Haven: Yale University Press, 1947.

Macleod, M. D. "Lucianic Studies since 1930." Forthcoming in *ANRW.*

MacMullen, R. *Enemies of the Roman Order: Treason, Unrest, and Alienation in the Empire.* Cambridge: Harvard University Press, 1966.

———. *Paganism in the Roman Empire.* New Haven: Yale University Press, 1981.

———. *The Roman Government's Response to Crisis,* A.D. 235–337. New Haven: Yale University Press, 1976.

Malherbe, A. J. "Self-Definition among Epicureans and Cynics." In *Jewish and Christian Self-Definition,* ed. B. F. Meyer and E. P. Sanders, 3:46–59. Philadelphia: Fortress, 1982.

Markus, R. A. "The Problem of Self-Definition: From Sect to Church." In *Jewish and Christian Self-Definition,* ed. B. F. Meyer and E. P. Sanders, 1:1–15. Philadelphia: Fortress, 1980.

Marrou, H. I. *Histoire de l'education dans l'antiquité.* Paris: Editions du Seuil, 1948. Translated by G. Lamb, as *A History of Education in the Ancient World.* New York: Sheed and Ward, 1956. Reprinted as *A History of Education in Antiquity.* Madison: University of Wisconsin Press, 1982.

McCarthy, B. P. "Lucian and Menippus." *Yale Classical Studies* 4 (1934): 3–55.

Mead, G. R. S. *Apollonius of Tyana, the Philosopher-Reformer of the First Century A.D.* London: Theosophical Publ. Soc., 1901. Reprinted as *Apollonius of Tyana, the Philosopher, Explorer, and Social Reformer of the First Century A.D.* Chicago: Ares, 1980.

Meeks, W. *The First Urban Christians: The Social World of the Apostle Paul.* New Haven: Yale University Press, 1983.

Meredith, A. "Asceticism—Christian and Greek." *JTS* 27 (1976): 313–32.

Messier, M. "Les Rapports avec autrui dans le 'Contre Celse' d'Origène." *Mélanges de science religieuse* 28 (1971): 189–94.

Meunier, M. *Apollonius de Tyane ou le séjour d'un dieu parmi les hommes.* Paris: B. Grasset, 1936. Reprint. Plan de la Tour: Editions d'Aujourd'hui, 1978.

Meyer, E. "Apollonius von Tyana und die Biographie des Philostratos." *Hermes* 52 (1917): 371–424 = *Kleine Schriften,* 2:131–91. Halle: M. Niemeyer, 1924.

Millar, F. *The Emperor in the Roman World.* Ithaca: Cornell University Press, 1977.

———. "Epictetus and the Imperial Court." *JRS* 55 (1965): 141–47.

————. *A Study of Cassius Dio.* Oxford: Clarendon Press, 1964.

Misch, G. *Geschichte der Autobiographie.* Vol. 1, *Das Altertum.* 3d ed. Frankfurt-am-Main: Schulte-Bulmke, 1949. Translated by E. W. Dickes, as *A History of Autobiography in Antiquity.* 2 vols. Cambridge: Harvard University Press, 1951. Reprint. Westport, Conn.: Greenwood, 1973.

Miura-Stange, A. *Celsus und Origenes: Das Gemeinsame ihrer Weltanschauung.* Zeitschrift für die neutestamentliche Wissenschaft und die Kunde der Älteren Kirche, Beiheft 4. Giessen: A. Töpelman, 1926.

Moles, J. "The Career and Conversion of Dio Chrysostom." *JHS* 98 (1978): 79–100.

Molthagen, J. *Der römische Staat und die Christen im zweiten und dritten Jahrhundert.* Hypomnemata Untersuchungen zur Antike und zu ihrem Nachleben 28. Göttingen: Vandenhoeck and Ruprecht, 1970.

Momigliano, A. Review of *Luciano: Un intellettuale greco contra Roma*, by A. Peretti. In *Rivista storica italiana* 60 (1948): 641–44 = *Quarto contributo alla storia degli studi classici*, 641–44. Rome: Edizioni di storia e letteratura, 1969.

Mommsen, T. *Römisches Strafrecht.* Systematisches Handbuch der Deutschen Rechtwissenschaft I.4. Leipzig: Duncker und Humboldt, 1899. Reprint. Aalen: Scientia-Verlag, 1990.

Morgan, J. R. Review of *Philostratus: Biography and Belles Lettres in the Third Century A.D.,* by G. Anderson. In *CR* 38 (1988): 235–36.

Murray, G. *Five Stages of Greek Religion.* 3d ed. Garden City, N.Y.: Doubleday, 1951.

Murray, R. *Symbols of Church and Kingdom: A Study in Early Syriac Tradition.* Corrected reprint. Cambridge: Cambridge University Press, 1977.

Nagel, P. *Die Motivierung der Askese in der Altenkirche und der Ursprung des Mönchtums.* Texte und Untersuchungen zur Geschichte der altchristlichen Literatur 95. Berlin: Akademie-Verlag, 1966.

Nautin, P. *Origène: Sa vie et son oeuvre.* Christianisme antique 1. Paris: Beauchesne, 1977.

Newman, R.J. "*Cotidie Meditare.* Theory and Practice of the *meditatio* in Imperial Stoicism." *ANRW* II.36.3 (1989): 1473–1517.

Nilsson, M. P. *Geschichte der griechischen Religion.* Vol. 2, *Die hellenistische und römische Zeit.* 2d ed. Handbuch der Altertumswissenschaft, Abt. 5, Teil 2, Band 2. Munich: Beck, 1961.

Nock, A. D. "Alexander of Abonouteichos." *CQ* 22 (1928), 160–62.

————. *Conversion: The Old and the New in Religion from Alexander the Great to Augustine of Hippo.* Oxford: Clarendon Press, 1933.

————. *Early Gentile Christianity and Its Hellenistic Background.* New York: Harper and Row, 1964.

————. "Oracles théologiques." *Revue des études anciennes* 30 (1928): 280–90 = *Essays in Religion and the Ancient World,* ed. Z. Stewart, 1:160–68. Corrected reprint. Oxford: Clarendon Press, 1986.

North, J. "Religious Toleration in Republican Rome." *Proceedings of the Cambridge Philological Society* 205 (1979): 85–103.

Noyen, P. "Divus Marcus, princeps prudentissimus et iuris religiosissimus." *Revue internationale des droits de l'antiquité,* 3d ser., 1 (1954): 349–71.

———. "Marcus Aurelius' Legislation and Government." Doctoral dissertation, Ghent, 1954.

———. "Marcus Aurelius the Greatest Practician [*sic*] of Stoicism." *Antiquité Classique* 24 (1955): 372–83.

Nutton, V. "The Patient's Choice: A New Treatise by Galen." *CQ*, n.s. 40 (1990): 236–57.

Obbink, D. "The Atheism of Epicurus." *GRBS* 30 (1989): 182–223.

Oliver, J. H. *Marcus Aurelius: Aspects of Civic and Cultural Policy.* Hesperia suppl. 13. Princeton: American School of Classical Studies at Athens, 1970.

Oliver, J. H., and R. E. Palmer. "Minutes of an Act of the Roman Senate." *Hesperia* 24 (1955): 320–49.

Olmstead, A. T. "The Mid-Third Century of the Christian Era." *Classical Philology* 37 (1942): 241–62; continued on 398–420.

Pack, R. "The Volatilization of Peregrinus Proteus." *American Journal of Philology* 67 (1946): 334–45.

Pagels, E. H. "Adam and Eve, Christ and the Church: A Survey of Second-century Controversies Concerning Marriage." In *The New Testament and Gnosis: Essays in Honor of Robert McL. Wilson,* ed. A. H. B. Logan and A. J. M. Wedderburn, 146–75. Edinburgh: T. and T. Clark, 1983.

———. *Adam, Eve, and the Serpent.* New York: Random House, 1988.

———. *The Gnostic Gospels.* New York: Random House, 1979.

Peek, W. "Epigramm auf Apollonius von Tyana." *Philologus* 2, Band 125 (1981): 297–98.

Pélagaud, E. *Un Conservateur au second siècle: Etude sur Celse et la première escarmouche entre la Philosophie et le Christianisme naissant.* Lyon: H. Georg, 1878.

Penella, R. J. *The Letters of Apollonius of Tyana: A Critical Text with Prolegomena, Translation and Commentary.* Mnemosyne suppl. 56. Leiden: E. J. Brill, 1979.

———. "Philostratus' Letter to Julia Domna." *Hermes* 107, no. 2 (1979): 161–68.

Peretti, A. *Luciano: Un intellettuale greco contra Roma.* Biblioteca di cultura 26. Florence: Nuova Italia, 1946.

Perkins, J. "The Apocryphal Acts and the Early Christian Martyrdom." *Arethusa* 18 (1985): 211–30.

———. "The Apocryphal *Acts of Peter*: A *Roman à Thèse?*" *Arethusa* 25 (1992): 445–55.

———. "The 'Self' as Sufferer." *Harvard Theological Review* 85 (1992): 245–72.

Peterson, E. *Der Monotheismus als politisches Problem: Ein Beitrag zur Geschichte der politischen Theologie in Imperium romanum.* Leipzig: Hegner, 1935.

Pétrement, S. *Le Dualisme dans l'histoire de la philosophie et des religions.* Paris: Gallimard, 1946.

Petzke, G. *Die Traditionen über Apollonius von Tyana und das Neue Testament.* Studia ad corpus Hellenisticum Novi Testamenti 1. Leiden: E. J. Brill, 1970.

Pichler, K. *Streit um das Christentum: Der Angriff des Kelsos und die Antwort der Origenes.* Regensburger Studien zur Theologie 23. Frankfurt-am-Main: D. Lang, 1980.

Pohlenz, M. *Die Stoa: Geschichte einer geistigen Bewegung.* 4th ed. with corrections, additions, and index by H.-J. Johann. 2 vols. Göttingen: Vandenhoeck and Ruprecht, 1970.

Puiggali, J. "La Démonologie de Philostrate." *Revue des sciences philosophiques et théologiques* 67 (1983): 117–30.

Rabbow, P. *Seelenführung: Methodik der Exercitien in der Antike.* Munich: Kösel-Verlag, 1954.

Rawson, B., ed. *The Family in Ancient Rome: New Perspectives.* Ithaca: Cornell University Press, 1986.

Raynor, D. H. "Moeragenes and Philostratus. Two Views of Apollonius of Tyana." *CQ,* n.s. 34 (1984): 222–26.

Reardon, B. P. *Courants littéraires grecs des IIe et IIIe siècles après J.-C* Annales littéraires de l'Université de Nantes 3. Paris: Belles Lettres, 1971.

——. "The Second Sophistic and the Novel." In *Approaches to the Second Sophistic: Papers Presented at the 105th Annual Meeting of the American Philological Association,* ed. G. W. Bowersock, 23–29. University Park, Pa.: A.P.A., 1974.

Reitzenstein, R. *Hellenistische Mysterienreligionen nach ihren Grundgedanken und Wirkungen.* 3d ed. Leipzig: B. G. Teubner, 1927. Reprint. Darmstadt: Wissenschaftliche Buchgesellschaft, 1980. Translated by J. E. Steely, as *Hellenistic Mystery-religions: Their Basic Ideas and Significance.* Pittsburgh Theological Monographs 15. Pittsburgh: Pickwick, 1978.

——. *Hellenistische Wundererzählungen,* Leipzig: B. G. Teubner, 1906. Reprint. Stuttgart: B. G. Teubner, 1974.

Remus, H. *Pagan-Christian Conflict over Miracle in the Second Century.* Philadelphia Patristic Monograph Series 10. Cambridge, Mass.: Philadelphia Patristic Foundation, 1983.

Renan, E. *Marc-Aurèle et la fin du monde antique.* Histoire des origines du christianisme 7. Paris: Calmann Lévy, 1882. Reprint. Paris: Le Livre de poche, 1984. Translated by W. Hutchinson, as *Marcus Aurelius.* London: Walter Scott, 1904.

Richardson, N. J., and P. Burian. "The Epigram on Apollonius of Tyana." *GRBS* 22 (1981): 283–85.

Riddle, D. W. *The Martyrs: A Study in Social Control.* Chicago: University of Chicago Press, 1931.

Rist, J. M. "Are You A Stoic? The Case of Marcus Aurelius." In *Jewish and Christian Self-Definition,* ed. B. F. Meyer and E. P. Sanders, 3:23–45. Philadelphia: Fortress, 1982.

——. "Beyond Stoic and Platonist. A Sample of Origen's Treatment of Philosophy (Contra Celsum 4.62–70). In *Platonismus und Christentum: Festschrift für Heinrich Doerrie,* ed. H.-D. Blume and F. Mann, 228–38. Jahrbuch für Antike und Christentum Ergänzungsband 10. Münster: Aschendorff, 1983.

——. "The Importance of Stoic Logic in the Contra Celsum." In *Neoplatonism and Early Christian Thought: Essays in Honor of A. H. Armstrong,* ed. H. J. Blumenthal and R. A. Markus, 64–78. London: Variorum, 1981.

——. "The Stoic Concept of Detachment." In *The Stoics,* ed. J. M. Rist, 259–72. Berkeley and Los Angeles: University of California Press, 1978.

———. *Stoic Philosophy*. Cambridge: Cambridge University Press, 1969.

Robert, L. *A travers l'Asie Mineur: Poètes et prosateurs, monnaies grecques, voyageurs et géographie*. Bibliothèque des Ecoles françaises d'Athènes et de Rome 239. Paris: de Boccard, 1980.

Robinson, C. *Lucian and His Influence on Europe*. Chapel Hill: University of North Carolina Press, 1979.

Robinson, J. M., and H. Koester, eds. *Trajectories through Early Christianity*. Philadelphia: Fortress, 1971.

Rosenbaum, H.-U. "Zur Datierung von Celsus 'ΑΛΗΘΗΣ ΛΟΓΟΣ." *Vig. Chr.* 26 (1972): 102–11.

Rostovtzeff, M. *The Social and Economic History of the Roman Empire*. 2d ed. 2 vols. Revised by P. M. Fraser. Oxford: Clarendon Press, 1957.

Rougier, L. *Celse contre les Chrétiens. La réaction païenne sous l'empire romaine. Le Discours vrai de Celse*. Paris: Copernic, 1977.

———. *Celse: Discours vrai contre les Chrétiens*. Paris: J.-J. Pauvert, 1965.

———. *Celse ou le conflit de la civilisation antique et du Christianisme primitif*. Paris: Editions du Siècle, 1925.

Rousseau, P. *Ascetics, Authority, and the Church in the Age of Jerome and Cassian*. Oxford: Oxford University Press, 1978.

Rutherford, R. B. *The Meditations of Marcus Aurelius: A Study*. Oxford: Clarendon Press, 1989.

Sandbach, F. H. *The Stoics*. 2d ed. Bristol: Bristol Press, 1989.

Schwartz, J. *Biographie de Lucien de Samosate*. Collection Latomus 83. Brussels: Latomus, 1965.

———. "La 'conversion' de Lucien de Samosate." *Antiquité Classique* 33 (1964): 384–400.

Scroggs, R. "The Sociological Interpretation of the New Testament: The Present State of Research." *New Testament Studies* 26 (1980): 164–79.

Sedgewick, H. D. *Marcus Aurelius: A Biography*. New Haven: Yale University Press, 1921. Reprint. New York: AMS, 1971.

Segal, A. F. "Hellenistic Magic: Some Questions of Definition." In *Studies in Gnosticism and Hellenistic Religions: Presented to Gilles Quispel on the Occasion of His 65th Birthday*, ed. R. van Den Broek and M. J. Vermaseren, 349–75. Leiden: E. J. Brill, 1981.

Sherwin-White, A. N. *The Letters of Pliny: A Historical and Social Commentary*. Corrected reprint. Oxford: Clarendon Press, 1985.

Sidebottom, H. "The Date of Dio of Prusa's Rhodian and Alexandrian Orations." *Historia* 41 (1992): 407–19.

Simpson, A. D. "Epicureans, Christians, Atheists in the Second Century." *TAPA* 72 (1941): 372–81.

Smith, J. Z. "Good News is No News: Aretalogy and Gospel." In *Christianity, Judaism, and Other Graeco-Roman Cults: Studies for Morton Smith at Sixty*, ed. J. Neusner, 1:21–38. Studies in Judaism in Late Antiquity 12. Leiden: E. J. Brill, 1975.

Smith, K. F. "Greek and Roman Magic." In *Encyclopaedia of Religion and Ethics*. New York: Scribner, 1955.

Smith, M. *Clement of Alexandria and a Secret Gospel of Mark*. Cambridge: Harvard University Press, 1973.

———. *Jesus the Magician*. New York: Harper and Row, 1978.

———. "On the History of the Divine Man." In *Paganisme, Judaïsme, Chris-*

tianisme: Influences et affrontements dans le monde antique. Mélanges offerts à Marcel Simon, 335–45. Paris: de Boccard, 1978.

———. "Prolegomena to a Discussion of Aretalogies, Divine Men, the Gospels and Jesus." *JBL* 90 (1971): 174–99.

———. Review of *The Charismatic Figure as Miracle Worker*, by D. Tiede. In *Interpretation* 28 (1974): 238–40.

Smith, M., and M. Hadas. *Heroes and Gods: Spiritual Biographies in Antiquity.* Religious Perspectives 13. New York: Harper and Row, 1965.

Smith, R. C., and J. Lounibos, eds. *Pagan and Christian Anxiety: A Response to E. R. Dodds.* Lanham, Md.: University Press of America, 1984.

Solmsen, F. "Philostratos (10)." *RE* 20.1 (1941): 136–74 = *Kleine Schriften* 2:92–118. Hildesheim: G. Olms, 1968.

———. "Some Works of Philostratus the Elder." *TAPA* 71 (1940): 556–72.

Sordi, M. *Il Cristianesimo e Roma.* Storia di Roma 19. Bologna: Cappelli, 1965.

———. *I cristiani e l'impero romano.* Di fronte e attraverso 118. Milan: Jaca Book, 1983. Translated by A. Bedini, as *The Christians and the Roman Empire.* Norman: University of Oklahoma Press, 1986.

———. "I nuovi decreti di Marco Aurelio contro i cristiani." *Studi Romani* 9 (1961): 365–78.

———. "Le polemiche intorno al Cristianesimo nel II secolo e la loro influenza sugli sviluppi della politica imperiale verso la Chiesa." *Rivista di Storia della Chiesa in Italia* 16 (1962): 1–28.

Spanneut, M. *Le Stoïcisme des Pères de l'Eglise de Clément de Rome à Clément d'Alexandrie.* 2d ed. Paris: Editions du Seuil, 1969.

Speigl, J. *Der römische Staat und die Christen: Staat und Kirche von Domitian bis Commodus.* Amsterdam: Hakkert, 1970.

Speyer, W. "Hierokles (I) (Sossianus Hierocles)." *Reallexikon für Antike und Christentum,* Lief. 113 (1989): 103–9.

———. "Zum Bild des Apollonius von Tyana bei Heiden und Christen." *Jahrbuch für Antike und Christentum* 17 (1974): 47–63.

Stanton, G. R. "The Cosmopolitan Ideas of Epictetus and Marcus Aurelius." *Phronesis* 13 (1968): 183–95.

———. "Marcus Aurelius, Emperor and Philosopher." *Historia* 18 (1969): 570–87.

———. "Marcus Aurelius, Lucius Verus, and Commodus: 1962–1972." *ANRW* II.2.2 (1975): 478–549.

Ste. Croix, G. E. M. de. *The Class Struggle in the Ancient Greek World.* Revised ed. Ithaca: Cornell University Press, 1989.

———. "Why Were the Early Christians Persecuted?" *Past and Present* 26 (1963): 6–38.

Strathmann, H. *Die Askese in der Umgebung der werdenden Christentums.* Leipzig: A. Deickert, 1914.

Syme, R. *Historia Augusta Papers.* Oxford: Clarendon Press, 1983.

Taggart, B. L. "Apollonius of Tyana. His Biographers and Critics." Ph.D. dissertation, Tufts University, 1972.

Tatum, J. *Apuleius and the Golden Ass.* Ithaca: Cornell University Press, 1979.

Theissen, G. *Lokalorit und Zeitgeschichte in den Evangelien: Ein Beitrag zur Geschichte der synoptischen Tradition.* Göttingen: Vandenhoeck und Ruprecht, 1989. Translated by L. M. Maloney, as *The Gospels in Con-*

text: Social and Political History in the Synoptic Tradition. Minneapolis, Minn.: Fortress, 1991.

———. *Soziologie der Jesusbewegung: Ein Beitrag zur Entstehungsgeschichte des Urchristentums.* Theologische Existenz heute, n.s. 194. Munich: Kaiser, 1977. Translated by J. Bowden, as *Sociology of Early Palestinian Christianity.* Philadelphia: Fortress, 1978.

———. *Studien zur Soziologie der Urchristentums.* 3d ed. Wissenschaftliche Untersuchungen zum Neuen Testament 19. Tübingen: Mohr, 1989. Translated by M. Kohl, as *Social Reality and the Early Christians: Theology, Ethics, and the World of the New Testament.* Minneapolis, Minn.: Fortress, 1992.

———. *Urchristliche Wundergeschichten: Ein Beitrag zur formgeschichtlichen Erforschung der synoptischen Evangelien.* Studien zum Neuen Testament 8. Gütersloh: Gütersloher Verlagshaus Mohn, 1974. Translated by F. McDonagh, as *The Miracle Stories of the Early Christian Tradition,* ed. J. Riches. Philadelphia: Fortress, 1983.

Tiede, D. *The Charismatic Figure as Miracle Worker.* SBL Dissertation Series 1. Missoula, 1972.

Tissot, Y. "Encratism et Actes Apocryphes." In *Les Actes Apocryphes des Apôtres: Christianisme et monde païen,* ed. F. Bovon et al., 109–19. Publications de la Faculté de théologie de l'Université de Genève 4. Geneva: Labor et Fides, 1981.

Tondriau, J. "L'Avis de Lucien sur la divinization des hommes." *Museum Helveticum* 5 (1948): 124–32.

Toynbee, J. M. C. "Dictators and Philosophers in the First Century A.D." *Greece and Rome* 13 (1944): 43–58.

Treggiari, S. *Roman Marriage: Iusti Coniuges from the Time of Cicero to the Time of Ulpian.* Oxford: Clarendon Press, 1991.

Trigg, J. W. *Origen: The Bible and Philosophy in the Third-Century Church.* Atlanta, Ga.: J. Knox, 1983.

Tsavari, I. "Une Edition récente des Lettres d'Apollonius de Tyane." Δωδώνη 16, no. 2 [Philol.] (1982): 205–25.

Ullman, W. "Die Bedeutung der Gotteserkenntnis für die Gesamtkonzeption von Celsus' Logos Alethes." In *Studia Patristica.* Vol. 14, *Tertullian, Origenism, Gnostica, Cappadocian Fathers, Augustiniana: Papers presented to the Sixth International Conference on Patristic Studies, Oxford 1971,* ed. E. A. Livingstone, 180–88. Texte und Untersuchungen 117. Berlin: Akademie-Verlag, 1976.

Veyne, P., ed. *Histoire de la vie privée.* Vol. 1, *De l'Empire romaine à l'an mil.* Paris: Editions du Seuil, 1985. Translated by A. Goldhammer, as *A History of Private Life.* Vol. 1, *From Pagan Rome to Byzantium.* Cambridge: Belknap Press of Harvard University Press, 1987.

Vööbus, A. *A History of Asceticism in the Syrian Orient: A Contribution to the History of Culture in the Near East.* 3 vols. Corpus Scriptorum Christianorum Orientalium (CSCO) 184, 197, 500; Subsidia 14, 17, 81. Louvain: CSCO, 1958–88.

Walzer, R. *Galen on Jews and Christians.* Oxford: Oxford University Press, 1949.

Weinreich, O. "Alexandros der Lügenprophet und seine Stellung in der Religiosität des IIe Jahrhunderts nach Chr." *Neue Jahrbücher für das klassischen Altertum* 47 (1921): 129–51.

Wifstrand, A. "Die wahre Lehre des Kelsos." *Société Royale de Lettres de Lund Bulletin / Kungliga Humanistika vetenskapssamfundet i Lund Aarsberättelse* 5 (1941–42): 391–431.

Wilken, R. L. *The Christians as the Romans Saw Them.* New Haven: Yale University Press, 1984.

———. "Pagan Criticism of Christianity: Greek Religion and Christian Faith." In *Early Christian Literature and the Classical Intellectual Tradition: In honorem Robert M. Grant,* ed. W. R. Schoedel and R. L. Wilken, 17–34. Théologie historique 53. Paris: Beauchesne, 1979.

———. "Toward a Social Interpretation of Early Christian Apologetics." *Church History* 39 (1970): 437–58.

Williams, W. "Individuality in the Imperial Constitutions. Hadrian and the Antonines." *JRS* 66 (1976): 67–83.

Wilmer, E. "Beiträge zur Alexandrinerrede (or. 32) des Dion Chrysostomos." Doctoral dissertation, Bonn, 1970.

Wilson, R. McL. "Alimentary and Sexual Encratism in the Nag Hammadi Texts." In *La tradizione dell'Enkrateia, motivazione ontologiche e protologiche: Atti del Colloquio internazionale, Milano 20–23 aprile 1982,* ed. U. Bianchi, 317–39. Rome: Edizioni dell'Ateneo, 1985.

Wimbush, V. L., ed. *Ascetic Behavior in Greco-Roman Antiquity: A Sourcebook.* Minneapolis, Minn.: Fortress, 1990.

Winden, J. C. M. van. "Notes on Origen, Contra Celsum." *Vig. Chr.* 20 (1966): 201–13.

Wlosok, A. *Rom und die Christen: Zur Auseinandersetzung zwischen Christentum und römischer Staat.* Der altsprachliche Unterricht, Reihe 13, Beiheft 7. Stuttgart: E. Klett, 1970.

Index